Also by Kiernan Ryan

Shakespeare (3rd Edition)
King Lear: Contemporary Critical Essays
Shakespeare: Texts and Contexts
Shakespeare: The Last Plays
New Historicism and Cultural Materialism: A Reader

Shakespeare's Comedies

Kiernan Ryan

palgrave
macmillan

First published 2009 by
PALGRAVE MACMILLAN

Palgrave Macmillan in the UK is an imprint of Macmillan Publishers Limited,
registered in England, company number 785998, of Houndmills, Basingstoke,
Hampshire RG21 6XS.

Palgrave Macmillan in the US is a division of St Martin's Press LLC,
175 Fifth Avenue, New York, NY 10010.

Palgrave Macmillan is the global academic imprint of the above companies
and has companies and representatives throughout the world.

Palgrave® and Macmillan® are registered trademarks in the United States,
the United Kingdom, Europe and other countries

ISBN-13: 978–0–333–59931–0   hardback
ISBN-10: 0–333–59931–4   hardback
ISBN-13: 978–0–333–59932–7   paperback
ISBN-10: 0–333–59932–2   paperback

This book is printed on paper suitable for recycling and made from fully
managed and sustained forest sources. Logging, pulping and manufacturing
processes are expected to conform to the environmental regulations of the
country of origin.

A catalogue record for this book is available from the British Library.

A catalog record for this book is available from the Library of Congress.

10 9 8 7 6 5 4 3 2 1
18 17 16 15 14 13 12 11 10 09

For Liz

Contents

Preface

I should begin by coming clean about the title of this book, lest it be accused of being misleading. As I acknowledge in the first and final chapters, Shakespearean comedy in its broadest definition includes the so-called problem plays (*Troilus and Cressida*, *Measure for Measure* and *All's Well That Ends Well*) and the romances (*Pericles*, *Cymbeline*, *The Winter's Tale* and *The Tempest*) as well as the first ten comedies Shakespeare wrote, with which this book is exclusively concerned. A full account of the subject would have to tackle all these plays, which is what I originally set out to do, until the demands of trying to do justice to the ten plays commonly referred to as the comedies disabused me of that fantasy. As the book developed in its present form, however, my sense of the coherence of these plays as a distinct body of work within the corpus of Shakespearean comedy grew, to the point where it seemed justifiable, rather than merely expedient, to think of them as diverse instances of a kind of comedy which Shakespeare quite consciously brought to an end with *Twelfth Night*, and to which he never returned. The long-standing resort to the terms 'problem plays' and 'romances' to classify Shakespeare's subsequent ventures in the same genre reflects the widespread feeling that *Twelfth Night* marks a sea-change in Shakespearean comedy, however difficult it might be to pinpoint the nature of the change and secure the distinctions between the three groups of plays. This consideration, coupled with the implicit case this study makes for treating Shakespeare's farcical and festive Elizabethan comedies as a discrete sequence – as the first phase of Shakespearean comedy – will go some way, I hope, towards meeting the objections that the title of the book invites.

That said, my overriding concern in writing this book has been to engage with each play first and foremost as a singular work of dramatic and poetic art, with its own idiosyncratic shape, structure, idiom and strategies as well as its own distinctive preoccupations and critical challenges. Accounts of Shakespearean comedy have been prone in the past to flatten the distinguishing features of individual plays to make them fit a generic formula, neglecting the things that are innovative or eccentric about them in their keenness to determine what they have in common. My own account in Chapter 4 of my book *Shakespeare*, not-withstanding its expansion in the third edition to include extended readings of particular comedies, is far from immune to this charge; and not the least objective in the pages that follow is to put that highly compressed thesis about the utopian vision of Shakespearean comedy to the test by letting each play speak for itself, and allowing family resemblances and shared obsessions to emerge along the way instead of being established in advance of a close encounter with the texts. With that aim in mind, I've resisted the temptation to preface the chapters on the plays with an introductory chapter which defines Shakespearean comedy, and to follow them with a chapter which draws retrospective conclusions about it, preferring to let the chapter on *The Comedy of Errors* double as an introduction and the chapter on *Twelfth Night* furnish the book's natural conclusion.

My desire to treat each play as a whole and tackle it on its own terms has had other consequences for this study too. If one is disinclined to immure Shakespeare's drama in its early modern milieu by shackling it to extraneous archival material, and if reducing it to a quarry for cultural historians more interested in maps, make-up or medicine than in the power of plays is no more appealing than conscripting it to endorse a particular critical theory or procedure, then most of what currently passes for Shakespeare criticism is of little value. My own response to this predicament, for better or for worse, has been to steer clear of current Shakespeare criticism as far as possible while writing this book. I've turned back instead to the great Shakespeare critics of the distant past, and to some neglected critics of the more recent past, for fresh inspiration and examples of how to write directly about a play, unconstrained by the obligation to buttress the account with displays of erudition, to cite everyone who once thought something similar, and to anchor each point in a footnote. To free this study of footnotes I've confined primary and secondary references to the bare minimum and to a separate section ('Works Cited') at the back of the book. There will doubtless be readers who would prefer me to have supplied fuller references in a conventional form and an explicit theoretical rationale for my approach to Shakespeare's comedies, situating it in relation to rival approaches and bolting it into place with an extended bibliography. But I hope most readers will find a critical study of Shakespeare unencumbered by the usual academic apparatus more congenial. Anyone interested in the origins of the critical approach I adopt in this book, and the theoretical arguments that underpin it, can find them spelled out in the third edition of *Shakespeare*, which also contains a fairly comprehensive list of Further Reading.

This is the point at which to confess that the chapter on *The Comedy of Errors* recycles, more or less verbatim, a substantial section of my account of that play in the third edition of *Shakespeare*, because I needed to make those points again and couldn't see any reason for putting them differently. I have also redeployed some ideas, and some phrases, from my brief reading of *The Merchant of Venice* in the same book in Chapter 6. Apart from these exercises in critical thrift, all the material in this study appears in print for the first time.

This book owes much to my undergraduate and graduate students at Royal Holloway, whose questions and constructive criticism have helped me to shape its ideas and sharpen its arguments. It owes a special debt, however, to my colleague Ewan Fernie for his constant encouragement and invaluable friendship throughout its writing. I'm also indebted, and not for the first time, to Kate Belsey, who provided enthusiastic support and characteristically astute advice at a crucial point. It's a pleasure to record at long last my gratitude to Margaret Bartley, who commissioned this study more years ago than I care to recall, and to Kate Haines at Palgrave, who coaxed me into completing it and supervised its publication so adroitly. My deepest debt is to Elizabeth Drayson, to whom this book is dedicated, with love.

1

Killing Time: *The Comedy of Errors*

The Magician's Hat

Which of Shakespeare's earliest comedies was his first venture into his favourite dramatic genre remains a matter of dispute, but there's no good reason to dissent from the still widespread view that *The Comedy of Errors* is the most plausible candidate. Even if cast-iron proof that *The Two Gentlemen of Verona* or *The Taming of the Shrew* preceded it were to be discovered, its seminal role in the evolution of Shakespearean comedy would remain secure. The play's own claim to precedence is inscribed in its title. It's not just that it's the only title of a comedy by Shakespeare that trumpets the term 'comedy'. It's also the choice of the word 'errors' to qualify the kind of comedy we're about to be served, and the prefacing of the phrase 'comedy of errors' with the definite article. By billing itself boldly as '*The* Comedy of Errors' rather than '*A* Comedy of Errors', the play announces itself as an instance of a whole genre or mode of comedy: this, like all its successors in one way or another, will be a comedy not merely of mistakes and confusions, but also of 'errors' in the word's original Latin sense of wandering, straying, transgressing. It will be a kind of comedy in which boundaries are crossed and categories confounded, in which abnormality is the norm and exceptions rule. In this respect, *The Comedy of Errors* is a prophetic paradigm of Shakespeare's subsequent adventures in the genre, the magician's hat from which he pulled ingenious permutations of the same core motifs and devices.

The multiple misconceptions bred by the absurdity of identical twin masters and identical twin servants inaugurate Shakespeare's preoccupation throughout the comedies with the vulnerability of perception and the fragility of identity. Ephesus furnishes the first in a long series

1

of licensed realms governed by the logic and the laws of dreams, which allow the characters to inhabit a parallel universe of alternative possibilities. The play's concurrent creation of a privileged temporal zone that holds the tyranny of clock-time at bay prefigures the outrageous liberties taken with time in the comedies that follow it. The riddling, raillery and preposterous wordplay in which the twin masters and servants indulge, playing havoc with the assumptions ensconced in normal discourse, pave the way for a cavalcade of impertinent clowns and quick-tongued lovers locked in badinage. And the haunting resolutions of the romances, in which Shakespeare bade the stage as well as comedy goodbye, are foreshadowed in the poignant reunion of the estranged twin sons with their long-lost mother and father at the close of *The Comedy of Errors*.

These are only the most conspicuous features in which the family resemblance of the comedies can be read and confirmation that *The Comedy of Errors* adumbrates Shakespeare's entire comedic career can be found. In 'the fairy land' (II.ii.192) of Ephesus, where the Antipholus twin from Syracuse and his faithful servant, Dromio, 'wander in illusions' (IV.iii.43) at the mercy of 'Lapland sorcerers' (IV.iii.11), not knowing whether they are 'Sleeping or waking' (II.ii.216), lie the seeds of the havoc wrought in the sylvan darkness of *A Midsummer Night's Dream* by Oberon and Puck, and the delusions spawned by the spellbound island over which Prospero and Ariel preside in Shakespeare's last masterpiece. (The fact that Shakespeare chose to observe in his final comedy the unities of time and place to which the first of his comedies alone also adheres is too remarkable to be dismissed as coincidence; it suggests irresistibly a valedictory return to his point of departure, as the wheel of Shakespearean comedy comes full circle.) The bewildering profusion of selves and misapprehensions to which cross-dressing consigns Rosalind in *As You Like It* and Viola in *Twelfth Night* is presaged by the identity crisis into which the Antipholus twins are pitched:

ADRIANA. I see two husbands, or mine eyes deceive me.
DUKE.   One of these men is *genius* to the other:
          And so of these, which is the natural man,
          And which the spirit? Who deciphers them?
                                        (V.i.333–6)

It's equally apparent that in the fractious Dromio twins, with their ribald puns, frantic logic-chopping and unbridled backchat, we behold the progenitors of clowns like Lancelot Gobbo in *The Merchant of*

Venice, wise fools like Touchstone (*As You Like It*), Feste (*Twelfth Night*) and Lavatch (*All's Well That Ends Well*), and smart-mouthed rogues like Lucio in *Measure for Measure* and Autolycus in *The Winter's Tale*. Nor is it any wonder that the moving restoration of Pericles to his daughter, Marina, and his wife, Thaisa, in the twilight of Shakespeare's career mirrors so closely the restoration of Egeon to his twin sons and his wife, Emilia, at its dawn, since both plays draw on the tale of Apollonius of Tyre, which Shakespeare culled from Gower's version in his *Confessio Amantis*.

'a very formidable anachronism'

I've always been most struck, however, by the curious character in *The Comedy of Errors* called Doctor Pinch. William Hazlitt was struck by him too, I was glad to discover, since Hazlitt's critical hunches invariably repay pursuit. His slight account of the comedy in *Characters of Shakespear's Plays* is uncharacteristically blind to its trailblazing brilliance, reproaching Shakespeare for being too deeply indebted to the farcical comedy of intrigue he found in his chief classical sources, the *Menaechmi* and the *Amphitruo* of Plautus. 'His own genius was strong enough to bear him up', insists Hazlitt, 'and he soared longest and best on unborrowed plumes.' But at the very end of the essay, almost as an afterthought, Hazlitt remarks: 'Pinch the conjuror is also an excrescence not to be found in Plautus. He is indeed a very formidable anachronism.' And he quotes part of the vivid portrait of Pinch sketched by an outraged Antipholus of Ephesus in the final scene of the play:

> They brought one Pinch, a hungry lean-faced villain,
> A mere anatomy, a mountebank,
> A threadbare juggler, and a fortune-teller,
> A needy, hollow-eyed, sharp-looking wretch,
> A living dead man. This pernicious slave,
> Forsooth, took on him as a conjurer,
> And gazing in mine eyes, feeling my pulse,
> And with no face, as 'twere, outfacing me,
> Cries out I was possessed.
>
> (V.i.238–46)

The vignette has indeed, as Hazlitt notes, the grotesque animation of a figure engraved by Hogarth. Doctor Pinch is plainly a kissing cousin of

the ragged, starved apothecary who materializes so memorably in his
'beggar's shop' stuffed with tortoises, alligators 'and other skins / Of
ill-shaped fishes' in the final act of *Romeo and Juliet* (V.i.37–84), written just a few years after *The Comedy of Errors*. Like the apothecary,
Pinch acquires an autonomous vitality out of proportion to his role in
the plot that houses him, and for equally elusive reasons, which Hazlitt
does not choose to unravel.

The character's peculiar resonance is rooted, I think, partly in the
fact that he expands into an 'excrescence', as Hazlitt calls him, a gratuitous outgrowth of the dramatist's imagination in excess of comedic
requirements; partly in the 'formidable' impression of anachronism he
makes on Hazlitt by transporting himself from the urban reality of
Elizabethan England into the archaic fantasy land of Ephesus; and
partly in his depiction as a self-styled sorcerer ('juggler'), a cut-price
magus who can conjure spirits and exorcise the possessed, and who thus
conspires with the theatrical forces of enchantment that command *The
Comedy of Errors*. Modern stagings of the play have not been slow to
cotton on to the character's innate theatricality, and time and again
gifted actors have stolen the show in the role of Pinch, as Robert
Helpmann did in the 1957 production at the Old Vic, and John
Woodvine did in Trevor Nunn's RSC production at Stratford in 1976.

The reason why this 'mere anatomy', this marginal 'mountebank',
can paradoxically seem so central is that he encapsulates key qualities
not only of *The Comedy of Errors*, but also of Shakespearean comedy as
it develops over the next two decades. To anatomize the cadaverous
charlatan Doctor Pinch is to cut to the heart not only of the show he is
prone to steal, but also of the comedy of errors that constitutes
Shakespearean comedy. For when Hazlitt homed in on the formidably
anachronistic part Pinch plays as an extrusive appendix to the plot of
The Comedy of Errors, he hit upon two crucial, indivisible features of
Shakespearean comedy embodied in the phoney exorcist: the dislocation of time and the compulsion to deviate from the action and the dialogue dictated by the plot.

'There's no clock in the forest'

The Comedy of Errors marks the outbreak of the relentless war waged by
Shakespearean comedy on conceptions of time that clamp people into
the predictable scripts of their culture. The comedies have no time for the
quantified, calibrated, sequential type of time mocked by Touchstone

in *As You Like It*, when he mirrors Jaques's posture of gloom in a
wicked parody, which Jaques himself recounts with relish to his fellow
exiles in Arden:

'Good morrow, fool,' quoth I. 'No, sir,' quoth he,
'Call me not fool till heaven hath sent me fortune.'
And then he drew a dial from his poke,
And looking on it with lack-lustre eye
Says very wisely 'It is ten o'clock.'
'Thus we may see', quoth he, 'how the world wags.
'Tis but an hour ago since it was nine,
And after one hour more 'twill be eleven,
And so from hour to hour we ripe and ripe,
And then from hour to hour we rot and rot;
And thereby hangs a tale.' When I did hear
The motley fool thus moral on the time
My lungs began to crow like chanticleer,
That fools should be so deep-contemplative,
And I did laugh sans intermission
An hour by his dial.

(II.vii.18–33)

'And thereby hangs a tale' indeed — the melancholy tale of acquiescence in the inexorable that the fool and the comedy he rules are bent
on subverting.

The third act of *As You Like It* furnishes another illuminating
instance of Shakespeare's assault on this temporal tunnel vision:

ROSALIND. I pray you, what is't o'clock?
ORLANDO.   You should ask me what time o' day. There's no clock
           in the forest.
ROSALIND. Then there is no true lover in the forest, else sighing
           every minute and groaning every hour would detect
           the lazy foot of time as well as a clock.
ORLANDO.   And why not the swift foot of time? Had not that
           been as proper?
ROSALIND. By no means, sir. Time travels in divers paces with
           divers persons. I'll tell you who time ambles withal,
           who time trots withal, who time gallops withal, and
           who he stands still withal.

(III.ii.293–304)

And Rosalind proceeds to do just that, conscripting a quartet of satirical examples to demolish the spurious objectivity of the clock and
demonstrate the relative nature of time, the ways in which our perception of its passing is warped by subjectivity and circumstance. All the
comedies engage in this conspiracy to unshackle the diversity of time in
order to unfold the diverse destinies we might pursue. 'There's no clock
in the forest' of Shakespearean comedy, because these plays are committed to liberating us from subjection to that temporal regime. This ambition is inseparable from making the space to cultivate difference and
letting language off the leash. Exactly how time and place and words
connive together in these plays, however, requires some teasing out.

Orlando's observation that 'There's no clock in the forest' takes us a
fair distance by itself, for it identifies the space of exile beyond the
state's jurisdiction with the suspension of conventional time and its
attendant obligations. Whether they are loitering in some *locus amoenus*
like Arden or stranded in Prospero's enchanted enclave, whether they
are sentenced to a life *en voyage* like Pericles or immured in the park of
the King of Navarre in *Love's Labour's Lost*, the protagonists of the
comedies are intent on *killing time*. These plays are full of figures whose
displacement from their habitat and daily routine has turned them into
footloose wanderers like Innogen in *Cymbeline*; urban strollers — prototypes of Walter Benjamin's *flâneur* — like Antipholus of Syracuse in
the mad marketplace of Ephesus; idlers in the interludes of romance
between or after battles, as in *Troilus and Cressida* and *Much Ado About
Nothing*; or loafers and languishers like most of the cast of *Twelfth Night*
and *As You Like It*, whose task is to spend their time filling in, hanging
about, kicking their heels and spinning things out, until the approach
of the denouement breaks the spell and lets them off the hook.

One of the deepest pleasures of Shakespearean comedy is its gift of
time and space we never thought we had. Small wonder that Celia concludes Act I of *As You Like It* with the couplet: 'Now go we in content, /
To liberty, and not to banishment' (I.iii.136–7). Punning, riddling and
repartee have a vital role to play in keeping this breathing space open by
treating our thraldom to clock-time with contempt. The verb that
neatly links such abuse of language and logic to the question of time
and place is *to extemporize*. The word means to improvise, to skip the
script and wing it, making it up as one goes along. Its root Latin meaning is to speak *out of time*, in a manner inappropriate to the moment,
which means talking out of turn, without respect for procedure and
decorum. At its most exuberant, Shakespearean comedy sometimes
seems to be simply a pretext for inspired extemporaneous nonsense and

pointless verbal virtuosity. And so it is, insofar as these impromptu digressions and pursuits of irrelevance are there to dilate the space of comedy and defer its surrender to the time that ticks outside the theatre. Procrastination is indeed the thief of time, and it's not hard to see why Hamlet exhibits his mastery of the art by assuming the mantle of Yorick and adopting the role of a jaundiced court jester, whose antic disposition and manic equivocations allow him to stall the tragedy and postpone the catastrophe.

'time's deformèd hand'

No comedy by Shakespeare is more tightly gripped by clock-time than *The Comedy of Errors*. The whole Plautine imbroglio evolves and unravels within the brief stay of execution granted Egeon by the Duke of Ephesus. The passing and lifting of the sentence mark the start and close of the play, so that everything that occurs in between is charged for the audience with a fatal urgency, to which most of the characters are oblivious. In this comedy, which observes the unities of time and place only to violate them, every second counts, and the hours are told at intervals throughout the play as time runs out and the confusions escalate:

> By this, I think, the dial point's at five.
> Anon, I'm sure, the Duke himself in person
> Comes this way to the melancholy vale,
> The place of death and sorry execution,
> Behind the ditches of the abbey here.
>   (V.i.119–23)

Nor is Egeon's deadline the only one to inflict anxiety on the persons of the play, which is packed with individuals bound to appointments by obligation, relationship or debt: 'Soon at five o'clock, / Please you,' the merchant of Ephesus promises Antipholus of Syracuse, 'I'll meet with you upon the mart, / And afterward consort you till bedtime' (I.ii.26–8); 'My wife is shrewish when I keep not hours' (III.i.2), complains Antipholus of Ephesus to his man Dromio; and the goldsmith Angelo is threatened with arrest by a second merchant for failing to pay off his debt by the agreed date: 'You know since Pentecost the sum is due', his creditor reminds him, 'Therefore make present satisfaction, / Or I'll attach you by this officer' (IV.i.1, 5–6).

The last quotation shows how inextricably the bonds of time and the bonds of debt are entwined; it's Egeon's inability to discharge on time the fine he owes the Duke for trespassing on Ephesian soil that will determine his death at the appointed hour. *The Comedy of Errors* exposes this conspiracy of time and debt expressly in order to undo it by logical legerdemain and sleight of speech:

> DROMIO S. No, no, the bell. 'Tis time that I were gone:
> It was two ere I left him, and now the clock strikes one.
> ADRIANA. The hours come back! That did I never hear.
> DROMIO S. O yes, if any hour meet a sergeant, a turns back for very fear.
> ADRIANA. As if time were in debt. How fondly dost thou reason!
> DROMIO S. Time is a very bankrupt, and owes more than he's worth to season.
> Nay, he's a thief, too. Have you not heard men say
> That time comes stealing on by night and day?
> If a be in debt and theft, and a sergeant in the way,
> Hath he not reason to turn back an hour in a day?
> (IV.ii.52–61)

Here the sly contention of the witty servant turns the tables on clock-time, reversing the power-relations that normally obtain between us and it. Commodified, linear time with a price-tag is the product of early modern capitalism at its most invasive and extortionate, colonizing human consciousness so completely as to redefine the landscape of the mind, moulding it into the mentality demanded by the market, upon whose site the exchanges of *The Comedy of Errors* take place. The usual assumption, which Dromio's fond reasoning rejects, is that we mortals stand in constant debt to time, paying back the borrowed, finite hours of our existence to our merciless creditor, until death arrives to terminate the agreement and leave us all square. If we do manage to filch a few extra hours for ourselves by putting things off and prevaricating, it's we who are indicted as the thieves of time. But, in this inspired piece of pointed nonsense, Dromio puts the plot on hold to switch the roles round and turn back the clock, creating the space to expand the future by throwing time into reverse.

Even though Dromio of Syracuse has the weight of the whole comedy behind him, he has his work cut out, for this is a world in which time appears to be omnipotent. When the lot of a man is compared to that of a woman, it may well seem that 'A man is master of his liberty', as Luciana observes; but in fact, as Luciana goes on to point out, 'Time is their mistress, and when they see time, / They'll go or come' (II.i.7–9). So pervasive does time's dominion seem, that it penetrates the body and inscribes itself, both literally and figuratively, in the flesh, as Dromio of Ephesus attests while chiding the man he mistakes for his master for not coming home to dine on time:

> The clock hath strucken twelve upon the bell;
> My mistress made it one upon my cheek [...]
> Methinks your maw, like mine, should be your clock,
> And strike you home without a messenger.
>   (I.ii.45–6, 66–7)

The experience of physical disfigurement by time is by no means reserved, however, for the play's drudges and dogsbodies. When Antipholus of Ephesus fails to recognize his own father, Egeus, in the final scene, the latter sighs:

> O, grief hath changed me since you saw me last,
> And careful hours with time's deformèd hand
> Have written strange defeatures in my face.
>   (V.i.298–300)

And when his voice rings no bell with this Antipholus either, Egeus lays the blame likewise on 'time's extremity', which has 'so cracked and splitted' his 'poor tongue' that he no longer sounds like himself.

It takes all the ingenuity at the comedy's command to undo the damage time habitually inflicts on its human subjects, but once again the twin servant from Syracuse seems up to it in this extemporized exchange with his master:

ANTIPHOLUS S.   Well, sir, learn to jest in good time. There's a time for all things.

DROMIO S.   I durst have denied that before you were so choleric.

ANTIPHOLUS S.   By what rule, sir?

DROMIO S.   Marry, sir, by a rule as plain as the plain bald pate of Father Time himself.

ANTIPHOLUS S.   Let's hear it.

DROMIO S.	There's no time for a man to recover his hair that grows bald by nature.
ANTIPHOLUS S.	May he not do it by fine and recovery?
DROMIO S.	Yes, to pay a fine for a periwig, and recover the lost hair of another man.
ANTIPHOLUS S.	Why is Time such a niggard of hair, being, as it is, so plentiful an excrement?
DROMIO S.	Because it is a blessing that he bestows on beasts, and what he hath scanted men in hair he hath given them in wit.
ANTIPHOLUS S.	Why, but there's many a man hath more hair than wit.
DROMIO S.	Not a man of those but he hath the wit to lose his hair.
ANTIPHOLUS S.	Why, thou didst conclude hairy men plain dealers, without wit.
DROMIO S.	The plainer dealer, the sooner lost. Yet he loseth it in a kind of jollity.
ANTIPHOLUS S.	For what reason?
DROMIO S.	For two, and sound ones too.
ANTIPHOLUS S.	Nay, not sound, I pray you.
DROMIO S.	Sure ones, then.
ANTIPHOLUS S.	Nay, not sure, in a thing falsing.
DROMIO S.	Certain ones, then.
ANTIPHOLUS S.	Name them.
DROMIO S.	The one, to save the money that he spends in tiring; the other, that at dinner they should not drop in his porridge.
ANTIPHOLUS S.	You would all this time have proved there is no time for all things.
DROMIO S.	Marry, and did, sir: namely, e'en no time to recover hair lost by nature.
ANTIPHOLUS S.	But your reason was not substantial, why there is no time to recover.
DROMIO S.	Thus I mend it: Time himself is bald, and therefore to the world's end will have bald followers.
ANTIPHOLUS S.	I knew 'twould be a bald conclusion.
	Enter [from the Phoenix] Adriana and Luciana
	But soft — who wafts us yonder?

                                                        (II.ii.64–112)

Dromio's cod logic — or rather, codpiece logic — wastes time wonderfully. In this absurd excursus, nominally devoted to proving that bald Father Time does indeed have us by the short and curlies, because 'there is no time for all things', servant and master swerve off into a double-act that romps with reason and frolics with language, as if they had all the time in the world — and in the meantime the plot can go and hang itself, until they are ready to return to it on cue with the question, 'But soft — who wafts us yonder?' There's a nice touch of poetic justice, too, in Time's being obliged to suffer the same sign of his ravages that he carves on the pates of male mortals — with a little help from venereal disease, as Dromio's bawdy equivocations suggest.

The Extemporal Vein

This unmotivated outbreak of smutty sophistry is a classic instance of the frivolous cross-talk and quibbling innuendo that are the hallmarks of Shakespearean comedy, the ridiculous discourse with which it feels most at home, and which Shakespeare will drop the plot for at the drop of a hat every chance he gets. Mining what Shakespeare's contemporary, the pamphleteer and novelist Thomas Nashe, called the 'extemporal vein' affords an expansive release from narrative consequence, an unbridled interlude in which words rebel against the tyranny of relevance and the clock's grim chronology, playing fast and loose with sound and sense for the sake of it. The pointlessness of such wordplay *is* the point. George Bernard Shaw was driven to distraction by Shakespeare's relentless verbal juggling, and long before him Samuel Johnson famously complained in his *Preface* to his edition of Shakespeare that the pun was the Bard's 'fatal Cleopatra', because he would cheerfully put a whole play in jeopardy for the sake of a play on words: 'A quibble is to Shakespeare what luminous vapours are to the traveller; he follows it at all adventures, it is sure to lead him out of his way and sure to engulf him in the mire.' And few critics since Shaw have had enough patience with the Bard's compulsive quibbling to pause and ask what its global role might be in the zany economy of Shakespearean comedy.

Most commentators, taking the flagrant incongruity of the comedies' quibbles at face value, slide over them to attend to the main business of the plays, whose advancement these *obiter dicta* have interrupted and delayed. But to neglect such passages is as misguided as it would be to reduce the meaning of a complex sentence to its main clause, as if the subordinate clauses and parentheses were not as vital to the articulation of its import as every punctuation mark. By their own secret alchemy, these giddy departures from sense and purpose accelerate the metamorphosis on which the comedy is intent. Relieved of the burden of pertinence, the discourse of the drama becomes buoyant and the dialogue is free to dance, however dark and painful the realities that lie beneath it may be. It's due in no small part to the subtle ministry of such absurdities that the miraculous finale of a play like *The Comedy of Errors* seems as inevitable as it is incredible. For the aimless deviations of the comedies from functional dialogue are ways of *spacing things out* that transform theatrical time, and thus our perception of these plays, by giving us glimpses of liberation from the constraints of the clock and the alienated life they entail.

Our enjoyment of these riffs of rampant banter stems not only from their transformation of our purchase on time, however. There's also an obscure erotic energy released when Shakespeare's language lights out on one of its sprees, especially when the spree engenders a spate of prurient puns. There's a clue to what's at stake here in a common synonym for speaking extempore or off the cuff: ad-libbing. *Ad lib* is short for *ad libitum*, the Latin phrase meaning 'according to one's pleasure' or 'as one pleases'. To talk out of turn with an unbridled tongue in Shakespearean comedy is to give time the slip through the slipperiness of language, and the pleasure of playing at one's own sweet will with words invariably involves a moment of libidinal delight.

Straying off the point and verbal diversions are as vital to the ends of Shakespearean comedy as physical disorientation and sanctioned transgression. *The Comedy of Errors* is, of course, about straying literally into taboo territory. After five fruitless years 'Roaming clean through the bounds of Asia' (I.i.133) in quest of his sons, Egeon crosses the forbidden border of Ephesus and incurs the penalty that triggers the action of the play and dictates its relentless tempo. The Antipholus who hails like his father from Syracuse is obliged to disguise his provenance from the Ephesians, lest his wealth be confiscated by this hostile nation as the price of his liberty. Having just disembarked in the harbour, he finds himself with time on his hands before he is due to dine and turn in for the night, and he resolves to take a stroll and do a little sightseeing:

Within this hour it will be dinner-time.
Till that I'll view the manners of the town,

Peruse the traders, gaze upon the buildings,
And then return and sleep within mine inn;
For with long travel I am stiff and weary.
                          (I.ii.11–15).

Unluckily for Antipholus, this is Shakespearean comedy, where to play
the *flâneur* is to play with fire. A few moments later, his intention takes
an ominous turn: 'I will go lose myself', he says, 'And wander up and
down to view the city' (I.ii.30–1). For losing himself in a deeper sense
is exactly what he will wind up doing, not least because that's what he
really wants to do, as his parting words intimate:

I to the world am like a drop of water
That in the ocean seeks another drop,
Who, falling there to find his fellow forth,
Unseen, inquisitive, confounds himself.
So I, to find a mother and a brother,
In quest of them, unhappy, lose myself.
                          (I.ii.35–40)

Instantly, the wrong Dromio twin appears, as if summoned by this
speech, and the carnival of errors arrives in earnest, bringing a train of
cruelty and treachery in its wake.

Dead Ringers

'This sympathizèd one day's error' (V.i.400), as Emilia calls it at the
end of the play, takes place, aptly enough, in the marketplace, the fluid
public space of traffic and exchange between the three abodes on its
boundary to which the characters resort. In this anarchic arena 'imaginary wiles' (IV.iii.10) run riot: identities fuse or dissolve, while secret,
adulterous desires and sadistic appetites can be satisfied with the ultimate impunity vouchsafed by comedy. Just as the doubling of meaning
and splitting of hairs through linguistic digression dilates time, so the
collision of duplicate twins through territorial transgression splits open
a rival reality in which alternative possibilities breed.

The identical twins device allows two different courses which the
same life might take to coexist for our contemplation. The rootless,
restless Antipholus of Syracuse endures a brief taste of domesticity as

the wedded master of a bustling household and pillar of the community, oppressively adored by a possessive wife:

> What, was I married to her in my dream?
> Or sleep I now, and think I hear all this?
> What error drives our eyes and ears amiss?
> Until I know this sure uncertainty,
> I'll entertain the offered fallacy.
>   (II.ii.185–9)

His Ephesian sibling suffers the converse fate of finding himself an alien
in his own domain: locked out of his home, betrayed by his wife and
servant, arrested for non-payment of debt, diagnosed as demonically
possessed, bound hand and foot, and left to languish 'in a dark and
dankish vault' (V.i.248). At the same time, his Syracusan alter ego fan-
tasizes in his stead about ditching his wife for her sister and openly voicing his forbidden feelings:

> She that doth call me husband, even my soul
> Doth for a wife abhor. But her fair sister,
> Possessed with such a gentle sovereign grace,
> Of such enchanting presence and discourse,
> Hath almost made me traitor to myself.
>   (III.ii.164–8)

Each Antipholus twin supplies a surrogate self for the other, allowing
both to metamorphose into someone 'much, much different from the
man he was' (V.i.46), as the bewildered Adriana puts it. This revelation
of the diverse lives latent within any life is magnified by its parodic replication in the ordeals undergone by the twin Dromios.

For Coleridge, the double helping of dead ringers served up by *The
Comedy of Errors* consigned the play, notwithstanding its title, to the
perfectly legitimate but inferior category of farce:

> A proper farce is mainly distinguished from comedy by the licence
> allowed, and even required, in the fable, in order to produce strange
> and laughable situations. The story need not be probable, it is
> enough that it is possible. A comedy would scarcely allow even the
> two Antipholuses; because, although there have been instances of
> almost indistinguishable likeness in two persons, yet these are mere
> individual accidents, *casus ludentis naturae* [accidents of playful

nature], and the *verum* [truth] will not excuse the *inverisimile* [lack of verisimilitude]. But farce dares add the two Dromios, and is justified in so doing by the laws of its end and constitution.

That farce propels the main action of the play and provides much of its pleasure can hardly be gainsaid. But Coleridge's contention that *The Comedy of Errors* doesn't qualify as a comedy, because it's premised on a mere freak of nature that stretches credulity to the limit, misses the point of the play's resort to wild improbability. Coleridge almost stumbles upon the point when he invokes the notion of a licence 'to produce strange and laughable situations', but it's his near-contemporary, the German critic Hermann Ulrici, who comes closest to grasping it in this passage from his account of the play in *Shakespeare's Dramatic Art*:

> the gradually increasing complication and perplexity, notwithstanding the obvious possibility of a mistake of identity, is not cleared up until the two pairs of twins are accidentally brought face to face. By all this the truth (not more comic than tragic) is most strikingly impressed upon us, that the knowledge and ignorance of man run so nicely into each other, that the boundary line almost disappears, and that the very convictions which we look upon as the most certain and best-grounded may, perhaps, turn out to be nothing but error or deception. [. . .] All are in a moment disturbed by a mere freak of nature, in violating the seemingly most unimportant of her laws, and in neglecting those differences of the outward man by which the senses distinguish individuals. So artificial is the constitution of our world, that the derangement of the minutest of its members is sufficient to throw the whole into disorder.

The rationally intolerable postulate of two sets of identical twins, far from placing the play beyond the pale of comedy in the ghetto of farce, is the mainspring of its success as the prototype of a new kind of comedy being pioneered by Shakespeare. As Ulrici recognizes, Shakespeare deliberately premises *The Comedy of Errors* on a ludicrous fluke in order to expose the strangeness and artificiality of 'the constitution of our world'. The play flouts credibility through a 'derangement' of that constitution to show how flimsy our fundamental assumptions really are, how little it takes to suggest that 'the very convictions which we look upon as the most certain and best-grounded' are in fact 'nothing but error or deception'.

The protagonists of *The Comedy of Errors* are trapped in an improbable predicament, which reveals the fragility of the identities and relationships they took for rock-solid realities, the arbitrariness of having become this person rather than another, dwelling here rather than elsewhere, married to this individual rather than to someone else or to no one. Nor does Shakespeare disguise the dark side of this revelation. On the contrary, he is at pains to dramatize the terror and the violence that can result from straying into a place where 'everyone knows us, and we know none' (III.ii.158), as Antipholus of Syracuse puts it. This being comedy, however, it's the empowering implications of the characters' estrangement from themselves and their world that prevail. The realization that people's identities and relationships are neither natural nor immutable also opens up the prospect of transforming them for the better. The conclusion of *The Comedy of Errors* in a poignant moment of reunion and restoration that embraces everyone gives us an inkling of what such a transformation might look and feel like: 'After so long grief, such festivity!' (V.i.409).

The Sorcery of the Stage

If we return now to 'Good Doctor Pinch' (IV.iv.48), that skeletal synecdoche of this seminal Shakespearean comedy, we can find both the destructive and the transformative impulses of the play etched in his portrait and his performance. Pinch is the living proof that everything Antipholus of Syracuse has heard about Ephesus is true:

> They say this town is full of cozenage,
> As nimble jugglers that deceive the eye,
> Dark-working sorcerers that change the mind,
> Soul-killing witches that deform the body,
> Disguisèd cheaters, prating mountebanks,
> And many suchlike libertines of sin.
> (I.ii.97–102)

As the archetypal Ephesian juggler and mountebank, Pinch is also, however, the incarnate quintessence of Shakespearean comedy, whose stock-in-trade is 'cozenage', the sorcery of the stage that deforms and disguises to change the mind by deceiving the eye. In return for remuneration, Pinch plays the part of 'conjurer' to perfection, staging a spectacle that makes his audience believe that his make-believe is real:

> I charge thee, Satan, housed within this man,
> To yield possession to my holy prayers,
> And to thy state of darkness hie thee straight:
> I conjure thee by all the saints in heaven.
>
> (IV.iv.55–8)

It's hard not to discern in the 'doting wizard' (IV.iv.59) a proleptic travesty of Prospero, especially when one bears in mind the other respects in which Shakespeare's first and his final experiment in comedy resemble each other. The comparison certainly accentuates the sinister aspect of Doctor Pinch, whom his victim, Antipholus of Ephesus, describes as 'a living dead man', a zombie-like creature 'with no face'. The description could serve as the devil's definition of an actor, whose fate is to animate the lifeless progeny of the imagination and thus possess no face of their own. In this respect Pinch's own fate might well give us pause, since it suggests a covert hostility on the part of the play towards its uncanny epitome:

> My master and his man are both broke loose,
> Beaten the maids a-row, and bound the Doctor,
> Whose beard they have singed off with brands of fire,
> And ever as it blazed they threw on him
> Great pails of puddled mire to quench the hair.
> My master preaches patience to him, and the while
> His man with scissors nicks him like a fool;
> And sure — unless you send some present help —
> Between them they will kill the conjurer.
>
> (V.i.170–8)

Nor, as we shall see, is Doctor Pinch the last *spiritus rector* of a Shakespearean comedy to be subjected to vindictive violence.

For the present, though, suffice it to say that the final key quality of *The Comedy of Errors* that Pinch dramatizes is its uneasiness about its own alchemical art, its capacity for disenchantment with its own powers of enchantment. It would clearly be perverse to inflate the importance of this hapless charlatan to the point where he eclipses the comedy in which he plays such a potent cameo role. The last word in

The Comedy of Errors is given, after all, to the reunited twin servants, who have been beaten black and blue throughout the play, but who voice in the play's concluding lines the egalitarian spirit that pervades Shakespearean comedy from the outset:

> DROMIO E. Methinks you are my glass and not my brother.
> I see by you I am a sweet-faced youth.
> Will you walk in to see their gossiping?
> DROMIO S. Not I, sir, you are my elder.
> DROMIO E. That's a question. How shall we try it?
> DROMIO S. We'll draw cuts for the senior. Till then, lead thou first.
> DROMIO E. Nay, then thus:
> We came into the world like brother and brother,
> And now let's go hand in hand, not one before another.
>
> (V.i.420–30)

Yet, as Hazlitt's account of the comedy testifies, even as this closing couplet resonates in the heart, the mind is drawn back to the egregious impostor Doctor Pinch as unerringly as the eye is drawn to the gargoyle squatting on the gutter of a cathedral. He lingers in the memory to remind us of the 'cozenage' in which *The Comedy of Errors* must collude in order to turn terror into delight.

2
'A kind of history': *The Taming of the Shrew*

'a character which most husbands ought to study'

In light of the last chapter's reflections on Doctor Pinch as an equivocal incarnation of Shakespearean comedy, it's no surprise that Hazlitt has Petruchio pegged as an infinitely more accomplished adept of the same spellbinding art: 'Everything flies before his will, like a conjuror's wand, and he only metamorphoses his wife's temper by metamorphosing her senses and all the objects she sees, at a word's speaking.' Insofar as the shrew he succeeds in taming is reviled as a woman possessed – a 'fiend of hell' (I.i.88), a 'hilding of a devilish spirit' (II.i.26) and 'the devil's dam' (III.iii.29) – Petruchio could clearly give Doctor Pinch some pointers on effective exorcism as well. But his superiority to the latter as a sorcerer only increases one's discomfiture at the fact that the metamorphoses he inflicts on Kate to bridle her will, turning sun into moon and man into woman through the wizardry of words, are the same kind as Shakespeare's theatre conjures up to bewitch its audience and make it believe in *The Taming of the Shrew*.

Not that Hazlitt experiences any such discomfiture. On the contrary, although he allows that 'The situation of poor Katherine, worn out by his incessant persecutions, becomes at last almost as pitiable as it is ludicrous', Hazlitt's overriding attitude to Petruchio's ploy is admiration, and he lauds him as a model of marital masculinity: 'It is a character which most husbands ought to study, unless perhaps the very audacity of Petruchio's attempt might alarm them more than his success would encourage them.' Denunciations of the ruses Petruchio employs to turn his bride 'from a wild Kate to a Kate / Conformable as other household Kates' (II.i. 271–2), and outrage at the sermon on submission Kate volunteers at the close of the play, are of more recent provenance, establishing

19

themselves as staples of critical opinion in the first flush of modern fem-
inism at the end of the nineteenth century. Seventy years on from
Hazlitt, in June 1888, George Bernard Shaw adopted the persona of an
appalled lady from Devon, with the blatantly unfeminine name of
Horatio Ribbonson, to write a letter to the *Pall Mall Gazette* protesting at the performance of *The Taming of the Shrew* he had just witnessed
in London. The production, wrote Shaw in this androgynous guise,
proved that the play 'is one vile insult to womanhood and manhood
from the first word to the last'. No 'civilized audience' should brook its
'brutality' or find 'the spectacle of a man cracking a heavy whip at
a starving woman' anything other than 'disgusting and unmanly'. And
the letter concludes: 'In the future I hope all men and women who
respect one another will boycott The Taming of the Shrew until it is
driven off the boards.'

   In fact, Shaw had more than a sneaking regard for the play and for
the anti-romantic personality of its proto-Shavian protagonist in particular. In a *Saturday Review* article of 6 November 1897, he praised it as
'a remarkable example of Shakespear's repeated attempts to make the
public accept realistic comedy. Petruchio is worth fifty Orlandos as
a human study.' Nevertheless, even without the camouflage of epistolary drag, Shaw wound up by concurring with the sentiments of his
Devonian alter ego a decade earlier:

> the last scene is altogether disgusting to modern sensibility. No man
> with any decency of feeling can sit it out in the company of a woman
> without being extremely ashamed of the lord-of-creation moral
> implied in the wager and the speech put into the woman's own
> mouth. Therefore the play, though still worthy of a complete and
> efficient representation, would need, even at that, some apology.

The only thing that requires an apology, however, is the myopia displayed by Shaw and the countless critics who have recycled these sentiments in the name of progressive gender politics down to this day.

   In sharp contrast to them, theatre and cinema audiences since Shaw's
time have found the play a continuous source of delight, exhibiting an
avid appetite for it that would have died off decades ago if it really boiled
down to a brutal, misogynistic fantasy. Far from becoming an obsolete
embarrassment, a politically incorrect period piece best left to gather
dust in some cranny of the canon, *The Taming of the Shrew* has spawned
a score of screen versions in North America and Europe (not to mention
spin-offs like the hit teen-flick *Ten Things I Hate About You*), making it

in this respect by far the most popular of all Shakespeare's comedies, rivalled only by the great tragedies in its cinematic appeal. Those who remain affronted by the patriarchal propaganda they impute to the play would doubtless construe that appeal as proof of the unbroken sway of patriarchy itself, which still has plenty of ideological work for *The Taming of the Shrew* to do. But it seems unlikely that a play preaching an outworn creed of sexual subjection would have lasted for so long, let alone exponentially increased its popularity, unless we are to ascribe to modern movie- and theatre-goers a slack-jawed gullibility which the enlightened denizens of academia have been spared. An alternative explanation may be that, having no theoretical or political axe to grind, most spectators of a screening or performance of *The Taming of the Shrew* are free to apprehend the subtler, more sophisticated vision inscribed in its poetic language and theatrical form.

Kicking against the Pricks

To take the measure of that vision and what's so remarkable about it, we need only glance back to Shakespeare's handling of the same thorny theme in *The Comedy of Errors*. In the first scene of Act II, Adriana, the unbiddable wife of Antipholus of Ephesus, finds herself on the receiving end of a lecture from her unwedded younger sister, Luciana, which is plainly a dry run for the more notorious one Kate delivers to her fellow fledgling brides to clinch her husband's wager and conclude *The Taming of the Shrew*. To Luciana's assertion that 'A man is master of his liberty', Adriana retorts, 'Why should their liberty than ours be more?' and triggers the following exchange:

> LUCIANA. Because their business still lies out o' door.
> ADRIANA. Look when I serve him so, he takes it ill.
> LUCIANA. O, know he is the bridle of your will.
> ADRIANA. There's none but asses will be bridled so.
> LUCIANA. Why, headstrong liberty is lashed with woe.
> There's nothing situate under heaven's eye
> But hath his bound in earth, in sea, in sky.
> The beasts, the fishes, and the wingèd fowls
> Are their males' subjects and at their controls.
> Man, more divine, the master of all these,
> Lord of the wide world and wild wat'ry seas,
> Indued with intellectual sense and souls,

> Of more pre-eminence than fish and fowls,
> Are masters to their females, and their lords.
> Then let your will attend on their accords.
> ADRIANA. This servitude makes you to keep unwed.
> LUCIANA. Not this, but troubles of the marriage bed.
> ADRIANA. But were you wedded, you would bear some sway.
> LUCIANA. Ere I learn love, I'll practise to obey.
> ADRIANA. How if your husband start some otherwhere?
> LUCIANA. Till he come home again, I would forbear.
> ADRIANA. Patience unmoved! No marvel though she pause:
> They can be meek that have no other cause.
> A wretched soul, bruised with adversity,
> We bid be quiet when we hear it cry.
> But were we burdened with like weight of pain,
> As much or more we should ourselves complain.
> So thou, that hast no unkind mate to grieve thee,
> With urging helpless patience would relieve me.
> But if thou live to see like right bereft,
> This fool-begged patience in thee will be left.
> LUCIANA. Well, I will marry one day, but to try.
>   (*CE*, II.i.7, 10–42)

Luciana seeks to muzzle her sister's mutinous spirit by reciting the authorized argument for the subordination of female to male within marriage: the wife's subjection to her husband's will is dictated by divine and natural law, and if she kicks against the pricks in vain pursuit of 'headstrong liberty', her inexorable reward will be to wind up 'lashed with woe'. However, even this incidental dialogue on the supremacy of doublet and hose can't let the patriarchal rationale advanced by Luciana pass unchallenged. Adriana is accorded the right to reply to her single sibling's reproof, and her contention that Luciana's posture of obedient forbearance is only possible because she knows nothing of the 'weight of pain' an 'unkind mate' can inflict is also couched in rhyming couplets, and thus has the same apodictic impact as her sister's rebuke. The line with which Luciana concludes the exchange – 'Well, I will marry one day, but to try' – certainly suggests that her elder sister's counter-argument from experience has struck home and shaken her confidence in the party line she has just been pushing.

So does Luciana's interjection in the encounter between Adriana and the Abbess in Act V, when the latter treats the former to another scolding for the shrewish jealousy she is tricked into confessing. Far from failing to berate her husband often enough for straying, Adriana assures the Abbess,

> It was the copy of our conference.
> In bed he slept not for my urging it.
> At board he fed not for my urging it.
> Alone, it was the subject of my theme.
> In company I often glancèd it.
> Still did I tell him it was vile and bad.
>
> ABBESS.   And thereof came it that the man was mad.
> The venom clamours of a jealous woman
> Poisons more deadly than a mad dog's tooth.
> It seems his sleeps were hindered by thy railing,
> And thereof comes it that his head is light.
> Thou sayst his meat was sauced with thy upbraidings.
> Unquiet meals make ill digestions.
> Thereof the raging fire of fever bred,
> And what's a fever but a fit of madness?
> Thou sayst his sports were hindered by thy brawls.
> Sweet recreation barred, what doth ensue
> But moody and dull melancholy,
> Kinsman to grim and comfortless despair,
> And at her heels a huge infectious troop
> Of pale distemperatures and foes to life?
> In food, in sport, and life-preserving rest
> To be disturbed would mad or man or beast.
> The consequence is, then, thy jealous fits
> Hath scared thy husband from the use of wits.
>
> LUCIANA. She never reprehended him but mildly
> When he demeaned himself rough, rude, and wildly.
> (*To Adriana*) Why bear you these rebukes, and
>   answer not?
>
> ADRIANA. She did betray me to my own reproof.
>
>   (*CE*, V.i.63–91)

There's no doubt that the dramatic deck is stacked at this point against Adriana, who meekly accepts the censure of the play's *dea ex machina* as her just deserts – although the audience knows that her chiding is by no means the main cause of her spouse's derangement. Yet here, too, where the spectators' satisfaction is staked on seeing a termagant trapped and chastened by a pious matriarch, Shakespeare makes room for a dissenting viewpoint. This time it's voiced by Luciana, who not only defends her sister's reproaches as mild and more than merited by her husband's behaviour, but also expresses her bewilderment at Adriana's unwonted reluctance to stick up for herself when she has every reason to.

In *The Taming of the Shrew* Shakespeare homes in on the topos of the scold bridled, which provides merely brief bouts of byplay in *The Comedy of Errors*, and exposes it to the full glare of his dramatic intelligence. Like the scenes from *The Comedy of Errors* just cited, whose chief aim is to curb Adriana's recalcitrance, *The Taming of the Shrew* takes its cue from patriarchal ideology at its most imperious. But it amplifies the muted voice of dissent in *The Comedy of Errors* to the point where it turns that ideology inside out, even as it seems to subscribe to it. To espouse such a reading of the play, however, is to incur the incredulity of critics wedded to the indictment of Shakespeare as 'the patriarchal Bard', whose bias towards his gender is nowhere more blatant than in the black farce of *The Taming of the Shrew*. Surely, such critics protest, nothing short of wilful misprision could rehabilitate such a flagrant vindication of crass misogyny: a play whose 'comedy' offers its audience the pleasure of watching a feisty, sharp-witted woman not merely brought to heel by a masterful male, who starves and brainwashes her into submission, but so completely subdued that she gladly enjoins those 'headstrong women' (V.ii.135), Bianca and the widow, to follow her example in her infamous final speech:

Thy husband is thy lord, thy life, thy keeper,
Thy head, thy sovereign, one that cares for thee,
And for thy maintenance commits his body
To painful labour both by sea and land,
To watch the night in storms, the day in cold,
Whilst thou liest warm at home, secure and safe,
And craves no other tribute at thy hands
But love, fair looks, and true obedience,
Too little payment for so great a debt.
Such duty as the subject owes the prince,
Even such a woman oweth to her husband,
And when she is froward, peevish, sullen, sour,
And not obedient to his honest will,
What is she but a foul contending rebel,
And graceless traitor to her loving lord?
I am ashamed that women are so simple

To offer war where they should kneel for peace,
Or seek for rule, supremacy, and sway
When they are bound to serve, love, and obey.
Why are our bodies soft, and weak, and smooth,
Unapt to toil and trouble in the world,
But that our soft conditions and our hearts
Should well agree with our external parts?
Come, come, you froward and unable worms,
My mind hath been as big as one of yours,
My heart as great, my reason haply more,
To bandy word for word and frown for frown;
But now I see our lances are but straws,
Our strength as weak, our weakness past compare,
That seeming to be most which we indeed least are,
Then vail your stomachs, for it is no boot,
And place your hands below your husband's foot,
In token of which duty, if he please,
My hand is ready, may it do him ease.

(V.ii.151–84)

For those who think this speech sums up the thrust of the play, the best that can be done to redeem it for the stage is to deliver it in a tone of voice and with an expression which suggest either that Kate is still in a stupefied trance or that she doesn't mean a word of it. But these strike me as strained, unconvincing strategies, for which the text provides no warrant whatsoever. If the play really *were* a repellent patriarchal parable, it would be braver and more honest to accept the fact and play it straight, allowing the dramatic interest to arise from its violent contradiction of the feminist precepts of the present. But the truth is that *The Taming of the Shrew* doesn't need to be saved from itself, because the comedy can't be collapsed into its final scene, let alone Kate's final speech, without distorting its import beyond recognition. If the play is stripped down to the main plot and flattened like a concertina into its finale, we might as well read the version in the Lambs' *Tales from Shakespeare*, which ends:

And to the wonder of all present, the reformed shrewish lady spoke as eloquently in praise of the wifelike duty of obedience, as she had practised it implicitly in a ready submission to Petruchio's will. And Katharine once more became famous in Padua, not as heretofore, as

Katharine the Shrew, but as Katharine the most obedient and
duteous wife in Padua.

But if we attend instead to the way *The Taming of the Shrew* as a whole
is shaped and worded by Shakespeare, it stands revealed as the much
more complex, exhilarating engagement with gender, love and marriage most people instinctively know it to be.

'let the world slide'

Consider, first of all, the implications of the Induction that frames, and
paves the way for, the play proper. In these two crucial scenes, which
moved Schlegel to remark in his *Lectures* that 'The prelude is still more
remarkable than the play itself', the drunken tinker Christopher Sly is
duped, on the whim of a passing nobleman, into believing himself to be
'a mighty Lord' (Ind.1.63) blessed with a beautiful wife, for whose
entertainment a travelling troupe of players put on the 'pleasant comedy' (Ind.2.126) of *The Taming of the Shrew*. The latter is thus a play
within a play, deliberately placed at one remove from us, and our
response to it is refracted through our understanding of the prelude that
precedes it. It's not just that there's a vast difference between viewing
the courtship of Kate and Petruchio as Shakespeare's *direct* dramatic
statement about the war between the sexes, and viewing it as a diversion
mounted to amuse a deluded tinker and his transvestite spouse as part of
an elaborate hoax. It's that *Shakespeare's* play is actually the comedy of
Kate and Petruchio, and of Bianca and her suitors, filtered through the
lens of the Induction, which we discount at our cost.

In case the point of the Induction escapes us, Sly spells it out at the
start in the phrase he will echo with a slight alteration as the players
begin their performance: 'let the world slide' (Ind.1.5). This alerts us
to the fact that we're about to enter a licensed realm, in which the dead
weight of custom and convention will be lifted from our shoulders,
whatever the play's title may connote to the contrary. Then we observe
an aristocrat hatch his somewhat sadistic wheeze of transmuting 'a poor
and loathsome beggar' (Ind.1.121) into a 'Thrice-noble lord' (Ind.2.115)
merely by dressing and treating him as one. That's all it takes, essentially,
to make a lord: the right kind of setting, the right sort of clothes and
accoutrements, and enough people to agree to regard you as one. No
sooner have we witnessed the brief nativity of a nobleman, than we are
invited to witness the fabrication of his no less noble spouse – 'a lady far

more beautiful / Than any woman in this waning age' (Ind.2.61-2) – without whom the metamorphosis of 'old Sly's son of Burton Heath' (Ind.2.17) would naturally be incomplete:

> Sirrah, go you to Barthol'mew, my page,
> And see him dressed in all suits like a lady.
> That done, conduct him to the drunkard's chamber,
> And call him 'madam', do him obeisance.
> Tell him from me, as he will win my love,
> He bear himself with honourable action
> Such as he hath observed in noble ladies
> Unto their lords by them accomplishèd.
> Such duty to the drunkard let him do
> With soft low tongue and lowly courtesy,
> And say 'What is't your honour will command
> Wherein your lady and your humble wife
> May show her duty and make known her love?'
> And then with kind embracements, tempting kisses,
> And with declining head into his bosom
> Bid him shed tears, as being overjoyed
> To see her noble lord restored to health,
> Who for this seven years hath esteemèd him
> No better than a poor and loathsome beggar. [. . .]
> I know the boy will well usurp the grace,
> Voice, gait, and action of a gentlewoman.
>   (Ind.1.103–21, 129–30)

When Bartholomew subsequently enters, 'dressed in all suits like a lady' and with a lady's entourage, to greet 'her' long-lost husband, the dialogue between them runs thus:

BARTHOLOMEW. How fares my noble lord?
SLY.   Marry, I fare well,
                 For here is cheer enough. Where is my wife?
BARTHOLOMEW. Here, noble lord. What is thy will with her?
SLY.   Are you my wife, and will not call me hus-
                     band?
                 My men should call me lord. I am your
                     goodman.
BARTHOLOMEW. My husband and my lord, my lord and husband;

>   I am your wife in all obedience.
> SLY.   I know it well.

(Ind.2.99–106)

The point hardly needs to be laboured, especially when it's been underscored by the advent of the players and their host's praise of their natural acting; and it would have needed even less labouring in
Shakespeare's time, when the theatrical impersonation of women by
boys was obligatory. Not only do we see the social roles of lord and
beggar, and the gender roles of husband and wife, exposed as cultural
constructions, as matters of mimicry, performance and perception,
before our eyes; we also behold a compressed burlesque, a proleptic
parody, of the theme of the play that follows the Induction: the artificial creation by a man of a meek, tractable wife, stereotypically endowed
'With soft low tongue and lowly courtesy'. Before the comedy's supposedly patriarchal plot is even under way, its predictable trajectory and
the system of sexual and social distinctions on which it depends are
unmasked as man-made and undermined.

'This representing of a play within a play (of which Shakespeare was
fond)', wrote Hazlitt in the *Examiner* of 18 May 1828, 'produces an
agreeable theatrical perspective – it is like painting a picture in a picture –
and intimates pointedly enough that all are but shadows, the pageants
of a dream.' But it intimates something far more pointed and profound
than that in *The Taming of the Shrew*, as the last lines of the Induction
advise us. Not sure what he should expect from the 'pleasant comedy'
that's about to commence, the transfigured tinker asks his brand-new
boy-bride, Bartholomew, 'Is not a comonty / A Christmas gambol, or
a tumbling trick?' To which Bartholomew replies, 'No, my good lord,
it is more pleasing stuff' – not the 'household stuff' (i.e., domestic
doings) that Sly would be pleased to watch, but 'a kind of history'.
'Well', says Sly, plainly none the wiser, 'we'll see't. Come, madam wife,
sit by my side / And let the world slip' (Ind.2.133–8). It's a marvellous
moment, not least because Shakespeare is offering us a rare, teasing definition of the art of comedy at the start of almost his first stab at it, and
in response to the query not of a cultivated gentleman, but of a 'simple
peasant' (Ind.1.133) from his own native Warwickshire. The task of
Shakespearean comedy is to let the world as it is slip and slide away to
reveal the way the world could be, if human affairs were subject to a less
divisive dispensation. In his editorial notes on *The Taming of the Shrew*,
Dr Johnson rightly harps on its 'diverting' quality, because creating a
diversion from normality, by releasing *us* from the cultural assumptions

to which the *characters* remain in thrall, is precisely what it's up to. Crude radical critics of the comedy see only stereotypes and hear only the voices of convention, oblivious to the play's conversion of androcentric farce into 'a kind of history', a history of life in Shakespeare's time that grants us glimpses of that life transformed.

Romance by Rote

Such critics have made it all too easy to overlook the play-within-the-play's scandalous affront to the norms of patriarchal class society in the Elizabethan era. Those norms are underwritten in word and deed by the protagonists of the subplot, whose romantic intrigue revolves around the wooing of Bianca, and flouted in the most contemptuous fashion by Petruchio's courtship and marriage of Kate, for which the subplot serves as a foil. 'Of this play', Johnson observes, 'the two plots are so well united that they can hardly be called two without injury to the art with which they are interwoven.' For a century, however, the subplot and the Induction were banished from the stage while Garrick's adaptation, *Catherine and Petruchio*, held sway in place of Shakespeare, and even when they are restored in performance today, they are commonly ignored by reviewers in favour of the main taming plot. But the subplot is as indispensable to a true understanding of *The Taming of the Shrew* as the Induction, because it's designed to give us the measure of the main plot's departure from the protocol that governed the conduct of the sexes in that period.

On his first glimpse of Bianca in Act I, Lucentio believes that he beholds, in stark contrast to her demonic sister, the perfect embodiment of the cardinal female virtues prescribed by the patriarchal dogma of the day: 'But in the other's silence do I see / Maid's mild behaviour and sobriety' (I.i.70–1). Just how mistaken his belief is becomes apparent as the play develops and Bianca morphs first into a very shrewd cookie in the game of courtship and finally into a full-grown shrew, a posture which is not the polar opposite but merely the flipside of mute, compliant maidenhood. Right at the outset, however, it's clear from the jaded rhetoric he uses that Lucentio is ensnared by a stale male fantasy rather than a flesh-and-blood woman. 'Tranio,' he cries to his manservant, 'I burn, I pine, I perish, Tranio':

> Tranio, I saw her coral lips to move,
> And with her breath she did perfume the air.
> Sacred and sweet was all I saw in her.
>
> (I.i.153, 172–4)

Lucentio is as constrained by clichés as his rivals for Bianca's hand, Gremio and Hortensio, who think and feel in platitudes, such as 'there's small choice in rotten apples' and 'He that runs fastest gets the ring' (I.i.133–4, 138–9). It's apt, therefore, that their competition for Baptista's younger daughter should exploit the charade of schooling her by rote in Latin and the lute in Act III, Scene i. For this scene, which has no known source and seems to be entirely Shakespeare's invention, underscores the subplot's conformity to the textbook roles and routines of heterosexual courtship. In so doing, it throws into relief Petruchio's utterly unorthodox mock-schooling of Kate.

At the same time, though, the cross-dressing of servant as master, whereby 'Tranio is changed into Lucentio' (I.i.235) simply by donning his clothes, conspires with the part of Petruchio's ploy that seeks to undo the distortions wrought by wealth and rank as well as by society's mating conventions. When Lucio goes so far as to say,

> Nor can we be distinguished by our faces
> For man or master. Then it follows thus:
> Thou shalt be master, Tranio, in my stead;
> Keep house, and port, and servants, as I should.
>   (I.i.198–201)

it's plain that the subplot, too, has learned the lesson of the Induction with a vengeance. When not even physiognomy can prise master and man apart, the criteria for establishing social superiority, and the rights to power and wealth that attend it, become perilously circumstantial, to say the least. If Tranio can pass on all counts – physically, linguistically and sartorially – for the son and heir of a grand Pisan merchant, then there are no innate or metaphysical grounds for regarding him as inferior to the latter or any less deserving of his advantages. Indeed, so contagious is the inference that begs to be drawn from Sly's mutation into 'a mighty lord' that it even infects the names of Petruchio's insolent servant, Grumio, and Bianca's wealthy old suitor, Gremio: the coincidence of consonants that makes them sound so alike insinuates that the disparity between their means and destinies hangs by a single vowel.

'a mad marriage'

When Petruchio arrives 'to wive it wealthily in Padua' (I.ii.72) and set the main plot in motion, his instinctive attraction, before he has even met her, to the woman Hortensio and Gremio decry as 'Katherine the curst' (I.ii.126, 127) marks the gulf that divides his mentality from theirs. A dab hand at ill-tempered railing himself, as Grumio knows to his cost, Petruchio is unfazed by the prospect of wooing 'an irksome brawling scold' (I.ii.186). On the contrary, he welcomes the idea of winning 'this wildcat' (I.ii.195), because a decorous, bourgeois trophy bride, a docile bimbo on a pedestal, is the last thing he wants for a wife. He wants a woman who's a match for him, and from the start he envisages their relationship precisely not as a brutal act of male domination, but as a passionate clash of equals resolved through mutual concession:

> I am as peremptory as she proud-minded,
> And where two raging fires meet together
> They do consume the thing that feeds their fury.
> Though little fire grows great with little wind,
> Yet extreme gusts will blow out fire and all.
> So I to her, and so she yields to me [. . .]
> (II.i.131–6)

That remarkable last line provides the key to the significance of the whirlwind courtship that then commences. In their first impromptu battle of wits, which they sustain for some hundred lines, the parity of Kate and Petruchio is proved by the ability of both to cap each other's quips and turn the cross-talk to their own advantage. This opening round of abusive badinage entails an exchange of mental and verbal prowess that enacts their equality theatrically through repartee. It also serves as a sustained euphemism for sexual congress, although there's nothing very euphemistic about the more graphic of the double entendres they feed each other, which leave little to the imagination:

> PETRUCHIO. Who knows not where a wasp does wear his sting?
> In his tail.
> KATHERINE. In his tongue.
> PETRUCHIO. Whose tongue?
> KATHERINE. Yours, if you talk of tales, and so farewell.
> PETRUCHIO. What, with my tongue in your tail? Nay, come again,
> Good Kate, I am a gentleman.
> (II.i.213–17)

Their erotic appetite for each other is immediate and intense, and Kate's virtuosity at coupling through quips makes her infinitely more admirable and desirable to Petruchio than she would have been, had she adopted the persona of the demure Petrarchan damsel like her sister.

Before we know it, the comedy has stolen our approval of a crazy relationship that sets itself against the world – 'If she and I be pleased, what's that to you?' (II.i.299) – and proceeds to play havoc with ortho-dox expectations and values. The hilarity of Petruchio's horseplay in the wedding scenes in Act III can't disguise the contempt his behaviour dis-plays for the sacrament of marriage, the church itself, and the shallow materialism of the mercantile culture the marriage is meant to cement. When this 'mad-brain rudesby' (III.ii.10) limps in late to his nuptials on a spavined nag, tricked out like a demented tramp in 'an old jerkin, a pair of old breeches thrice-turned' and 'a pair of boots that have been can-dle-cases' (III.ii.43–4), the point he's making to the good people of Padua couldn't be more obvious. But just in case they might miss it, he spells it out for them: 'To me she's married, not unto my clothes' (III.ii.117). And just in case *we* might underestimate its importance as well, Shakespeare has Tranio reinforce it again: 'He hath some meaning in his mad attire' (III.ii.124). Moreover, a few dozen lines earlier, on first hearing of Petruchio's appearance in his 'mad attire', Tranio had mused, 'Yet oftentimes he goes but mean-apparelled' (III.ii.71), which suggests that Petruchio's disdain for ostentatious consumerism is ingrained and has not been contrived merely for the occasion.

The sanctity of the marriage ceremony and those ordained to con-duct it receive equally short shrift from Petruchio, as the appalled Gremio reports:

>   when the priest
> Should ask if Katherine should be his wife,
> 'Ay, by Gog's woun's,' quoth he, and swore so loud
> That all amazed the priest let fall the book,
> And as he stooped again to take it up
> This mad-brained bridegroom took him such a cuff
> That down fell priest, and book, and book, and priest.
> 'Now take them up,' quoth he, 'if any list.'
> TRANIO.   What said the vicar when he rose again?
> GREMIO.   Trembled and shook, forwhy he stamped and swore
> As if the vicar meant to cozen him.
> But after many ceremonies done
> He calls for wine. 'A health,' quoth he, as if
> He had been aboard, carousing to his mates
> After a storm; quaffed off the muscatel

And threw the sops all in the sexton's face,
Having no other reason
But that his beard grew thin and hungerly
And seemed to ask him sops as he was drinking.
This done, he took the bride about the neck
And kissed her lips with such a clamorous smack
That at the parting all the church did echo,
And I seeing this came thence for very shame,
And after me, I know, the rout is coming.
Such a mad marriage never was before.
(III.iii.31–55)

A groom prepared to physically assault the priest and sexton is unlikely to tarry at his bride's behest for 'the bridal dinner' (III.iii.91), which is an opportunity for her community to parade its largesse and indulge its appetite, and consequently leaves Petruchio cold: 'Go to the feast, revel and domineer, / Carouse full measure to her maidenhead. / Be mad and merry, or go hang yourselves' (III.iii.96–8). Nor has his opinion of them in this regard changed by the end of the comedy: 'Nothing but sit, and sit, and eat, and eat' (V.ii.12), he sighs as he takes his place for the final feast.

Feigning to fend off an attempt to stop him sweeping his bride away from the church, Petruchio declares:

I will be master of what is mine own.
She is my goods, my chattels. She is my house,
My household-stuff, my field, my barn,
My horse, my ox, my ass, my anything,
And here she stands, touch her whoever dare.
(III.iii.101–5)

Only the most perverse critic, or the most obtuse production, could read or perform this speech as a straightforward male-chauvinist manifesto. If the savage mockery that fuels the wedding fiasco is not enough to make the penny drop, the speech's ludicrous literalism and hyperbole should be, especially when Petruchio delivers it as part of the chivalric melodrama he's just concocted out of sheer devilment:

Grumio,
Draw forth thy weapon, we are beset with thieves.
Rescue thy mistress if thou be a man.

Fear not, sweet wench. They shall not touch thee, Kate.
I'll buckler thee against a million.

(III.iii.107–11)

In a move which is perfectly consistent with his behaviour throughout the wedding sequence, Petruchio quotes Padua's conception of wives as commodities right back at it, but in parodically amplified and distorted terms.

At the same time, the play loses no opportunity to confirm that the relationship between the partners in this 'mad marriage' is taking another direction altogether. Identical diction and symmetrical phrasing surreptitiously ascribe to the couple a transposition of qualities that places them on a par with each other. 'Why, he's a devil, a devil, a very fiend', exclaims Gremio as he reels from Petruchio's demolition of the sacrament of matrimony; 'Why she's a devil, a devil, the devil's dam', echoes Tranio in response (III.iii.28–9). 'Mistress, what's your opinion of your sister?' inquires Lucentio of Bianca. 'That being mad herself she's madly mated', replies the latter, setting Gremio up to snap the couplet shut: 'I warrant him, Petruchio is Kated' (III.iii.115–17). The realization that 'Petruchio is Kated', that he has absorbed her demonized characteristics, adds a crucial dimension to our understanding of *The Taming of the Shrew*. Indeed, if Petruchio's servant, Curtis, is to be believed, 'he is more shrew than she' (IV.i.76) – a remark which reminds us that the term 'shrew' in Shakespeare's day could be used of either sex, though it was applied more often to women. In the act of mimicking Kate's shrewish disposition and mirroring it back to her as a grotesque caricature, Petruchio also enters her territory and surrenders his identity to hers, sharing her shrewishness even as he travesties it through exaggeration. 'He kills her in her own humour' (IV.i.161), observes Petruchio's servant, Peter: the ruse he employs to change and subdue her paradoxically unites them and seals their alliance against the consensus that surrounds them.

'to kill a wife with kindness'

The play uses the template of the taming game in order to subvert the assumptions on which the rules of that game rest. The abortive honeymoon of Act IV in Petruchio's country house puts this beyond question. Petruchio's systematic baffling of Kate proves to be anything but a boorish act of brainwashing. It's his invitation to his bride to partner him in the spoof of their predicament that he's been staging with such gusto since the moment he met her. The aim of the exercise is indeed 'to kill a wife with kindness' (IV.i.194) in the sense of destroying all semblance of the bourgeois wife Kate would otherwise become, and the humdrum marriage to which both of them would otherwise be condemned. To this end, Petruchio imposes on *both of them* a despotic regime of privations that derails their marriage at the outset, and prevents it from running the accustomed course, including consummation. Shakespeare takes pains to stress that the enterprise is a joint one and the denial of food, sleep and sexual satisfaction equally shared. 'Since of ourselves ourselves are choleric', declares Petruchio, expressly employing the first-person plural, 'we'll fast for company' (IV.i.160, 163); and what's more, he assures us, 'all is done in reverent care of her' (IV.i.190).

Kate is understandably bamboozled to begin with by her husband's treatment of her:

> Beggars that come unto my father's door
> Upon entreaty have a present alms,
> If not, elsewhere they meet with charity.
> But I, who never knew how to entreat,
> Am starved for meat, giddy for lack of sleep,
> With oaths kept waking and with brawling fed,
> And that which spites me more than all these wants,
> He does it under name of perfect love [. . .]
>
> (IV.iii.4–12)

But the sudden enlargement of her sympathy to accommodate the plight of beggars, especially on the part of a spoilt little rich girl, 'who never knew how to entreat' until now, makes the method in Petruchio's madness plain once again. The beliefs that buttress the marital dispensation can't be unravelled without unravelling the system of values that locks that dispensation into place.

That's why Petruchio makes such a meal of the scene with the tailor, at the end of which he hammers home the reversal of values heralded by his ragamuffin's outfit at the wedding:

> Well, come, my Kate. We will unto your father's
> Even in these honest, mean habiliments.
> Our purses shall be proud, our garments poor,
> For 'tis the mind that makes the body rich,
> And as the sun breaks through the darkest clouds,
> So honour peereth in the meanest habit.

What, is the jay more precious than the lark
Because his feathers are more beautiful?
Or is the adder better than the eel
Because his painted skin contents the eye?
O no, good Kate, neither art thou the worse
For this poor furniture and mean array.
                              (IV.iii.167–78)

By beggaring them both, for a time, of food, sleep, fine clothes and sexual pleasure, Petruchio's ruse exposes them to the levelling perspective
opened by the beggar Sly in his borrowed robes, and widened by Grumio
right at the start of Act IV: 'but thou know'st, winter tames man,
woman, and beast, for it hath tamed my old master, and my new mistress,
and myself' (IV.i.19–22). A play whose vision is expansive enough to discount the culturally imposed hierarchies dividing not only master, mistress and servant, but also men, women and animals, has little trouble
mounting an even-handed critique of the roles of husband and wife.

Thus, when the taming game of Act IV culminates in Kate's agreement to contradict the evidence of her senses, calling the day the night
and an elderly man a 'Young budding virgin' (IV.vi.38) at Petruchio's
whim, the thrust of the whole parodic pantomime should be apparent
even to the play's most hostile spectators. Petruchio has been acting
out before Kate a cartoon version of the irrational domestic tyranny
that both husbands and wives are prone to display: the perversity and
absurdity of either party's being subjected to the diktats of the other.
This comedy knows that male shrews and female shrews are mirror-
images of each other, the identical twin offspring of an institution that
designates the woman the chattel of the male. It cannot, nor does it
wish to, dramatize a portrait of emancipated marital bliss beyond patriarchy. But what it can and does do is burlesque the codes that twist couples into Herods and harridans, and dramatize the potential of women
and men to live together on terms undisfigured by domination.

Whether critics recognize it or not, Kate certainly understands and
accepts Petruchio's invitation in this final scene of Act IV to collude in
his burlesque of the marital bind with which they must reach some
accommodation, since their world offers no other form of liaison. So
much is clear from the tone of her first wry capitulation to his ridiculous
reasoning:

Then God be blessed, it is the blessèd sun,
But sun it is not when you say it is not,

And the moon changes even as your mind.
What you will have it named, even that it is,
And so it shall be still for Katherine.

                    (IV.vi.19–23)

But her knowing concurrence in his *reductio ad absurdum* of male
supremacy is put beyond question when she picks up her cue and conspires with Petruchio in public to tease Vincentio:

Pardon, old father, my mistaking eyes
That have been so bedazzled with the sun
That everything I look on seemeth green.
Now I perceive thou art a reverend father.
Pardon, I pray thee, for my mad mistaking.

                    (IV.vi.46–50)

There's no mistaking that private joke about being 'bedazzled with
the sun', which signals Kate's acknowledgement that they are now a
double-act. Nor can there be any doubt about the intimate tenderness
of the relationship to which they have won through, not by bowing to
convention but by flouting it together:

KATHERINE. Husband, let's follow to see the end of this ado.
PETRUCHIO. First kiss me, Kate, and we will.
KATHERINE. What, in the midst of the street?
PETRUCHIO. What, art thou ashamed of me?
KATHERINE. No, sir, God forbid; but ashamed to kiss.
PETRUCHIO. Why then, let's home again. Come sirrah, let's away.
KATHERINE. Nay, I will give thee a kiss. Now pray thee love, stay.
                  They kiss.
PETRUCHIO. Is not this well? Come, my sweet Kate.
                  Better once than never, for never too late.

                    (V.i.132–41)

Which brings us back to Kate's infamous final speech commending
wifely submission, a speech whose significance should be less easy to
misconstrue in the light of all that has led up to it. Her protracted
rebuke is directed specifically, of course, at Bianca and the widow, who
have already swapped compliance for defiance, reinforcing the norm of
male domination by merely reversing it. It's also a covert act of solidarity
with Petruchio, designed to ensure that he wins the wager and confounds

the presumptuous gibes of his fellow grooms. But it is, above all, a *tour de force* of ironic iteration in the same extravagant vein as Petruchio's travesty of courtship and marriage, and it enlists the same mimetic strategy. Kate's speech is emphatically not ironic, however, in the sense that the character doesn't really mean what she's saying, or in fact thinks the very opposite, and thus remains an untamed shrew at heart after all. To take that tack, as so many well-meaning productions have done, is as misguided as to read it straight, as an embarrassing testimony to Shakespeare's male chauvinism. The irony here is of an incomparably subtler kind, which can keep two or more conflicting attitudes continuously in play.

In the context of the final scene and the comedy as a whole, Kate's hyperbolic homily on behalf of husbands is a performed citation, a sustained cultural quotation, which opens a space between speaker and speech, creating a slippage between them. The extremity and excess of its argument, and its incongruity with the character of its proponent, place the whole patriarchal apologia in italics as a scripted construction of its world and time rather than Kate's spontaneous subscription to an eternal verity. Although the case Kate makes for male supremacy and female subservience is thereby opened to scrutiny and sceptical critique, it's not by any means negated, though. On the contrary, it's hard to think of a more eloquent testimony to its pervasive, persuasive power in the dramatic literature of the day. But that's precisely what makes Kate's speech so extraordinary. Even as it crowns the comedy's sly undoing of the discourse of male domination, it demonstrates how deeply entrenched that discourse remains in the minds and hearts of women as well as men. Like the entire play it brings to a close, which wrests the prospect of liberation from a parable of oppression, it leaves us under no illusion that a world fit for Kate and Petruchio still lies well beyond their reach.

3
Dancing Leviathans: *The Two Gentlemen of Verona*

The Curse of Shakespeare Criticism

The fact that *The Two Gentlemen of Verona* stars twice as many gentlemen of Verona as *The Taming of the Shrew* has not, alas, led to its being valued twice as highly as the comedy through which their fellow citizen Petruchio romps so successfully. On the contrary, none of Shakespeare's comedies has had a rougher ride from the critics, who have found little to praise and a lot to fault in it from the eighteenth century down to the present. Its stage history over the same span of time, and particularly in the last century, when it was rarely produced and even more rarely to anything like acclaim, has nothing much to write home about either – apart from the sole feature that has secured the play a nook in audiences' affections, the broad comic double-act of motley and mutt performed by Launce and the incontinent Crab. Not even Shaw could resist them: 'The scenes between Launce and his dog brought out the latent silliness and childishness of the audience as Shakespear's clowning scenes always do', he wrote of Augustin Daly's production of 1895: 'I laugh at them like a yokel myself.'

Two Gentlemen has, to be sure, received due credit for being a seed-bed of characters, motifs and devices destined to blossom in the mature Elizabethan comedies a few years later, and to bloom afresh in the problem plays and romances that succeeded them. The play is Shakespeare's first crack at the kind of romantic comedy that he was to make his own, and that he perfected in *As You Like It* and *Twelfth Night*. Julia, the first of his witty transvestite heroines, is the plucky forerunner of Portia, Rosalind, Viola and Innogen, all of whom purloin the garb of the opposite sex to serve, win or reclaim the man they love; and the name she assumes, Sebastian, is the name Shakespeare adopts for Viola's identical twin brother in *Twelfth Night*. Julia's faithless beau, Proteus, is likewise the blatant prototype of those equally shallow cads, Claudio in *Much Ado About Nothing* and Bertram in *All's Well That Ends Well*. The competing claims of masculine friendship and heterosexual courtship, between which Proteus is torn, crop up again as a thorny dilemma in *The Merchant of Venice*, where Bassanio fails Portia's love-test by surrendering her ring at Antonio's behest; indeed, the ring motif itself in *The Merchant* owes as much to *Two Gentlemen* as the alliance of mistress and maid forged by Portia and Nerissa to poke fun at men, as Julia's and Lucetta's review of Julia's suitors in Act I, Scene ii makes plain. And the 'shadowy desert, unfrequented woods' (V.iv.2) to which Valentine repairs when exiled from Silvia in Milan, and where he dwells as the leader of a band of outlaws in the mould of Robin Hood, foreshadow not only the woods to which the lovers flee in *A Midsummer Night's Dream*, but also the Forest of Arden, where the banished Duke Senior and his loyal lords 'live like the old Robin Hood of England [. . .] and fleet the time carelessly, as they did in the golden world' (*AYLI*, I.i.110–13).

Nor is the special sylvan space or 'green world' of transformation, recognition and reunion the least or the last of the features for which Shakespearean comedy is beholden to the ingenuity of *The Two Gentlemen of Verona*. The task of tracing them all, in all their intricacy, would require a chapter to itself. That thought alone ought to give the play's detractors pause, and prompt them to wonder whether there might be more than meets the eye to a comedy that Shakespeare himself kept drawing on throughout his theatrical career. But such considerations have been eclipsed by the consensus that the play is the work of a tyro of the dramatic craft, whose immaturity is immediately apparent in the glaring gaffes and inconsistencies with which the text is riddled.

Dr Johnson was among the first to be irked by the comedy's cavalier, illogical geography. It's not just that 'the author conveys his heroes by sea from one inland town to another in the same country', as Johnson points out in his editorial notes; it's that we're never certain whether the main action is taking place in Verona, Milan or Padua, so that Shakespeare 'has by mistaking places left his scenery inextricable'. In Johnson's opinion, 'The reason of all this confusion seems to be that he took his story from a novel which he sometimes followed and sometimes forsook, sometimes remembered and sometimes forgot.' Subsequent exasperated editors have piled a score of further alleged blunders on top of Shakespeare's loose sense of location. Thus, to cite only the more blatant, Julia starts the play possessed of a father who inexplicably disappears in Act II; Proteus uses Valentine's servant, Speed, to deliver a letter to Julia in the opening scene, evidently forgetting that he has a servant of his own in the shape of Launce; Sir Eglamour is named as one of Julia's suitors in Act I, Scene ii, but then turns in acts IV and V into the quite different man who aids Silvia in her escape from her father's court; in Act III, Scene i, Proteus and Launce enter hot on the heels of the departing Duke, who has just banished Valentine, and proceed to discuss the banishment and its aftermath with the latter as though several hours had intervened; later in the same scene, Launce tells us he thinks his master is 'a kind of knave' (III.i.261), though there's no way he could have learned of Proteus's treachery – one of several examples of characters displaying an inexplicable knowledge or foreknowledge of events; in Act IV, Scene iv, Julia, masquerading as Proteus's page, gives a letter to Silvia which she instantly takes back because it's the wrong one, and the nature of this letter, let alone the point of the mistake, is never explained; and this conundrum is compounded by its replication in the final scene of the play (V.iv), where Julia mistakenly gives Proteus the ring he gave her when they parted instead of the one he charged her to deliver to Silvia, which she hastily produces too late to forestall (if not expressly to precipitate) the ensuing revelations.

The most egregious instance of the comedy's ineptitude, however, is commonly agreed to occur immediately before this confusing incident. Not content with forgiving Proteus completely for his betrayal of their friendship and brutal assault on Silvia, Valentine reaffirms the supremacy of that bond by handing his beloved over to the man he's just stopped from raping her. Small wonder that George Eliot, after rereading the play in the spring of 1855, wrote : '[it] disgusted me more than ever in the final scene where Valentine, on Proteus's mere begging pardon when he has no longer any hope of gaining his ends, says: "All that was mine in Silvia I give thee"! – Silvia standing by.' Even Charles and Mary Lamb, whose *Tales from Shakespeare* normally proves so adept at smoothing over or sidestepping the less palatable episodes in the plays, were too affronted by Valentine's 'sudden flight of heroism' to let it pass without reproof:

> Julia, who was standing beside her master as a page, hearing this strange offer, and fearing Proteus would not be able with this new-found virtue to refuse Silvia, fainted, and they were all employed in recovering her: else would Silvia have been offended at being thus made over to Proteus, though she could scarcely think that Valentine would long persevere in this overstrained and too generous act of friendship.

But the contention that *The Two Gentlemen of Verona* is fatally flawed by the ham-fisted incompetence of a prentice hand doesn't stand up to scrutiny. Shakespearean drama in general, and Shakespearean comedy and romance in particular, are notoriously prone to temporal and topographical anomalies, absurd improbabilities, sheer impossibilities, flat contradictions, attacks of amnesia, and wildly incongruous conclusions. Why *Two Gentlemen* should be singled out as unduly hobbled by violations of verisimilitude and consistency that are tolerated in *Measure for Measure* or *The Winter's Tale* is by no means clear. More importantly, even if one were to grant that this play furnishes more instances of such violations than most of the others, it would be beside the point to take it to task for them. Shakespeare's comedies invite us to abandon expectations of verisimilitude and consistency at the theatre door, and enter a universe in which rationality and the laws of likelihood can be dispensed with at will or suspended altogether.

Realism is the curse of Shakespeare criticism, which is never more misguided than when it mistakes for haste, error or negligence in the comedies what are actually cues to switch our imaginations to another frequency. If realism is the frame of mind that keeps us in line with the status quo, that reconciles us to the reality of the way things are, then Shakespearean comedy constitutes a sustained assault on that tyrannous mentality in the name of how things should be. Shakespeare, in Coleridge's wonderful phrase, 'shakes off the iron bondage of space and time' in order to arouse in us 'faculties which have no relation to time or place' as they are usually perceived. The confusions of place to which Johnson took exception in *Two Gentlemen*, and which he ascribed to the author's carelessness, are symptoms of this unshackling, as are the liberties the same play takes in telescoping time, in making some characters suddenly privy to the playwright's perspective, in merging others under the same name, and in obliging its protagonists to speak and act unpredictably or implausibly.

Just like *The Taming of the Shrew*, *The Two Gentlemen of Verona* seeks to 'let the world slide' into the dream-logic of a dramatist struck by the strangeness of human affairs in their present arrangement. The cracks in the play's credibility are not the signs of its immaturity, but the measure of its alienation from an alienated world. When characters and events fail to make sense in a familiar way, it's time to wonder if they make sense in an unfamiliar way, which owes nothing to accepted attitudes and forms of conduct and everything to dissatisfaction with the current constitution of reality. Reconsidered from this angle, *The Two Gentlemen of Verona* reveals itself to be not, as Hazlitt for once mistakenly thought, 'little more than the first outlines of a comedy loosely sketched in', but an accomplished comedy whose agenda exerts its own peculiar fascination.

'metamorphosed with a mistress'

Top of that agenda is excoriating the outmoded code of courtship and the equally obsolete cult of masculine friendship, in which the eponymous protagonists of the play are incarcerated to everybody's cost. As Hermann Ulrici observed a century and a half ago in *Shakespeare's Dramatic Art*, although love is viewed in *Two Gentlemen* as 'the foundation and ruling spring of life', it is marred by 'instability and rottenness' and exposed in all its forms as 'weak, foolish, perverse, and self-indulgent'. Before the play is barely under way, the love-votary Proteus is infected by the love-heretic Valentine's image of love as an 'eating canker', which blasts in the bud 'all the fair effects of future hopes' (I.i.43, 50). In fact, the blighting of Proteus's life seems to be already well advanced:

> Thou, Julia, thou hast metamorphosed me,
> Made me neglect my studies, lose my time,
> War with good counsel, set the world at naught;
> Made wit with musing weak, heart sick with thought.
> (I.i.66–9)

By the start of the second act, the virus has Valentine at its mercy as well. Now that he, too, is 'metamorphosed with a mistress' (II.i.29), it's his turn to be the butt of the ridicule Speed directed at Proteus in Act I, when he derided his precious Julia as a mere 'laced mutton' (I.i.95), a common tart. Valentine's behaviour is debunked by Speed as a collage of clichés, a threadbare repertoire of third-hand postures, which are about as convincing as his bosom buddy's:

> you have learned, like Sir Proteus, to wreathe your arms, like a
> malcontent; to relish a love-song, like a robin redbreast; to walk
> alone, like one that had the pestilence; to sigh, like a schoolboy
> that had lost his ABC; to weep, like a young wench that had buried
> her grandam; to fast, like one that takes diet; to watch, like one
> that fears robbing; to speak puling, like a beggar at Hallowmas.
> (II.i.18–24)

Silvia's 'exquisite' beauty is dismissed by Speed first as the 'painted' product of cosmetic deceit (II.i.51–7), and then, in a startling twist of thought, as deformity. 'How long hath she been deformed?' asks the puzzled Valentine. 'Ever since you loved her', retorts Speed. 'I have loved her ever since I saw her,' counters Valentine, 'and still I see her beautiful.' 'If you love her', Speed replies, displaying a wisdom well beyond Valentine's reach, 'you cannot see her' (II.i.61–5); Speed's paradoxical point being that love fostered by sight alone isn't love at all, but an effect of visual distortion, an effect of the disfigurement inflicted on the beloved's physiognomy by the lover's infatuated eye.

Just how remote Valentine is from spontaneity and the command of his emotions becomes apparent in the bizarre conclusion of this scene, which Speed welcomes in an aside as an 'excellent motion' (II.i.89) or puppet-play. The star of this side-show, the 'exceeding puppet' (II.i.89) Valentine, gives Silvia the love-letter he has written at her request to help her woo a 'secret, nameless friend' (II.i.98), obtusely oblivious to the fact that the letter is meant for him and Silvia has been pulling his strings. The jest, as Speed quips in another aside, is as 'invisible/As a nose on a man's face or a weathercock on a steeple' (II.i.127–8):

> O excellent device! Was there ever heard a better? –
> That my master, being scribe, to himself should write the letter.
>   (II.i.131–2)

But it takes another two dozen lines of patient explanation by Speed before the truth dawns on his curiously passive, almost somnambulant master, who seems to be acting and reacting on automatic pilot. Valentine gives the same hypnotized impression in Act III, Scene i, when the Duke locks him into a clockwork cross-examination and he sleepwalks into divulging his imminent elopement with Silvia and the means by which he aims to effect it. It may be that a similar mesmerized state of mind supervenes at the denouement, when Valentine exclaims aside, 'How like a dream is this I see and hear!' (V.iv.26), shortly before obeying the inane imperative to sacrifice Silvia to a perfidious friendship. What all three moments unquestionably have in common is a sense of the character's detachment from the lines he's mouthing and the motions he's going through.

Proteus fares no better after Speed has finished twitting him for his amorous affectations in Act II, when Launce takes over the task of cutting his master down to size in our eyes. The brief valedictory interlude of Scene ii, in which Proteus and Julia part after exchanging rings as a pledge of fidelity, is immediately robbed of its poignancy by the show-stealing entrance of the lachrymose Launce and his impassive pooch.

Launce's virtuoso monologue on his tearful farewell to his family, during which 'this cruel-hearted cur [. . .] sheds not a tear nor speaks a word' (II.iii.9, 30–1), provides a comic prose paraphrase of the more elevated leave-taking we've just witnessed. It punctures the rarefied mood of refined anguish evoked by Proteus and Julia with a sharp reminder of a parallel plebeian realm in which feet smell and breath stinks. Julia's 'tide of tears', upon which Proteus lamely puns (II.ii.14–15), is matched in volume by 'the unkindest tide' that feeds Launce's hyperbolic quibbling on the same word (II.iii.36–53); the exact verbal echo, amplified by reiteration, underscores the symmetry of the two scenes and Shakespeare's parodic design. That design includes Crab's unwitting, mute mimicry of Julia's speechless exit, which is odd enough for Proteus to harp upon as he strives to rationalize it: 'What, gone without a word?/Ay, so true love should do. It cannot speak' (II.ii.16–17); and again, in an aside as he exits himself: 'Alas, this parting strikes poor lovers dumb' (II.ii.21). The subliminal conflation of Julia with a truly dumb creature, who has, as Launce laments, 'no more pity in him than a dog' (II.iii.10–11), goes beyond satirical belittlement to hint at more troubling emotions secreted by Julia's silence.

Launce returns to deflating the pretensions of his social superiors in Act III, Scene i. Valentine's metaphysical monologue on the dissolution of identity entailed by his banishment from Silvia – 'To die is to be banished from myself, / And Silvia is my self' (III.i.171–2) – falls flat on its face when Launce insists on taking Valentine's depiction of himself as 'nothing' literally (III.i.198–204), declaring him 'vanished' instead of 'banished' (III.i.215, 216). Having disposed of that posture, he colludes with Speed to debunk his betters' obsession with hidden letters, Valentine's rash disclosure of his secret love to Proteus, and the high-flown habit of blazoning the beloved's virtues (III.i.260–371). For a moment, Julia and Silvia are toppled from their Petrarchan pedestals by Launce's earthbound *inamorata*, whose sour breath, toothlessness and freedom with her favours are outweighed in the end by her having 'more wealth than faults' (III.i.344).

Not the least part of Launce's task in *Two Gentlemen* is to make sure we don't forget that there's a world elsewhere, the workaday world inhabited by most of Shakespeare's audience, to which the romantic fantasies of those perched at the top of the pecking order are alien. Indeed, Launce's *pièce de résistance* in Act IV, which Hazlitt hailed as 'a perfect treat in the way of farcical drollery and invention', scarcely manages to mask the hostility of *hoi polloi* towards the class they were born to serve and obey. When Crab, as Launce recounts it, 'thrusts me himself into the

company of three or four gentleman-like dogs under the Duke's table'
(IV.iv.16–18) to relieve himself and foul the whole chamber with the
stench of dog-piss, his covert mission is to act as a canine surrogate for his
master, as the latter's tell-tale use of the ethical dative ('thrusts *me* himself') intimates. That Launce takes the blame for Crab's transgression –
''twas I did the thing you wot of' (IV.iv.26–7) – puts the surrogacy
beyond question, and paves the way for the outrageous image of human
defilement in which the monologue culminates: 'Nay, I remember', says
Launce to Crab, 'the trick you served me when I took my leave of
Madam Silvia. Did not I bid thee still mark me, and do as I do? When
didst thou see me heave up my leg and make water against a gentlewoman's farthingale?' (IV.iv.33–7). Not even Silvia, 'Holy, fair, and
wise', who 'excels each mortal thing / Upon the dull earth dwelling'
(IV.ii.40, 50–1), is safe from the denigration the clown deals out to the
genteel in the guise of a reproof of his errant pet.

  It's not hard to imagine the frisson of scandalized delight that would
have passed through the play's original audience at the thought of a servant pissing on a lady's dress. Nor is it difficult to understand why
Alexander Pope's editorial pen, anxious to preserve Augustan standards
of decorum, itched to delete such scenes, which he regarded as 'com-
pos'd of the lowest and most trifling conceits, to be accounted for only
from the gross taste of the age he liv'd in; *Populo ut placerent*'. Please
the people they undoubtedly did, and often for more subversive reasons
than Pope realized, as the unruly bladders of Launce and Crab demonstrate. But even Johnson couldn't share Pope's desperate hope that
some of them had been scripted by an inferior hand or 'interpolated by
the players', because they were so palpably integral to the work's concerted vision: 'When I read this play,' Johnson confessed, 'I cannot but
think that I discover both in the serious and ludicrous scenes the language and sentiments of Shakespeare.'

Letters, Secrets and Illiterate Loiterers

The burden of exposing the ludicrousness of their masters' love-lives
doesn't rest solely on the shoulders of Launce and Speed. As members
of the class that commands, Silvia and Julia may be fair game for the
derogatory impertinence of servants, but, as women subject to the sway
of the dominant gender, they can be equally scathing about their suitors' self-delusions and reliance on jaded rhetoric. In the opening act,
Julia's instinctive first response to Proteus's love-letter is to tear it to
shreds, saying, 'This bauble shall not henceforth trouble me. / Here is

a coil with protestation' (I.ii.99–100). And when Valentine tells Silvia that Proteus 'Had come along with me, but that his mistress / Did hold his eyes locked in her crystal looks', Silvia refuses to take him figuratively, teasing him for resorting to such a trite metaphor: 'Nay, then he should be blind, and being blind / How could he see his way to seek out you?' (II.iv.86–7, 91–2). Moreover, just as Launce's unshakeable loyalty to Crab and, indeed, his affable camaraderie with Speed, throw the brittleness of the two gentlemen's bond into relief, so the initiative and resourcefulness in love displayed by Julia and Silvia, and the respect and even tenderness each shows for the other woman's feelings, highlight the conspicuous shortage of these qualities in their male counterparts for most of the comedy.

That's not to say, however, that Julia and Silvia are free of the assumptions that fetter their lovers' perception of themselves and the women they woo; on the contrary, their ironic intelligence and capacity for disenchantment make the stress inflicted by their powerless plight all the more acute. It's through the women that Shakespeare dramatizes the emotional cost of being steered by discourses of desire over which one has no final control. The high price they pay for living under such unsolicited pressure is most evident in the second scene of Act I, in which Julia's contemptuous shredding of Proteus's missive precipitates a protracted schizoid fit. It's hard to think how else one might describe the way she splits herself into two antagonistic selves, torn between a violent rejection of the suit inscribed in the epistle and an equally violent compulsion to punish herself by proxy for ripping Proteus's deathless prose to bits:

Look, here is writ 'Kind Julia' – unkind Julia,
As in revenge of thy ingratitude
I throw thy name against the bruising stones,
Trampling contemptuously on thy disdain.
And here is writ 'Love-wounded Proteus'.
Poor wounded name, my bosom as a bed
Shall lodge thee till thy wound be throughly healed;
And thus I search it with a sovereign kiss.
But twice or thrice was 'Proteus' written down.
Be calm, good wind, blow not a word away
Till I have found each letter in the letter
Except mine own name. That, some whirlwind bear
Unto a ragged, fearful, hanging rock
And throw it thence into the raging sea.
                                        (I.ii.110–23)

Her engrossed animation of the personified names and the totemic power they assume in her imagination are almost as alarming as the ferocity of her self-hatred. Once the depth of Julia's self-division is recognized, the puzzles posed by her tendering of the wrong letter in Act IV, Scene iv, and the wrong ring in Act V, Scene iv, are puzzles no more. When Julia says to Silvia, 'Pardon me, madam, I have unadvised / Delivered you a paper that I should not' (IV.iv.120-1), takes it back and leaves us in the dark as to its contents, the effect – as with the muddling of the rings in Act V – is to betray the presence of a secret self, which resists absorption into the role prescribed by the plot.

In Act IV, Silvia duplicates Julia's response to her first letter from Proteus by shredding the one the perfidious dolt sends her, because she knows that it's 'stuffed with protestations, / And full of new-found oaths, which he will break / As easily as I do tear his paper' (IV.iv.126–8). Silvia, too, is split into the substance and the shadow of herself, when Proteus resorts to courting her portrait ('To that I'll speak, to that I'll sigh and weep' (IV.ii.119)), whose 'senseless form' even Julia apostrophizes instead of the flesh and blood woman it depicts (IV.iv.194–202). Silvia's deafening silence during the play's finale, when she is shunted back and forth between men oblivious to her presence, is at once a sign of her impotence and – like Julia's wordless exit when she parts from Proteus – a symptom of her dislocation from the 'discourse of disability' (II.iv.107) that hobbles both women and men in the warped world of *The Two Gentlemen of Verona*.

'A curious essay', remarks Edward Dowden in *Shakspere: A Critical Study of His Mind and Art*, 'might be written upon the silences of some of the characters of Shakspere.' It might indeed, because silence offers, amongst other things, a refuge from, and resistance to, the power of a dominant discourse to dictate the way people think, feel and act. So, too, does secrecy, as the mysterious, undivulged letter Julia takes back from Silvia attests. The discursive regime of *Two Gentlemen* exerts intense pressure on the play's tiny cast (the smallest in the entire Shakespearean canon) to spill the beans about what they are up to. The haste Valentine makes to confide fatally in Proteus, and the ease with which the Duke winkles his elopement plan out of him, furnish ample proof of that. In such a confined, claustrophobic universe intent on transparency, not telling and obfuscation are indispensable resources.

Launce gives Speed an object lesson in their effectiveness in Act II, when he plays fast and loose with the word 'understand' to make sure that Speed does no such thing, and crowns his confounding of the latter with the line, 'Thou shalt never get such a secret from me but by a parable' (II.v.34–5). Launce makes the same point through parody in Act III: 'He lives not now that knows me to be in love, yet I am in love, but a team of horse shall not pluck that from me, nor who 'tis I love; and yet 'tis a woman, but what woman I will not tell myself' (III.i.262–6); whereupon, of course, he immediately tells Speed, allowing him to read aloud 'the catalogue of her conditions' (III.i.271) and then denouncing him for doing so as 'An unmannerly slave, that will thrust himself into secrets' (III.i.370–1). The same scene is also packed with examples of a closely allied obstructive strategy: the clown's compulsion to 'mistake the word' like the 'old vice' of the mystery plays (III.i.279), milking gags from the scrambling of plain communication. From the insubordinate standpoint of Launce and Speed, to be dubbed an 'illiterate loiterer' (III.i.289) is to join the ranks of the comedy's true elite.

Illiterate loitering alone, however hawk-eyed such sniping from the sidelines may be, cannot liberate Launce and Speed from the language-game that defines the horizon of the characters' universe. But it leaves us in no doubt about how tightly all the *dramatis personae* are constrained by the rules of that game and the limits of that universe. When Speed assures Valentine, 'All this I speak in print, for in print I found it' (II.i.159), or when Launce quips bawdily to Speed, 'Why, stand-under and under-stand is all one' (II.v.29), or demands that Speed 'Rehearse that once more' (III.i.346–7) to give him a second run at a feed-line, we're being prompted to attend to dramatic speech as a textually produced oral performance, a circumscribing script which is being slowed down and magnified for self-conscious scrutiny.

On her first appearance in Act II, Silvia gangs up with Speed to heckle Valentine in a sustained pursuit of this reflexive effect:

VALENTINE. No, madam. So it stead you I will write –
Please you command – a thousand times as much.
And yet. . .
SILVIA. A pretty period. Well, I guess the sequel.
And yet I will not name it. And yet I care not.
And yet, take this again.
She offers him the letter
And yet I thank you,
Meaning henceforth to trouble you no more.
SPEED. (*aside*) And yet you will, and yet another yet.
(II.i.106–13)

For half a minute the needle sticks in the script and all three characters get stuck with their creator on the same two conjunctions. The passage furnishes a paradigm of the plight all the characters share to one degree or another: a plight never more apparent than when the wittiest of them steal a glimpse of freedom from it by turning into textual commentators and literary critics.

The Two Gentlemen of Verona conveys a pervasive impression of individuals entangled in a web of words, irrevocably trapped in a text which is determined to call the shots. From the opening scene, in which Proteus and Valentine both buttress their contentions with the tag 'writers say' (I.i.42, 45), it's evident that this is a play whose protagonists do not own the words they speak, because they are obliged to spout recycled sentiments and automated arguments. It's no accident that, as Johnson observed, *Two Gentlemen* 'abounds in γνωμαὶ [maxims] beyond most of his plays'. Nor is it a coincidence that Valentine's affirmative answer to the question 'Have you the tongues?' (IV.i.32) – the fact that he is 'by [his] own report / A linguist' (IV.i.54–5) – is what swings his election as captain of the outlaws, who know that talking other people's language is the ultimate weapon in the world they prey upon.

Even Speed and Launce at their most impromptu must take their linguistic cues from the diction of others, as Launce's punning on the 'tide of tears' Proteus ascribed to Julia in the previous scene demonstrates. In fact, there are moments in the play when it seems as if some quirky imperative of language itself is dictating the characters' conversations, irrespective of their intentions or the exigencies of the plot. Such a moment occurs in the two clowns' comic duet on the merits and demerits of Launce's secret love: '*Item*,' reads Speed, 'she hath no teeth.' 'I care not for that, neither', responds Launce, 'because I love crusts', and the last word of his reply produces, by some loopy anagrammatic logic, the very next quality Speed proffers for appraisal: '*Item*, she is curst' (III.i.331–3).

Authentic communication is a rare commodity in a play where speech is almost entirely restricted to monologue, duologue or the aside inserted as a comment. The intricate orchestration of several voices in dynamic dialogue is inconceivable for a comedy which begins its third act with the entrance of the Duke, Thurio and Proteus solely in order that Thurio can be dismissed by the Duke in the first line before he even opens his mouth. In the course of the 20 scenes that comprise the play, each of which tends to form an insular tableau, the two pairs of lovers rarely meet before the final act and, when they do (in II.i, II.ii, II.iv and IV.iv), their duets seem oddly perfunctory or stilted. They appear more often apart from each other, talking about their love alone or to someone else, and investing it, ironically, with a vitality it never possesses when they are physically together on stage. Valentine's soliloquy bewailing his banishment from

Silvia (III.i.170–87) provides an illuminating instance of this paradox, which is equally apparent in the play's portrayal of the two gentlemen's much-vaunted friendship: their amity comes alive in Proteus's tormented soliloquy on his treachery (II.vi) in a way it never does when they actually converse. It's not surprising, in light of this, that the reunions and reconciliations of both friends and lovers in the final scene have a hollow ring.

Nothing underlines the isolation of the protagonists from each other and their own emotions more emphatically than their contagious resort to letters to communicate, even when the circumstances render a letter quite redundant. The profusion and prominence of letters in this play, the most epistolary comedy Shakespeare ever penned, is truly remarkable. The traumatic impact of Proteus's love-letter on Julia in Act I, Scene ii, where the torn words of the missive become autonomous figures in their own right, has already been discussed. The very next scene finds Proteus musing on Julia's written response – 'Sweet love, sweet lines, sweet life! / Here is her hand, the agent of her heart' (I.iii.45–6) – whose contents he only just keeps secret from his father by lying about its author. The following scene (II.i) culminates in Silvia's ruse to dupe Valentine into wooing her at one remove: instead of Valentine expressing his feelings directly to her in person or on paper on his own initiative, he winds up writing a love-letter on Silvia's behalf, and at her instigation, to an anonymous recipient, whom he fails to realize must be himself. His bone-headed bafflement at Silvia's insistence on handing back to him the *billet-doux* he has just handed her accentuates the circuitous absurdity of their courtship.

In Act II, Scene iv, Proteus's appearance in person in Milan is preempted by the Duke's report, only seconds before, of a letter from Valentine's friends announcing the 'good news' (II.iv.50) of his arrival. The opening scene of Act III pivots on the Duke's discovery and declaiming of the superfluous poetic epistle to Silvia that Valentine has concealed beneath his cloak en route to his rendezvous with the woman herself; the burden of the foreshortened sonnet is Valentine's envy of the 'herald thoughts' he has sent in place of himself to 'harbour where their lord should be' (III.i.144, 149). Within a hundred lines we get a ribald action-replay of this incident, as Speed reads out loud the secret 'paper' (III.i.280) that anatomizes Launce's paramour, before exiting with the exclamation: 'Pox of your love-letters!' (III.i.368–9). In next to no time the efficacy of that curse becomes apparent in Julia's bungled delivery of two letters to Silvia, the first of which she reclaims unopened, while the second suffers the same fate at Silvia's hands as Proteus's first letter to Julia.

'the dog is himself, and I am the dog'

'Thy letters may be here,' says Proteus to Valentine, 'though thou art hence' (III.i.247). This plague of epistles is the product of a comedic world consumed by surrogacy, bristling with proxies and substitutes for the real thing. Like letters, the rings that Proteus and Julia exchange, and that play such a decisive part in triggering the denouement, stand in for their owners in their absence, usurping the identity of those they supplant. Silvia's portrait, likewise, takes the place of the person it replicates, not only in the mind of the languishing Proteus, but also in the envious eyes of Julia, who has herself been displaced by the persona of Sebastian, who in turn serves as a surrogate for Proteus in his wooing of Silvia:

> Come, shadow, come, and take this shadow up,
> For 'tis thy rival.
> > *She picks up the portrait*
> > > O thou senseless form,
> Thou shalt be worshipped, kissed, loved, and adored;
> And were there sense in his idolatry
> My substance should be statue in thy stead.
> > > > > > (IV.iv.194–8)

Just as Julia longs to supplant Silvia as the object of Proteus's desire, so Proteus pines to occupy Valentine's place in Silvia's heart. Julia's noble self-sacrifice in wooing Silvia on Proteus's behalf – 'How many women would do such a message?' (IV.iv.88) – is explicitly prefigured by Launce's shouldering of the blame for Crab's incontinence: 'How many masters would do this for his servant?' (IV.iv.28–9). Crab himself is offered in vain to Silvia by Launce as a poor substitute for the stolen dog he was supposed to give her as a present from Proteus. The play's obsession with replacement and replication is exquisitely captured and mocked in Launce's stand-up routine on the problem of stand-ins:

> Nay, I'll show you the manner of it. This shoe is my father. No, this left shoe is my father. No, no, this left shoe is my mother. Nay, that cannot be so, neither. Yes, it is so, it is so, it hath the worser sole. This shoe with the hole in it is my mother, and this my father. A vengeance on't, there 'tis. Now, sir, this staff is my sister, for, look you, she is as white as a lily and as small as a wand. This hat is Nan our maid. I am the dog. No, the dog is himself, and I am the dog. O, the dog is me, and I am myself. Ay, so, so.
> > > > > > (II.iii.13–23)

'Thou shalt never get such a secret from me but by a parable' (II.v.34–5), says Launce a couple of scenes later, and, if the secret of the play is hidden anywhere in his lines, it's in this teasing parable about the ambiguity of representation itself, the theatrical craft that Launce and Crab incarnate before our eyes.

The speech encapsulates in a comic key the rampant estrangement to which all the characters are prey in a comedy where everyone is beside themselves, because no one can simply be themselves. When they are not being displaced by a token in the shape of a letter, a ring or a portrait, they are being taken for someone else or slipping into the skin of their soul-mate, their romantic rival, their social superiors or even man's best friend: 'No, the dog is himself, and I am the dog.' Well might the exiled Valentine cry, 'Repair me with thy presence, Silvia' (V.iv.11), but he cries in vain for a simulacrum, whose elusive identity provides the subject of the play's haunting song, 'Who is Silvia?' – the lyrical counterpart of Launce's struggle to work out who's who. The callousness of this surrogacy syndrome is apparent in the indiscriminate ease with which Silvia is exchanged for Valentine's redeemed friendship, then dropped and swapped for Julia by Proteus: 'What is in Silvia's face but I may spy / More fresh in Julia's, with a constant eye?' (V.iv.113–14).

The mentality that can reduce a woman to a silent cipher to be abused, switched or bartered is the same mentality that can turn anything or anyone into a commodity to be traded on the early modern market. Insofar as Shakespeare's joint-stock theatre company is a thriving child of the early modern market economy, it shares in that mentality, turning actors into the puppets of the plots and speeches that comprise the products of the playhouse. The instability of identity, self-division and alienation suffered by the characters in *The Two Gentlemen of Verona* are the endemic effects of a culture with which Shakespeare's theatre by its nature is deeply complicit. Turning people into other people, lives into parts, talk into texts, and reality into representation is the stock-in-trade of his drama.

But at the same time, as Launce's tomfoolery with his shoes and staff proves every time it's performed, the confounding of identity through comedy can also be a source of exhilaration and delight. For the dispensation that spawns the dislocated, soluble selves of Shakespeare's comedic vision also sparks the desire his comedy displays for equality and community – for what the last line of *The Two Gentlemen of Verona* triumphantly hails as 'One feast, one house, one mutual happiness' (V.iv.171). The surrogacy syndrome in *Two Gentlemen* is at once the sign of ubiquitous reification and the sign of a liberating dissolution of difference. The chain of substitution that binds all the characters in the comedy to each other through semblance, displacement, analogy and parody cancels the hierarchical distinctions that otherwise divide them. Beneath the surface of the play a covert democracy of counterparts takes shape, a clandestine regime founded on the ethics of empathy fostered by representation.

Julia's extraordinary, poignant speech to Silvia, in which she feigns a recollection of taking part in a play, takes us straight to the heart of the matter:

>   at Pentecost,
> When all our pageants of delight were played,
> Our youth got me to play the woman's part,
> And I was trimmed in Madam Julia's gown,
> Which servèd me as fit, by all men's judgements,
> As if the garment had been made for me;
> Therefore I know she is about my height.
> And at that time I made her weep agood,
> For I did play a lamentable part.
> Madam, 'twas Ariadne, passioning
> For Theseus' perjury and unjust flight;
> Which I so lively acted with my tears
> That my poor mistress, movèd therewithal,
> Wept bitterly; and would I might be dead
> If I in thought felt not her very sorrow.
>
> SILVIA.   She is beholden to thee, gentle youth.
> Alas, poor lady, desolate and left.
> I weep myself to think upon thy words.
>   (IV.iv.155–72)

In the original Elizabethan production of *Two Gentlemen*, Julia's speech would have entailed a boy actor playing the part of Julia, who in turn is masquerading as the page Sebastian, who here invents a memory of being 'trimmed in Madam Julia's gown' in order to perform before the latter the 'lamentable part' of 'Ariadne, passioning / For Theseus' perjury and unjust flight', which is, of course, a coded transposition of Julia's own predicament, as the audience alone appreciates.

The mind-bending embedding of roles within roles leaves the border between representation and reality terminally blurred. But it also fuses the actor, Julia, Sebastian, Ariadne, Silvia and the spectator as avatars of the same self in an act of compassionate identification. Julia's imaginary impersonation, as Sebastian, of the grief-stricken Ariadne produces the empathetic pain not only of herself as imaginary spectator ('would I might be dead / If I in thought felt not her very sorrow'), but also of Silvia ('I weep myself to think upon thy words') as the auditor of Julia's fabricated anecdote. The whole passage serves as a trenchant parable about the power of theatrical representation, which is predicated on equivalence and likeness, to obliterate the barriers between individuals by finding the points at which their emotions and attitudes coincide.

It also bears eloquent witness to the wealth of insights into the art of Shakespearean comedy that still lie buried in *The Two Gentlemen of Verona*, and to the fascination this unjustly neglected comedy exerts in its own right when it's allowed to work its singular magic. An intimation of what that magic entails, and an implicit admonition not to underestimate its potency, are smuggled into four unforgettable lines and placed in the mouth of Proteus midway through the play:

> For Orpheus' lute was strung with poets' sinews,
> Whose golden touch could soften steel and stones,
> Make tigers tame, and huge leviathans
> Forsake unsounded deeps to dance on sands.
>
> (III.ii.77–80)

4
'Merry days of desolation':
Love's Labour's Lost

'heirs of all eternity'

If the romantic male leads of *The Taming of the Shrew* and *The Two Gentlemen of Verona* get away with murder from a matriarchal point of view, the quartet of academic aristos who rhyme their way through *Love's Labour's Lost* have no such luck. The female foursome at whom they set their caps lead them a merry dance from first to last, which leaves them unrequited, and which makes them pay, one might almost say, for the indignities inflicted on the heroines of the *Shrew* and *Two Gentlemen* by Petruchio, Proteus and Valentine. The fantasy of reaping intellectual immortality from the repression of the flesh – 'The mind shall banquet, though the body pine' (I.i.25) – is no sooner floated by the King of Navarre than it sinks like a stone, scuppered by the forgotten advent of the Princess of France. The superior wit of the Princess and her ladies-in-waiting gives them the whip hand over the royal dilettante and his forsworn confederates, whose glib overtures are dashed by acerbic mockery, and whose last-minute bid for marital bliss founders on the rocks of death, distrust and deferral.

It's an extraordinary end to an extraordinary play. Before his career in romantic comedy is four plays old, Shakespeare reverses the patriarchal poles of the form he is creating and defies its demand for a conjugal resolution. Small wonder that *Love's Labour's Lost* vanished from the English stage for 200 years until it was revived at Covent Garden in 1839, and had to wait until the latter half of the twentieth century to be fully appreciated and as regularly performed as it continues to be in the twenty-first. None of Shakespeare's comedies confounds more effectively the still

56

widespread view that they are congenitally disposed to disempower women and protract the subjection of placket to codpiece.

The rough ride the play has in store for the four male protagonists begins in earnest when they confront their French nemeses at the start of Act II. The first act has already seen their oaths begin to unravel and the King's edict undermined. In the opening scene the King invites Berowne, Dumaine and Longueville to join him in conquering time and death, to become 'heirs of all eternity' by waging 'war against [their] own affections / And the huge army of the world's desires' and making their court 'a little academe, / Still and contemplative in living art', that will be 'the wonder of the world' (I.i.7, 9–10, 12–14). The King's exhortation has barely left his lips before Berowne is bemoaning the futility of signing up to such 'barren tasks, too hard to keep – / Not to see ladies, study, fast, not sleep' (I.i.47–8). Three years of swatting and mortifying the flesh, he protests, will gain them nothing 'Save base authority from others' books' (I.i.87). The news of the arrival of 'th'ad-mirèd Princess' (I.i.138), which forces Navarre to suspend his prohibi-tion of discourse with women 'on mere necessity' (I.i.146), prompts Berowne's sardonic prediction that 'Necessity will make us all forsworn / Three thousand times within this three years' space' (I.i.147–8). Further proof of the impotence of the royal decree is furnished moments later by Costard, who has been arrested at Armado's request for consorting with Jaquenetta, and in the next scene by Armado, who confesses his love for the selfsame 'base wench' (I.ii.57–8), first to his page Moth and then to the damsel herself. In Costard and Armado the play caricatures the impending fate of their superiors.

At the start of the single long scene that constitutes Act II, the audi-ence might be forgiven for inferring that the course of true love may yet run smooth for our four cerebral gallants. What Maria, Katherine and Rosaline report in turn of Longueville, Dumaine and Berowne respec-tively is flattering enough to make the Princess exclaim: 'God bless my ladies, are they all in love, / That every one her own hath garnishèd / With such bedecking ornaments of praise?' (II.i.77–9). But Navarre's refusal to let the Princess through 'his forbidden gates' (II.i.26) to enjoy the hospitality of his court provokes a spiky first exchange between them, from which the romantic liaisons promised by the plot never recover.

As Navarre peruses the French king's demand for a hundred thou-sand crowns, which naturally foments more friction, Rosaline engages Berowne in a bout of barbed repartee which sets the pattern for the subsequent encounters between all four pairs of potential lovers. Each

rhyming riposte drives a wedge between both parties, even as it seals
their affinity by making them sound alike:

> BEROWNE. Your wit's too hot, it speeds too fast, 'twill tire.
> ROSALINE. Not till it leave the rider in the mire.
>
> (II.i.119–20)

Rosaline caps every one of Berowne's quips and counter-quips, compelling his ego to retire wounded from the fray not once, but twice in
swift succession. Nor is Berowne, 'the merry madcap lord' (II.i.215),
the sole casualty of this opening skirmish in the 'civil war of wits'
(II.i.226) that has been declared. If Berowne's humour can be discounted as shallow, heartless wordplay ('Not a word with him but a jest',
observes Maria – 'And every jest but a word', adds Boyet (II.i.216)), his
sovereign's attraction to the Princess seems equally vulnerable to the
charge of superficiality latent in Boyet's view of him:

> Methought all his senses were locked in his eye,
> As jewels in crystal, for some prince to buy,
> Who, tendering their own worth from where they were glassed,
> Did point you to buy them along as you passed.
> His face's own margin did quote such amazes
> That all eyes saw his eyes enchanted with gazes.
>
> (II.i.242–7)

That 'margin' metaphor suggests not only that the King's face can
be read like the tomes he wants to bury himself in, but also that he's
turning into a text-book example of the transfixed lover, primed for
romance by rote. In the exquisite soliloquy with which he closes Act
III, Berowne spells out with mock dismay the doom to which he, too,
has been consigned by his reluctant crush on Rosaline, 'A whitely wanton with a velvet brow, / With two pitch-balls stuck in her face for eyes'
(III.i.191–2). The sworn foe of the 'giant dwarf, Dan Cupid, / Regent
of love-rhymes, lord of folded arms, / Th'anointed sovereign of sighs
and groans' (III.i.175–7), is now forced to serve as a humble 'corporal
of his field' (III.i.182), and consequently condemned, like his brothers-
in-arms, to the same stale verbal routines and behavioural clichés: 'Well,
I will love, write, sigh, pray, sue, groan' (III.i.199).

Unfortunately for 'the Prince and his bookmates' (IV.i.99), the
women they proceed to woo remain immune to the affected passion that
has infected their wooers. The postures they strike and the verses they

recite cut no ice with the objects of their affection, who remain coolly contemptuous of the pantomimes of desire the men perform for them. Just how impervious the fair maids of France will prove to the seductive ploys of their suitors is foreshadowed by the Princess's upbraiding of Boyet in Act II – 'my beauty, though but mean, / Needs not the painted flourish of your praise' (II.i.13–14) – and confirmed when she playfully scolds the Forester at the start of Act IV for failing to flatter her:

> Nay, never paint me now.
> Where fair is not, praise cannot mend the brow.
> Here, good my glass, take this for telling true.
>   *She gives him money*
> Fair payment for foul words is more than due.
>   (IV.i.16–19)

After honing their derision on Armado's letter to Jaquenetta and prac-tising their put-downs on Boyet, the formidable Princess and her court-wise companions are poised to disabuse the lords of their misprision in the final act of the comedy.

That their work will be cut out for them is made plain two scenes later, when the four lords catch each other out in the act of perjury and are forced to acknowledge that their devotion to scholarship has been supplanted by their 'Sweet fellowship in shame' (IV.iii.46). The mutual humiliation of exposure releases them from hypocrisy and a pointless pledge, but leaves them imprisoned in the prescribed tropes and para-doxes of the poems they declaim. Berowne musters all the resources of the 'painted rhetoric' the Princess scorns to show that he 'needs it not' (IV.iii.237) in order to prove Rosaline's supremacy. The dialectical ingenuity he deploys to turn cosmetic prejudice upside down and demonstrate that 'No face is fair that is not full so black' (IV.iii.251) is certainly commendable. And his triumphant paean to the power of love and of women is irresistibly eloquent:

> And when love speaks, the voice of all the gods
> Make heaven drowsy with the harmony.
> Never durst poet touch a pen to write
> Until his ink were tempered with love's sighs.
> O, then his lines would ravish savage ears,
> And plant in tyrants mild humility.
> From women's eyes this doctrine I derive.
> They sparkle still the right Promethean fire.

They are the books, the arts, the academes
That show, contain, and nourish all the world,
Else none at all in ought proves excellent.
Then fools you were these women to forswear,
Or keeping what is sworn, you will prove fools.
For wisdom's sake – a word that all men love –
Or for love's sake – a word that loves all men –
Or for men's sake – the authors of these women –
Or women's sake – by whom we men are men –
Let us once lose our oaths to find ourselves,
Or else we lose ourselves to keep our oaths.
                              (IV.iii.320–38)

But, notwithstanding the complete *volte-face* of Berowne's contention that women, not books, 'show, contain, and nourish all the world', and his crowning concession that 'we men are men' by virtue of women, these particular men still have a lesson to learn about love.

'the sign of she'

The difference of the women's perspective on Cupid is implied in the intimation of mortality that clouds Katherine's dialogue with Rosaline in the opening lines of Act V, Scene ii. The god of love, sighs Katherine, can be 'a shrewd unhappy gallows, too'. 'You'll ne'er be friends with him', replies Rosaline, 'a killed your sister.' 'He made her melancholy, sad, and heavy', Katherine recalls, 'And so she died' (V.ii.12–15). The women's attitude to love is tempered by the knowledge that it sometimes turns sour and proves terminal. Their realism in matters of the heart sees straight through the mating dance mounted to charm them. They remain unswayed by the lords' rich gifts and ridicule their verses as 'A huge translation of hypocrisy / Vilely compiled, profound simplicity' (V.ii.51–2). There's a jagged edge of anger to Rosaline's response in particular – 'That same Berowne I'll torture ere I go' (V.ii.60) – and unquestioned agreement that their frivolous suitors deserve everything they are about to get: 'So shall we stay, mocking intended game, / And they well mocked depart away with shame' (V.ii.154–5).

What the lords should really be ashamed of, they discover, is not their infidelity to their academic oaths, but the spuriousness of their attachment to the women they are wooing. This is the lesson the ladies teach them through the subterfuge of swapping identities with each other.

The botched masque of the Muscovites brings home to the masquers the blunt truth that their undying devotion to their mistresses is arbitrary and rootless. As Berowne explains to his crestfallen *confrères*: 'The ladies did change favours, and then we, / Following the signs, wooed but the sign of she' (V.ii.468–9). Berowne makes a clean breast of his folly to Rosaline, swearing to forswear the phoney verbiage that has choked the voice of genuine feeling:

> Taffeta phrases, silken terms precise,
>> Three-piled hyperboles, spruce affectation,
> Figures pedantical – these summer flies
>> Have blown me full of maggot ostentation.
> I do forswear them, and I here protest,
>> By this white glove – how white the hand, God knows! –
> Henceforth my wooing mind shall be expressed
>> In russet yeas, and honest kersey noes.
>
>> (V.ii.406–13)

But his affected use of the Gallicism '*sans*' a second later compels him to concede that he still has 'a trick / Of the old rage' (V.ii.416–17) and that the plague of pretension is not so easily shaken off.

For Rosaline and the rest of the ladies, it's too late anyway for the lords to make amends and start afresh, as Berowne proposes. The verbal fencing in which the couples engaged while disguised seems to have killed whatever intimacy might have blossomed between them. 'The tongues of mocking wenches are as keen / As is the razor's edge invisible' (V.ii.256–7), Boyet comments on a clash between one couple, which illustrates how lethal the undertow of women's wit can be: when Longueville begs 'One word in private with you ere I die', Katherine closes the couplet with the chilling line: 'Bleat softly, then. The butcher hears you cry' (V.ii.254–5). When Monsieur Mercadé appears with news of the real death of the Princess's father, 'The scene begins to cloud' (V.ii.714) in earnest, and any lingering illusions of redemption the lords might harbour are soon shattered.

The festive respite of shared hilarity provided by the Pageant of the Nine Worthies gives way to funereal gloom. The imminent departure of the Princess and her train for France prompts Navarre to one last desperate plea: 'Now, at the latest minute of the hour, / Grant us your loves' (V.ii.779–80). But the Princess's reply, 'A time, methinks, too short, / To make a world-without-end bargain in' (V.ii.780–1), forces the King and his companions to face up to the final home truth the women have to teach them. The men's romantic advances were regarded by the latter merely 'As bombast and as lining to the time' (V.ii.773), because they deserved nothing more. Why should the Princess, Rosaline, Katherine and Maria take seriously suitors who do not take them seriously enough to acknowledge their otherness and respect their singularity? How could an impulsive commitment founded on mutual ignorance ever hope to survive and thrive?

Hence the ladies' demand that the lords show their true mettle by undergoing trials of their love's constancy and capacity to endure. Navarre must buttress his words with deeds and 'go with speed / To some forlorn and naked hermitage / Remote from all the pleasures of the world', to see 'If this austere, insociable life / Change not [his] offer made in heat of blood' (V.ii.786–8, 791–2). In the interim, the bereaved Princess pledges, she will 'shut / [her] woeful self up in a mourning house' (V.ii.799–800) to grieve for her father. Dumaine and Longueville get off much more lightly, being required only to serve their prospective paramours 'true and faithfully' (V.ii.817) till the stipulated fairy-tale term of 'A twelvemonth and a day' (V.ii.813) has expired. The harshest penance is reserved by Rosaline for Berowne, whose 'gibing spirit' (V.ii.844), accustomed to the 'shallow laughing hearers give to fools' (V.ii.846), must be exorcised by daily visits to 'the speechless sick' (V.ii.837), whom he must force to smile despite their pain. 'To move wild laughter in the throat of death?' exclaims Berowne. 'It cannot be, it is impossible. / Mirth cannot move a soul in agony' (V.ii.841–3).

The four couples and the audience are robbed of the satisfaction of the form's staple finale, which Shakespeare sabotages in order to dramatize the gulf that divides realism from romance, the bleak realm of probability from the dreamscape of fiction:

> BEROWNE.   Our wooing doth not end like an old play.
>   Jack hath not Jill. These ladies' courtesy
>   Might well have made our sport a comedy.
> KING.   Come, sir, it wants a twelvemonth an' a day,
>   And then 'twill end.
> BEROWNE.   That's too long for a play.
>   (V.ii.860–4)

The fourfold resolution of the romantic plot is made subject to taxing conditions and postponed forever to an imaginary point in time beyond the horizon of *Love's Labour's Lost*. In this respect the play provides a pre-emptive critique of the great romantic comedies Shakespeare will go on to pen, including his next one, *A Midsummer Night's Dream*, which ensures, in sharp contrast to *Love's Labour's Lost*, that 'Jack shall have Jill, / Naught shall go ill, / the man shall have his mare again, and all shall be well' (*MND*, III.iii.45–7). But it also adumbrates the subtler caveats those plays enter about the limits of comedy, even as they satisfy the expectations they arouse. That said, something else seems to be achieved by the abortive denouement of *Love's Labour's Lost*, which ends up delivering, paradoxically, a more profound satisfaction than the one it frustrates through death. The expectation of romantic failure embedded in the title of the comedy is, after all, fulfilled, leaving the audience with no reason to demand their money back. The question is, what deeper drive is the play obeying, what deeper need is it meeting, by derailing the conventional closure of comedy?

'gravity's revolt to wantonness'

There's a clue in the word 'defer' itself, which means to submit humbly to, or respectfully yield precedence to, as well as to put off, postpone or delay until another occasion. The double meaning of the term highlights the play's twin drives to enforce the surrender of male will to female wisdom and hold the resolution of their relationship in perpetual abeyance. The comedy's compulsion to procrastinate is indivisible from its urge to invert and undo structures of domination, of which patriarchy is only the most prominent in the amorous universe of *Love's Labour's Lost*. The *femmes fatales* of the French court wrest the initiative from their noble swains and turn the tables on them by trading 'mock for mock' (V.ii.139) and defeating 'sport by sport' (V.ii.152). But they are no less vulnerable than their suitors to the levelling insinuations of the subplot and the speech that springs from their own lips.

The account of Costard's illicit rendezvous with Jaquenetta and Armado's infatuation with the selfsame dairymaid provide blatant parallels with the plight of their betters, which undercut the latter's presumption of superiority from the outset. The ubiquity of the instinct that animates courtier and clown, native nobility and Spanish knight alike, betrays a concerted purpose beneath the obvious disparities. 'Necessity will make us all forsworn', predicts Berowne, 'For every man with his affects is born' (I.i.147, 149). Or as Costard puts it a few speeches later after being caught *in flagrante*: 'Such is the simplicity of man to hearken after the flesh' (I.i.215). That sexual attraction scorns the barriers raised by rank is comically underscored by Armado's passion for a 'dey-woman'

(I.ii.124) far beneath his station. Happily he finds a 'mighty precedent' (I.ii.111) for his transgression of class boundaries in the ballad of 'the King and the Beggar' (I.ii.104–5), to which Shakespeare makes sure he returns in his preposterous epistle to his beloved later in the play: 'The magnanimous and most illustrate King Cophetua set's eye upon the penurious and indubitate beggar Zenelophon, and he it was that might rightly say "*Veni, vidi, vici*"' (IV.i.64–7).

The love-struck male's posturing is as deftly punctured from below by Moth as it is from above by the needling wit of the Princess and Rosaline. The satirical master-class in moping to which he treats Armado echoes the diagnosis of Valentine's love-sickness delivered by Moth's counterpart, Speed, in *The Two Gentlemen of Verona* (II.i.17–30):

> No, my complete master; but to jig off a tune at the tongue's end, canary to it with your feet, humour it with turning up your eyelids, sigh a note and sing a note, sometime through the throat as if you swallowed love with singing love, sometime through the nose as if you snuffed up love by smelling love, with your hat penthouse-like o'er the shop of your eyes, with your arms crossed on your thin-belly doublet like a rabbit on a spit, or your hands in your pocket like a man after the old painting, and keep not too long in one tune, but a snip and away. These are complements, these are humours; these betray nice wenches that would be betrayed without these, and make them men of note – do you note? *men* – that most are affected to these.
>
> (*LLL*, III.i.10–24)

Just like Speed's plebeian cartoon of upper-class affectation, Moth's send-up generates, through its homespun diction, iterative rhythms and syntactical suspense, a visual exuberance that invites us to relish the object of ridicule and place it appreciatively beyond contempt.

Their thraldom to programmed emotions and attitudes is not the only aspect of the masters' conduct that has to run the gauntlet of comic prose paraphrase or farcical appropriation. As the quotation from Armado's missive to his mistress attests, their elevation of books, language and learning above the body, love and life is on a hiding to nothing too. Berowne blows the gaff on the whole misbegotten enterprise 50 lines into the play, when he gets the King to confirm that 'study's god-like recompense' is to discover 'Things hid and barred [. . .] from common sense' (I.i.57–8). That gives Berowne the perfect cue for a lecture on the vanity of severing themselves from the shared appetites and attachments of their kind in quest of recondite knowledge. After all, he reminds them:

> These earthly godfathers of heaven's lights,
>   That give a name to every fixèd star,
> Have no more profit of their shining nights
>   Than those that walk and wot not what they are.
>   (I.i.88–91)

The everyday experience of ordinary folk, whose age-old pool of wisdom every class can tap, furnishes the benchmark of sanity, the measure of what really matters, and the basis for debunking those whose thoughts and words presume to set them apart as superior.

The debunking kicks off in the same scene with Costard, 'That unlettered, small-knowing soul' (I.i.245) as Armado dubs him, playing havoc with the latter's verbose indictment of him by constantly interrupting, and then running rings round the royal edict with his impertinent equivocations. The lewd thrust of those equivocations is conscious in Costard's case, given his role as the fly fool, confident of the audience's approval: 'This "maid" will not serve your turn, sir', declares the King, to which Costard retorts, unabashed, 'This maid will serve my turn, sir' (I.i.286–7). Such calculated ribaldry deflates the learned discourse of officialdom by coupling it with the coarsest libidinal impulses. But the deflation is equally hilarious when the double entendres are unwitting and savoured by the spectators at the expense of the characters, as in this snatch of dialogue between the unctuous curate, Nathaniel, and the pathologically pedantic schoolmaster, Holofernes:

NATHANIEL.   Sir, I praise the Lord for you, and so may my Parishioners; for their sons are well tutored by you, and their daughters profit very greatly under you. You are a good member of the commonwealth.

HOLOFERNES.   *Mehercle*, if their sons be ingenious they shall want no instruction; if their daughters be capable, I will put it to them.
                                                   (IV.ii.73–9)

Such innuendo seems positively refined, however, when set beside Costard's cloacal garbling of '*ad unguem*' as '*ad dunghill*, at the fingers' ends' (V.i.73–4), which Armado unconsciously trumps with an even cruder gag combining sodomy and scatology: 'for I must tell thee it will please his grace, by the world, sometime to lean upon my poor shoulder and with his royal finger thus dally with my excrement, with my mustachio' (V.i.96–9).

Not even royalty is safe from the script's delight in the indecorous doings of the bowels and genitals, which hold high birth in as little esteem as over-education. Nor is that delight the sole preserve of the lower ranks of *Love's Labour's Lost* or the male *dramatis personae*. In the wake of 'gravity's revolt to wantonness' (V.ii.74) the lords of Navarre are in the same class as 'the rational hind Costard' (I.ii.113) when it comes to contriving indecent jests:

> BEROWNE. O, if the streets were pavèd with thine eyes
> Her feet were much too dainty for such tread.
> DUMAINE. O vile! Then as she goes, what upward lies
> The street should see as she walked overhead.
>   (IV.iii.276–9)

But they are outclassed by Boyet's 'mad wenches' (II.i.257), when they team up with him and Costard to generate a stream of salacious euphemisms for copulation, masturbation and ejaculation. The routine starts off obliquely enough with Rosaline's song 'touching the hit it' (IV.i.123), the act of intercourse, but Maria is soon feeding the men ambiguous metaphors from archery, whose seamy side triggers a fusillade of graphic one-liners. So gross do the jokes become that, when Costard brings the sequence to a climax with the line 'Then will she get the upshoot by cleaving the pin', even Maria feels obliged to rebuke him for going too far: 'Come, come, you talk greasily, your lips grow foul' (IV.i.135–6). But Costard is undaunted by the reproof, and when Boyet and Maria depart, leaving him alone on the stage, he can't resist sharing his pride in the calibre of their quips with the audience: 'O' my troth, most sweet jests, most incony vulgar wit, / When it comes so smoothly off, so obscenely, as it were, so fit!' (IV.i.141–2).

Berowne's part may be by far the biggest in the play, with nigh on 600 lines in five scenes, but Costard's downstage, choric intimacy with the audience in that parting speech highlights the crucial role he plays in the comedy as a whole. Such forward movement as this dilatory drama possesses it owes chiefly to Costard, who crops up in every scene except Act II, Scene i, usually halfway through or near the end, to nudge its apology for action on. It's no accident that the character who cherishes the play's obscenity and vulgarity serves as its fulcrum, because

Love's Labour's Lost is covertly governed from below throughout. When 'the magnificent Armado' (I.i.188) closes the play's second scene by appealing for divine poetic inspiration, he pre-empts the lords' embracing of the same vocation two acts later: 'Assist me, some extemporal god of rhyme, for I am sure I shall turn sonnet. Devise wit, write pen, for I am for whole volumes, in folio' (I.ii.174–6). Likewise, in the polysyllabic circumlocutions to which Armado is prone, and in the linguistic nit-picking of that human lexicon Holofernes, the arid eccentricity to which Navarre's 'little academe' aspires can be found prefigured and lampooned.

Staying the Odds

The nincompoops of Navarre, in short, provide the blueprint for its blue-bloods, reversing within the theatre the sequence of emulation that obtains beyond its walls. To realize this is to grasp at least part of the point of the riddling rhyme that Armado and Moth recite twice in Act III, and that has left the best efforts of editors baffled. Armado hails Moth's lame joke about the clown, 'here's a costard broken in a shin', as 'Some enigma, some riddle', which demands an '*envoi*' or valedictory couplet to complete it (III.i.68–9). Costard naturally mistakes 'enigma' for 'enema' and a cue for more lavatorial humour, while Moth compounds the confusion by pretending he thinks '*envoi*' means '*salve*', a greeting rather than a farewell. 'No, page,' Armado corrects him, 'it is an epilogue or discourse to make plain / Some obscure precedence that hath tofore been sain' (III.i.79–80). The 'obscure precedence' or 'moral' he cites to 'example it' is:

> The fox, the ape, and the humble-bee
> Were still at odds, being but three.

For which Moth improvises the '*envoi*':

> Until the goose came out of door
> And stayed the odds by adding four.
> (III.i.80–4, 88–9)

This miniature beast-fable in verse, over which the play pores at such length, anticipates the transformation of a trio of fools into a quartet in the eavesdropping scene, when Dumaine's arrival 'stays the odds' by turning the King, Berowne and Longueville into 'four woodcocks in a dish!' (IV.iii.79). The symmetry of the two episodes is underscored a hundred lines later, when Dumaine notes that 'Now the number is even' and Berowne says, 'True, true; we are four' (IV.iii.209). The more profound purpose served by the nonsense rhyme, however, is to encapsulate the levelling logic of *Love's Labour's Lost* as a whole, the logic enshrined in Berowne's admonition that 'justice always whirls in equal measure' (IV.iii.360).

That such egalitarian sentiments should slip from the lips of Berowne is entirely appropriate, because Berowne has been a double agent, masquerading as a member of the aristocracy, all along. The fact that his eloquence has such frequent recourse to proverbial lore, the demotic discourse of common sense – 'More sacks to the mill! (IV.iii.78) – is a dead giveaway in a play that employs more proverbs than any of Shakespeare's comedies. (The total is 189, of which about a quarter belong to Berowne.) Berowne's exit line at the end of Act III, 'Some men must love my lady, and some Joan' (III.i.200), self-mockingly invokes the proverb, 'Joan is as good as my lady' and is echoed in the refrain of Winter's song at the end of the play, 'While greasy Joan doth keel the pot' (V.ii.904, 912). His kinship with Costard is sealed when the latter's pet saying, 'sit thee down, sorrow' (I.i.302–3), pops out of Berowne's mouth in a sentence that slyly fuses their dramatic roles: 'Well, set thee down, sorrow; for so they say the fool said, and so say I, and I the fool' (IV.iii.3–5). The iconoclastic animus of the royal jester is given scope when Berowne unmasks his monarch's hypocrisy – 'To see a king transformèd to a gnat!' (IV.iii.164) – and then demotes all four of them from noblemen to 'pickpurses in love' who 'deserve to die' (IV.iii.207).

The sharpest social and moral distinctions evaporate in the shared heat of procreation, whose imperative is irresistible:

> As true we are as flesh and blood can be.
> The sea will ebb and flow, heaven show his face.
> Young blood doth not obey an old decree.
> We cannot cross the cause why we were born,
> Therefore of all hands must we be forsworn.
>   (IV.iii.213–17)

The creed of creation to which Berowne testifies gathers all the characters of *Love's Labour's Lost* into its indulgent, indiscriminate embrace. From a priapic perspective, every man in the play is one of 'affection's men-at-arms' (IV.iii.288) and may be regarded, like Holofernes, as 'a good member of the commonwealth' (IV.ii.76) of comedy. Nor can the

Princess and her ladies escape inclusion in the 'Sweet fellowship of shame' (IV.iii.46) to which their shameless flirtation and taste for sexual innuendo bind them. The fellowship of shame is sweet because, as Dumaine puts it, 'none offend where all alike do dote' (IV.iii.124), where everyone is swept up in the same dance of desire, whether they like it or not. The carnality of human kind is the comedy's centre of gravity, for gravity will ever revolt to wantonness, its perennial *point de repère*.

In the same carnival spirit, the motions of the human mind at its most rarefied, as it voices thought through language, are desublimated and refigured as an equally basic physical appetite. 'Sir', says Nathaniel to Holofernes, apologizing for Dull's travesties of their pompous Latin tags, 'he hath never fed of the dainties that are bred in a book. / He hath not eat paper, as it were, he hath not drunk ink' (IV.ii.24–6). The verbally intoxicated pair are requited, however, for their condescension to the good constable by Moth's astute aside: 'They have been at a great feast of languages and stolen the scraps.' Costard concurs: 'O, they have lived long on the alms-basket of words', and crowns their conversion of speech into food by exploiting the fact that Moth's name (pronounced 'Mote' in Elizabethan English) makes him a personified pun on the French for 'word' (*mot*): 'I marvel thy master hath not eaten thee for a word, for thou art not so long by the head as *honorificabilitudinitatibus*. Thou art easier swallowed than a flapdragon' (V.i.36–42).

Notwithstanding Moth's and Costard's digs at the play's learned dunces, and their disdain for Dull, every character is an equally welcome guest at the 'great feast of languages' Shakespeare has laid on in *Love's Labour's Lost*. Each of them plays an essential instrument in its symphony of sound and sense, and when the orchestra's in full swing it becomes hard to tell them apart. The ladies bandy backchat in the same key as the clowns. Berowne parrots proverbs to the same tune as Costard. Holofernes's observation that Armado 'draweth out the thread of his verbosity finer than the staple of his argument' (V.i.16–17) hits the schoolmaster's note perfectly too. And Holofernes's hymn to his own 'foolish extravagant spirit, full of forms, figures, shapes, objects, ideas, apprehensions, motions, revolutions' (IV.ii.67–8) could have been sung just as well by Berowne, whose promise to purge himself of 'figures pedantical' (V.ii.408) concedes his affinity with the play's talking textbook. Their shared consumption of words dissolves the differences between the *dramatis personae* as surely as the hunger for food or the craving for love.

Not the least striking paradox of *Love's Labour's Lost* is that Shakespeare's first and only comedy devoted exclusively to life at court should be so swayed by the tide of plebeian assumptions and values. No comedy in the canon is more self-consciously heightened, patterned and stylized, as its conspicuous symmetries and resort to more rhymes than any other play by Shakespeare might suggest. None is more keen to cultivate, by its ostentatious parade of rhetorical tropes, metrical diversity, concealed sonnets, and prodigious vocabulary (only *Hamlet* boasts a larger number of new words), the illusion of a refined, closed world spun purely out of words, floating far above the vulgar engrossments of ordinary life. Yet none succumbs more fully to the vision it finds vested in the common lot of humanity, a vision which cuts across rank and, at the close of the play, anchors us all in the seasons of the earth, the creatures of the countryside, and the simple labours of the people:

SPRING. (*sings*)   When daisies pied and violets blue,
                                  And lady-smocks, all silver-white,
                          And cuckoo-buds of yellow hue
                                  Do paint the meadows with delight,
                          The cuckoo then on every tree
                          Mocks married men, for thus sings he:
                                  Cuckoo!
                          Cuckoo, cuckoo – O word of fear,
                          Unpleasing to a married ear.

                          When shepherds pipe on oaten straws,
                                  And merry larks are ploughmen's clocks;
                          When turtles tread, and rooks and daws,
                                  And maidens bleach their summer smocks,
                          The cuckoo then on every tree
                          Mocks married men, for thus sings he:
                                  Cuckoo!
                          Cuckoo, cuckoo – O word of fear,
                          Unpleasing to a married ear.

WINTER. (*sings*)   When icicles hang by the wall
                                  And Dick the shepherd blows his nail,
                          And Tom bears logs into the hall,
                                  And milk comes frozen home in pail;
                          When blood is nipped, and ways be foul,
                          Then nightly sings the staring owl:
                          Tu-whit, tu-whoo! – a merry note,
                          While greasy Joan doth keel the pot.

> When all aloud the wind doth blow,
>> And coughing drowns the parson's saw,
> And birds sit brooding in the snow,
>> And Marian's nose looks red and raw;
> When roasted crabs hiss in the bowl,
> Then nightly sings the staring owl:
> Tu-whit, tu-whoo! – a merry note,
> While greasy Joan doth keel the pot.
>   (V.ii.879–912)

In retrospect, the whole play has been paving the way for the view of things voiced in these haunting songs it bows out with. In the fifth act itself, the burlesque of grandeur in the shambolic Pageant of the Nine Worthies, its rude disruption by news of Jaquenetta's pregnancy, and the swift eclipse of that news of new life by the shadow of death, ensure that our expectations are on the same wavelength as the lyrics of Winter and Spring. But nothing in the comedy really prepares us for the uncanny antiphony of the songs, through which the shallow dalliance of the court is displaced by the hard graft of the rural working class at home and in the field in all weathers. *Love's Labour's Lost* may commence with a king, deferentially ceding its first words to Navarre, but its last words are devoted to the humdrum toil of ploughmen, shepherds and housewives, to Dick and Tom, to red-nosed Marian and 'greasy Joan', with whom we are placed on familiar, first-name terms.

'Some enigma, some riddle'

They are not quite its last words, though. The age-old bird songs have conjured up and left us with vivid images of a workaday world, remote from the one in which the comedy has been set. They have situated the aristocratic enclave of Navarre in a broader social and natural context and in a longer temporal perspective, which expose its fragility and transience. And they have re-enacted, through their stark juxtaposition of spring and winter, the icy blighting of budding romance by Mercadé's tidings of death. But they also capture the uneasy ambiguity at the heart of the play that reverberates in its dying moments. It's obscurely odd that spring rather than summer is opposed to winter, and that Spring's song does not follow Winter's, as the sequence of the seasons would dictate. It's more disquieting, however, that the joyful spring scene is tainted by men's fear of their marriage being marred by adultery, although this is offset in Winter's ditty by the 'merry note' of the 'staring owl' and the thought of roasted apples bobbing in a bowl of ale to warm the blood nipped by the bitter cold. This unsettling sense of ambivalence is amplified by the terse prose speech with which Armado cryptically concludes the play when Spring and Winter have finished singing: 'The words of Mercury are harsh after the songs of Apollo. You that way, we this way' (V.ii.913–14).

The first of these two sentences is couched in terms designed to lend it a Delphic resonance. It can readily be construed as Armado's pretentious apology for his prosaic announcement, following 'the dialogue that the two learned men have compiled in praise of the owl and the cuckoo' (V.ii.872–3), that the play is done and its cast must depart. It can also be taken as an oblique allusion to the harsh words of death's messenger, Mercadé, which sabotaged the sweet love song the lords had hoped to be singing at the end of Act V. But, like all oracular pronouncements, let alone one that invokes Mercury, the god of hermeneutics himself, it solicits further interpretation, refusing to be reduced to these readings. This sibylline effect is enhanced in the Quarto edition of the play published in 1598, where the line is set in larger type than the rest of the play's dialogue, accorded no speech prefix, and thus assigned to nobody. The obscurity of the line is compounded, moreover, by the sentence that follows it, 'You that way, we this way', which was only added in the Folio edition of 1623, when the whole speech was attached to Armado. For it's by no means clear to whom the pronouns 'you' (the onstage audience? the theatre audience? the ladies of France?) and 'we' (the cast of the pageant? the cast of the comedy? the lords and their entourage?) are meant to refer. It's also worth noting that, of all the comedies, which conclude as a rule with rhymed speech, only *Twelfth Night* ends with a song; and that of the early comedies only *The Merry Wives of Windsor* ends with a prose speech and *The Two Gentlemen of Verona* with an unrhymed speech in verse. The very end of *Love's Labour's Lost*, in short, is eccentric on all counts – so much so that it seems to hint at 'Some enigma, some riddle' (to poach Armado's phrase) that the comedy is reluctant to unravel.

During the last century *Love's Labour's Lost* proved a happy hunting ground for scholars intent on reading it as an encrypted repository of cabbalistic lore. Frances Yates, the pre-eminent authority on occult philosophy in the age of Shakespeare, devoted a whole book, *A Study of 'Love's Labour's Lost'*, to this task. The play affords, in my view, no basis whatsoever for imputing to it such arcane designs, but in the light of those equivocal pagan songs and that abstruse closing speech, it's easy to understand why some have been tempted to think that it might. The comedy has a hermetic air about it, created not just by its conclusion, but also by its habit of holding things back that it will not divulge or implying much more than it's prepared to impart. The Princess's cry, 'Avaunt, perplexity!' (V.ii.298), goes unheeded by the play.

At the simplest level, its secretive spirit is apparent in its reluctance to put the paternity of Jaquenetta's baby beyond doubt. Costard is understandably keen to foist fatherhood on his rival with a pun on the hidalgo's archetypal trait: 'The child brags in her belly already' (V.ii.669–70). And the Braggart, as the good Don is regularly dubbed in the speech prefixes and stage directions of the Quarto and Folio texts, is nobly disposed to shoulder the responsibility for Jaquenetta's condition and 'hold the plough for her sweet love three year' (V.ii.870). But the truth of the matter remains as irretrievable as the full story of Berowne's first meeting with Rosaline long before the play begins, or the death of Katherine's love-sick sister from a broken heart. A similar teasing tact produces those moments in the play when the characters '*talk apart*' (as the stage directions put it) and become inaudible to the audience. That Berowne's 'One word in secret' (V.ii.236) with Rosaline stays a secret, and that we're not allowed to hear the 'brace of words' (V.ii.520) Armado utters in private to the King, is all the more striking in a comedy so eager to make us privy, through eavesdropping and mis-directed missives, to its characters' most intimate thoughts. Then again, perhaps it's not so surprising in a play whose romantic plot has so much to say about respecting the singularity of individuals.

Subtler instances of the converse effect – of connoting more than Shakespeare is inclined to spell out – arise from the Pageant of the Nine Worthies, whose unintentional debasement of its illustrious subjects secretes a poignant accommodation of the dead within the community of comedy. Holofernes's justified rebuke of his well-bred audience for jeering his Judas Maccabeus off the stage has often been applauded: 'This is not generous, not gentle, not humble' (V.ii.622). But it's the next line, delivered by Boyet, that haunts the mind with intimations that confound its speaker's intention and defy paraphrase: 'A light for Monsieur Judas. It grows dark, he may stumble' (V.ii.623). The same strange compassion, indeed a kind of tenderness, suffuses Armado's disarming reproof of the lords 30 lines later for heckling his Hector: 'The sweet war-man is dead and rotten. Sweet chucks, beat not the bones of the buried. When he breathed he was a man' (V.ii.652–4).

Such passages slip the confines of their context to hint at an agenda hidden in the deepest reaches of the play and manifest only in the pains it takes to shroud itself. Ultimately elusive though it may be, that agenda plainly embraces the razing of hierarchies and safeguarding the inscrutability of the self. These aims seem inseparable from the play's stylistic evasion of certainty and its structural reluctance to conclude. The 'Sweet smoke of rhetoric' (III.i.61) that swirls round the comedy is created by its relentless resort to euphemism, periphrasis, redundancy, repetition, tautology, paradox and riddle – in short, to any rhetorical ruse that will hamstring straight statement and keep the completion of meaning at bay. What Walter Pater called the 'curious foppery of language' in *Love's Labour's Lost* – its indulgence in fantastic verbal excess and wilful obfuscation – serves the same end as suspending its ending. 'The catastrophe is a nuptial' (IV.i.76), writes Armado to Jaquenetta, but this comedy knows that to conclude with a nuptial would indeed be a catastrophe in a sense unintended by the fatuous 'phantasim' (IV.i.98). For to do so would be to close down, and consign to the past as complete, what the play has striven to keep unresolved and thus forever open to the future.

That *Love's Labour's Lost* is the longest comedy Shakespeare wrote before 1602, and that its last scene, at just over 900 lines, is the longest last scene of all his plays, speaks volumes about its desire not to end by putting an end to desire. To keep alive the audience's longing for forms of fulfilment that lie beyond the reach of the present, consummation must be postponed and the play's *promesse de bonheur* left unfulfilled. Shakespeare's decision not to bring *Love's Labour's Lost* to a conventional close, but 'To dash it like a Christmas comedy' (V.ii.462), just as the ladies dash the masque of the Muscovites, might appear to set it apart from his other romantic Elizabethan comedies, such as *As You Like It* and *Twelfth Night*, in which couples do wed or the prospect of marriage seems assured. But on closer inspection, the earlier play's violation of comedic decorum turns out to be merely an exaggerated version of what Shakespearean comedy as a rule seeks to do: to transform our anticipation of pleasure into the pleasure of anticipation. The fact that *Love's Labour's Lost* is also the first of the three plays by Shakespeare whose plots seem to have been forged entirely in their author's imagination, since they appear to have no main source (the others being *A Midsummer Night's Dream* and *The Tempest*), only strengthens its credibility as a trailblazer for the comedies that would succeed it.

The chief legacy of *Love's Labour's Lost* to its successors is a vision to which the discourse of riddle and paradox alone can do justice. For a quotation that encapsulates the essence of that vision it's tempting to turn to Berowne, whose facility with that discourse is indubitable – 'Light, seeking light, doth light of light beguile' (I.i.77) – and does indeed conceal the 'unutterable longing' that Pater detects in it, and that permeates the play as a whole. In his essay on *Love's Labour's Lost* in *Appreciations*, Pater goes so far as to discern in the 'versatile, mercurial' figure of Berowne 'something of self-portraiture' on the dramatist's part, 'a reflex of Shakespeare himself', standing aloof from 'the other persons of the play', even as he epitomizes its spirit. But, although Berowne certainly dominates the play by virtue of having the most lines to speak, it's to his self-confessed doppelgänger that we must look for lines that enshrine the complex utopianism of Shakespearean comedy.

'I suffer for the truth, sir', declares Costard after being indicted for consorting with Jaquenetta, 'and therefore, welcome the sour cup of prosperity, affliction may one day smile again; and till then, sit thee down, sorrow' (I.i.299–303). The prospect of imprisonment inspires him to utter an equally sublime absurdity:

COSTARD.   Well, if ever I do see the merry days of desolation that
           I have seen, some shall see.
MOTH.   What shall some see?
COSTARD.   Nay nothing, Master Moth, but what they look upon.
           It is not for prisoners to be too silent in their words,
           and therefore I will say nothing.

                                                        (I.ii.151–6)

Costard's mockery of sagacity and oracular profundity renders what he says genuinely wise and deep. To return to these lines in light of the end of *Love's Labour's Lost* is to grasp in the guise of inanity the comedy's covert mission: to hasten the day when the face of affliction will smile once more and desolation will be turned to delight.

5
The Seventh Man: *A Midsummer Night's Dream*

Echoes and Affinities

In *A Midsummer Night's Dream* Shakespearean comedy takes a quantum leap, creating something richer and stranger than the English stage had ever seen before. With its precursor, *Love's Labour's Lost*, and *The Tempest*, which it foreshadows, the play shares the distinction of deriving the core story it dramatizes from nowhere but Shakespeare's own imagination, in sharp contrast to his normal practice of making the tales of others serve his turn.

Scholarship has, of course, detected all kinds of influences, borrowings, echoes and allusions in diverse features of the *Dream*. From Chaucer's *Knight's Tale*, for example, Shakespeare lifted the figures of Theseus and his conquered Amazon bride, Hippolyta, whose nuptial celebrations supply the framing device of the play. The courtly Elizabethan comedies of John Lyly, particularly *Gallathea*, may well have taught Shakespeare a trick or two about developing dramatic action through the interplay of self-contained groups of characters. To Lyly's *Midas*, moreover, *A Midsummer Night's Dream* doubtless owes as much as it does to *The Golden Ass* of Apuleius for Bottom's metamorphosis. Bottom's only begetter would also have found the legend of the hapless King Midas in Arthur Golding's version of Ovid's *Metamorphoses*, which provided him with the story transformed by the mechanicals into 'A tedious brief scene of young Pyramus / And his love Thisbe' (V.i.56–7). The original Latin version of the *Metamorphoses* plainly spawned the idea for the name Titania, while Oberon's name was probably plucked by Shakespeare from a recent play by Robert Greene, *The Scottish History of James IV*, in which Oberon brings on fairies dancing in rounds.

These and many more traces of Shakespeare's omnivorous reading have been tracked down in *A Midsummer Night's Dream*, but none of them can account for its unprecedented use of the conceit of a dream to fuse three disparate plots within three disparate realms into a single dramatic narrative. In its creation of a unique theatrical universe, as hospitable to 'hempen homespuns' (III.i.71) as it is not only to Duke Theseus, Hippolyta and the aristocratic Athenian lovers, but also to the immortal denizens of fairyland, Shakespeare's imagination was once more flying solo, but this time towards a horizon beyond which lay a vision of humanity transfigured.

That's not to deny the manifest debts of *A Midsummer Night's Dream* to Shakespeare's previous incursions into the kingdom of comedy. On the contrary, the play's redeployment of themes and techniques tried and tested in the first four comedies confirms the emergence of a distinctive complex of concerns that is the hallmark of his ventures in this vein. To see key ingredients of *A Midsummer Night's Dream* already brewing in those plays is to become intimate with the proclivities of its author's mind, to catch it in the act of disclosing what habitually attracts it, and thus what matters to it most.

The main action of the *Dream* is suspended, like that of *The Comedy of Errors*, between a verdict and a reprieve, which charges the play with tension. In *The Comedy of Errors* we can likewise observe, by virtue of the identical twins device, Shakespeare's first stab at dramatizing the treacherous instability of erotic attachment that torments the two pairs of lovers, and blights the union of the fairy king and queen, in *A Midsummer Night's Dream*. The Syracusan Dromio's baffled response to the insanity that surrounds him in Ephesus may even have sparked the thought of placing the fate of 'human mortals' (*MND*, II.i.101) literally at the mercy of the 'king of shadows' (*MND*, III.ii.348) and his kind in the later play:

> This is the fairy land. O spite of spites,
> We talk with goblins, oafs, and sprites.
> If we obey them not, this will ensue:
> They'll suck our breath or pinch us black and blue.
> (*CE*, II.ii.192–5)

A few lines earlier, the same Dromio's equally bewildered master muses on his translation into Adriana's husband, in terms that suggest how deeply rooted in Shakespearean comedy is the coupling of fairyland and the visions forged in slumber: 'What, was I married to her in my dream? / Or sleep I now, and think I hear all this?' (*CE*, II.ii.185–6). From these lines to Lysander's 'My lord I shall reply amazèdly, / Half sleep, half waking' and Demetrius's 'It seems to me / That yet we sleep, we dream' (*MND*, IV.i. 145–6,191–2) at the end of their nocturnal ordeal is no distance at all; the fascination with the credibility of the dream-state has simply expanded to embrace the entire play.

It's in *The Taming of the Shrew*, however, that Shakespeare first floats the notion of using a dream as a sustained structural trope and a licence for subversive transmutation. For the blueprint for 'Bottom's Dream' (*MND*, IV.i.212) of being the cosseted prince consort of the fairy queen, we need look no further than Christopher Sly's waking dream of transformation from 'a poor and loathsome beggar' (*TS*, Ind.1.121) into a pampered aristocrat with a doting well-bred wife – a dream from which Sly, unlike Bottom, has the good fortune not to be roused:

> Am I a lord, and have I such a lady?
> Or do I dream? Or have I dreamed till now?
> I do not sleep. I see, I hear, I speak.
> I smell sweet savours, and I feel soft things.
> Upon my life, I am a lord indeed,
> And not a tinker, nor Christopher Sly.
> (*TS*, Ind. 2.67–72)

Oberon and Puck delude Bottom just as the Lord and his retinue dupe the drunken tinker. The plebeian victims of these deceptions are both involved, moreover, in the performance of a play within their play, with the signal difference that whereas Sly is confined to the role of onstage spectator of a 'comonty' (*TS*, Ind.2.133), Bottom hogs the limelight as the noble romantic protagonist of his 'sweet comedy' (*MND*, IV.ii.40). And Puck's closing invitation to the audience to regard the whole of the play they have just seen as a 'weak and idle theme, / No more yielding but a dream' (*MND*, Epil.5–6) doubtless owes something to the *Shrew*'s insinuation that the comedy of Kate and Petruchio is not only mounted as an apt amusement for a 'simple peasant' (*TS*, Ind.1.133), but might also be merely 'Sly's Dream' of male supremacy, a fantasy as flimsy and implausible as the sleep of any henpecked peddler might concoct.

Sly is by no means Nick Bottom's only antecedent in the corpus of Shakespearean comedy. The indomitable weaver and the whole 'crew of patches' (III.ii.9) to which he belongs can trace their immediate ances-try in part to the twin Dromios, the butts of their betters' abuse in *The Comedy of Errors*, and in part to the impertinent servants and clowns in

The Two Gentlemen of Verona and *Love's Labour's Lost*. Like the latter – Launce and Speed, Costard and Moth – Bottom & Co. provide an irreverent, parodic perspective on the shenanigans of their social superiors, although, unlike them, they do so quite unwittingly. The question Launce directs to his canine accomplice, Crab – 'When didst thou see me heave up my leg and make water against a gentlewoman's farthingale?' (*TGV*, IV.iv.36–7) – leaves its calculated innocence before a knowing audience in no doubt. The pointed irony of Costard's response to being caught in the act with Jaquenetta – 'Such is the simplicity of man to hearken after the flesh' (*LLL*, I.i.214–15) – is equally palpable. At the same time, Costard is also liable to utter phrases of inspired absurdity that resonate beyond the scope of his intention, and lines such as 'if ever I do see the merry days of desolation that I have seen, some shall see' (*LLL*, I.ii.151–2) foreshadow the unconscious profundity of Bottom's malapropisms and his mangling of Corinthians as he grapples with the import of his 'most rare vision': 'The eye of man hath not heard, the ear of man hath not seen, man's hand is not able to taste, his tongue to conceive, nor his heart to report what my dream was' (*MND*, IV.i.202, 208–11).

To weave the lovers' tangled web of fierce romantic rivalry, friendship betrayed and misdirected desire in *A Midsummer Night's Dream*, Shakespeare picked up the threads of the conflict that brought Valentine, Silvia, Proteus and Julia to the brink of catastrophe in *The Two Gentlemen of Verona*. In Proteus's abrupt desertion of the devoted Julia following his sudden infatuation with his best friend's beloved, Silvia, and in Valentine's resort, after his banishment from Milan, to the 'unfrequented woods' (*TGV*, V.iv.2) where Proteus, Silvia and Julia join him, we can see the prototypes of Demetrius ditching Helena to woo Hermia; Lysander dropping Hermia to pursue Helena; both men's fixation on the same woman – first Hermia, then Helena; the bonds of Hermia's and Helena's friendship sundered by sexual envy; and the flight of all four lovers to 'the wood, a league without the town' (*MND*, I.i.165). In the *Dream*, however, the affective complications are multiplied, the emotional heat intensified, and Hermia has no idea just how strange the 'stranger companies' (I.i.219) they will encounter beyond the pale of Athens are going to be.

The 'trial' inflicted on the lovers in *A Midsummer Night's Dream* is, as Hermia perceives, 'a customary cross, / As due to love as thoughts, and dreams, and sighs, / Wishes, and tears, poor fancy's followers' (I.i.152, 153–5). The play's critique of romantic codes sealed by custom and sanctified by poetic convention carries on from where *The Two Gentlemen of*

Verona and *Love's Labour's Lost* left off. The speech and behaviour of
Hermia, Lysander, Helena and Demetrius prove to be as programmed
by stereotypes and shackled by clichés as anything Proteus and Julia,
Silvia and Valentine, or the four forsworn lords of Navarre's 'little academe' (*LLL*, I.i.13) say or do. The lovers' plight and discourse are likewise burlesqued by Bottom's troupe in 'Pyramus and Thisbe' in a
manner patently indebted to the travesties of true romance perpetrated
by Launce, Speed, Costard and Armado, not to mention Petruchio's
savage satirical caricature of conventional courtship and marriage.
Latent in the latter, too, and in the marriage of Adriana and Antipholus,
lies the *Dream*'s depiction of the violence simmering beneath the surface of marital and premarital intimacy alike. 'Hippolyta, I wooed thee
with my sword,' admits Theseus, 'And won thy love doing thee
injuries' (I.i.16–17). It's not difficult to discern in the impending wedlock of the Duke of Athens, and in the bitter connubial feud between
the fairy king and queen, which Oberon resolves through coercion,
echoes of the marriages portrayed in *The Taming of the Shrew* and *The
Comedy of Errors*.

In its broad design and trajectory, the play to which *A Midsummer
Night's Dream* bears the closest family resemblance is *Love's Labour's
Lost*. Apart from their creative kinship as two of Shakespeare's trio of
'sourceless' plays, they are linked by their dramatic dialogue with each
other about the upshot of romantic comedy. The denouement of *Love's
Labour's Lost*, which 'doth not end like an old play. / Jack hath not Jill'
(V.ii.860–1), may call the *Dream*'s conjugal conclusion into question,
but *A Midsummer Night's Dream*, which keeps Puck's promise that
'Jack shall have Jill' (III.iii.45), responds by rebuking the realism that
frustrates the fulfilment of desire in the earlier play. Just like *Love's
Labour's Lost*, however, *A Midsummer Night's Dream* commences with
an aristocratic ruler, whose decree instigates a convoluted romantic farce
focused on noble couples, but closes by evoking the labour and lore of
the humble rural populace: the haunting songs of Winter and Spring, in
which the owl and the cuckoo sing of Dick the shepherd, greasy Joan
and raw-nosed Marian, are matched by the entrance of Robin
Goodfellow with his broom, 'Whilst the heavy ploughman snores, / All
with weary task fordone' (V.ii.3–4), to herald the advent of the fairies,
whose blessing draws on the ancient fund of folk superstition that
Shakespeare's audience shared. As in *Love's Labour's Lost*, too, the finale
of the *Dream*'s romantic plot expands to accommodate a theatrical performance by the clowns in the cast that debunks the learned pretensions and
poetical refinement of the cultivated elite. That said, however crucial the

poignant buffoonery of the Pageant of the Nine Worthies may be to the final effect of *Love's Labour's Lost*, the impact of 'Pyramus and Thisbe' on the vision of *A Midsummer Night's Dream*, with its complex meditation on its own dramatic art, is incomparably more profound.

In the end, though, after all the evidence of its debts to Shakespeare's previous comedies has been reviewed, it's the fundamental difference of *A Midsummer Night's Dream* from the plays that blazed a trail for it that stands out. The repertoire of tropes and techniques they share is undeniable. But ultimately it's of no more help than a list of the bits poached from other authors when it comes to explaining what makes *A Midsummer Night's Dream* so marvellous. Any attempt to pluck out the heart of the play's mystery is doubtless doomed to fail for ignoring Bottom's warning: 'Man is but an ass if he go about t'expound this dream' (IV.i.204). Nevertheless, it may be possible to move a little closer to cracking the secret of the spell that Shakespeare's most enchanting comedy continues to cast.

'accidents of the same substance'

Foremost among the factors responsible for the *Dream*'s startling originality is the feature already touched upon: its creation of a manifold dramatic vision through the sustained interaction of three incongruous groups of characters, each with its own distinctive ethos and discourse. Shakespeare's previous comedies had concentrated on unravelling the amorous intrigues in which their high-ranking heroes and heroines found themselves snared. Into this dominant culture of wealth, command, education and leisure, the lower orders, in the shape of slaves, servants, pages, clowns and sundry menials, had been invited to play the fool, but on the strict understanding that their part in the play was subordinate, and their task of mirroring and mocking their masters secondary to the resolution of the main romantic plot. Far-reaching though its ramifications for the play as a whole might be, such plebeian impertinence, whether overt or oblique, was conceived as an extemporal interlude, a jocular aside within the statement made by the principal *dramatis personae*. But in *A Midsummer Night's Dream* the ruling-class characters, around whose fate Shakespearean comedy had hitherto revolved, are elbowed aside and forced to give equal room within the comedy not only to 'rude mechanicals / That work for bread upon Athenian stalls' (III.ii.9–10), but also to supernatural creatures, to whose existence and hold over humankind they are oblivious.

The result left Samuel Pepys contemptuous when he saw the play performed in 1662: 'and then to the King's Theatre, where we saw *Midsummer nights dreame*, which I had never seen before, nor shall ever again, for it is the most insipid ridiculous play that ever I saw in my life'. But, as John Middleton Murry observed in his superb riposte to Pepys three centuries later, 'Each of the three main elements of the play – the love, the fairy, and the clowning – was too naïve for Pepys' sophistication, and the combination of them too subtle for his naivety'. That combination is the key to the play's complex perspective, whose subtlety is as much a matter of structure as of standpoint. By making way for the worlds of fairy sprites and artisans, and obliging the high-born heroes and heroines of romantic comedy to share the stage with them, *A Midsummer Night's Dream* creates a vision which defies explicit paraphrase, and which could not be communicated in any other way.

The democratic impetus of this bold innovation isn't difficult to discern. Despite the gulf that yawns between their species and their ranks, the Athenian sons of toil and the ethereal citizens of Oberon's realm harbour a curious kinship, which unites them in a common cause against the presumption of Theseus and the lovers that their tale is the only one that counts. As Murry remarks, '[Shakespeare's] clowns and his fairies are accidents of the same substance'. When Bottom comforts himself by crooning 'The ousel cock so black of hue, / With orange-tawny bill' (III.i.118–19), he might as easily be a fairy, singing a fairy song. Conversely, Puck, that 'lob of spirits' (II.i.16), with his grotesque mutations, compulsive misprision and slapstick turns, may be seen as the counterpart of the human ass whose braying bewitches Titania, and whose outrageous hamming delights the Duke: 'I jest to Oberon, and make him smile / When I a fat and bean-fed horse beguile, / Neighing in likeness of a filly foal' (II.i.44–6). It's not simply for humorous effect that 'Bully Bottom behaves like a fairy gentleman', as Murry notes, 'when he is in the proper company': 'Monsieur Cobweb, good monsieur, get you your weapons in your hand and kill me a red-hipped humble-bee on the top of a thistle; and, good monsieur, bring me the honeybag' (IV.i.10–13). From such courteous speech it's clear that, to quote Murry once more,

> Bottom knows his manners in Shakespeare's fairy world; but it is much to be doubted whether he would be at ease in anybody else's. For the truth is that Shakespeare's fairies had their origin in the brains of Shakespeare's clowns. They are of one family, and they meet like brothers.

The fairyland of *A Midsummer Night's Dream* is essentially an eclectic figment of the popular imagination, which is why Nick Bottom is instantly at home in it and instinctively attuned to its etiquette. Notwithstanding the exotic provenance of their names, their intimacy with India, and their familiarity with the legendary figures of classical antiquity, including Theseus himself, Oberon and Titania belong as naturally to the native pagan pantheon as Mustardseed, Cobweb, Peaseblossom and 'that shrewd and knavish sprite / Called Robin Goodfellow', who 'frights the maidens of the villag'ry' (II.i.33–5) and ensures that simple folk justice is seen to be done:

> And the country proverb known,
> That 'every man should take his own',
> In your waking shall be shown.
>> Jack shall have Jill,
>> Naught shall go ill,
> the man shall have his mare again, and all shall be well.
>> (III.iii.42–8)

It's by grace of Oberon's goblin henchman that a humble weaver, 'The shallowest thick skin of that barren sort' (III.ii.13) is 'translated' (III.i.113) into the cherished paramour of a fairy monarch, who promises to release him from human bondage: 'I will purge thy mortal grossness so / That thou shalt like an airy spirit go' (III.i.152–3). It's thanks to Puck, too, as the instrument of Oberon's benign sorcery, that the violent catastrophe stalking the four lovers is averted and the way paved for both couples to join Theseus and Hippolyta at the altar. The Duke of Athens can claim no credit for deflecting the lovers' fate from the disastrous course on which it was set before Oberon intervened. Oberon alone knows, and can guarantee, that

> When they next wake, all this derision
> Shall seem a dream and fruitless vision,
> And back to Athens shall the lovers wend
> With league whose date till death shall never end.
>> (III.ii.371–4)

All Theseus can do is ratify the fairy *fait accompli* that confronts him the morning after 'the story of the night' (V.i.23) before.

Unbeknownst to Theseus, moreover, his own future happiness is as much in the gift of the beings in whom he does not believe as the happiness of the couples he invites to share his wedding day:

> OBERON. Now until the break of day
> Through this house each fairy stray.
> To the best bride bed will we,
> Which by us shall blessèd be,
> And the issue there create
> Ever shall be fortunate.
> So shall all the couples three
> Ever true in loving be,
> And the blots of nature's hand
> Shall not in their issue stand.
> Never mole, harelip, nor scar,
> Nor mark prodigious such as are
> Despisèd in nativity
> Shall upon their children be.
> With this field-dew consecrate
> Every fairy take his gait
> And each several chamber bless
> Through this palace with sweet peace;
> And the owner of it blessed
> Ever shall in safety rest.
>
> (V.i.31–50)

The destiny of the Duke of Athens and his privileged subjects is determined by forces beyond his ken and beyond his control. The real power in the play is revealed as residing not with the supreme civic authority, who assumes he possesses it, but with the unseen sovereign, whose followers perform the closing bridal lustration for the eyes of the audience alone.

The Art of Implication

The noble protagonists of the comedy are doubly displaced, in other words, from the high ground they would otherwise occupy at the centre of our concern. Their displacement doesn't rob their plot of significance, but it does force it to take its turn in the spotlight and be upstaged by stories from worlds that are alien to it. This levelling effect is achieved, furthermore, by structural means rather than by argument or assertion; it's a feat of form, not a product of persuasion. Nowhere does any character so much as insinuate that Theseus's presumption of omnipotence is deluded and his earthly powers subject to the sway of unearthly entities. Instead, those powers are curbed and eclipsed by the sublime coda that Shakespeare appends to the comedy, dislocating the closure Theseus seems to have clinched with the perfect valedictory couplet:

> This palpable-gross play hath well beguiled
> The heavy gait of night. Sweet friends, to bed.
> A fortnight hold we this solemnity
> In nightly revels and new jollity.   *Exeunt*
>   *Enter Robin Goodfellow with a broom*
>   (V.i.360–3)

With that stage direction, as G. K. Chesterton observed, 'one touch is added which makes the play colossal': the rational edifice on which Theseus's version of *A Midsummer Night's Dream* rests is rocked to its foundations. The absolute authority assumed by the ruler of Athens is impugned not by explicit contention, but by formal implication, by the inferences that the play's supplementary ending invites the audience to draw.

Nor is this the first feigned denouement staged by the play to produce a calculated derangement of comedic form. Having decreed that 'in the temple by and by with us / These couples shall eternally be knit' (IV.i.179–80), Theseus exits from Act IV on lines that have the distinct ring of a closing couplet: 'Away with us to Athens. Three and three, / We'll hold a feast in great solemnity' (IV.i.183–4). There, as far as the love-plot is concerned, the comedy might well conclude, since no further dramatic action is required to complete it, once the Athenian aristocrats have left the stage. The one remaining expectation to be satisfied is the performance of 'Pyramus and Thisbe' before Theseus and his bride, and to house this Shakespeare manufactures an entire fifth act, which serves no further narrative purpose. The subtler purposes it does serve deserve detailed explication in due course; the broad point to note here is the way Act V of *A Midsummer Night's Dream* is hijacked by the 'hempen homespuns' (III.i.71), whose farcical reminder of the tragedy this comedy might have been becomes the focus of the Athenian court's nuptial festivities. The vulgar, parodic jig that normally followed a performance in the Elizabethan public theatre invades, in effect, the play proper and colonizes the finale usually reserved for resolving the noble protagonists' plight. As a consequence, *A Midsummer*

Night's Dream culminates in a comic turn that allows 'Hard-handed men that work in Athens' (V.i.72) to steal the show from the nobility in the final act, relegating them to the role of bystanders, heckling from the sidelines. The carping and quipping at the mechanicals' expense may take its toll on our affectionate empathy with their efforts. But the derision they attract from their on-stage audience is not merely offset, but arguably outweighed, by Shakespeare's decision to contrive an extraneous last act governed by their 'tragical mirth' (V.i.57).

The annexation of Act V to mount the mechanicals' unwitting spoof is the climax of a process of sly usurpation, which is all the more effective for being inconspicuous. Disregarding the further subdivisions some modern editors see fit to add, *A Midsummer Night's Dream* consists of only seven scenes, fewer than any other Shakespeare play: two in Athens, three in the wood, and then two back in Athens again. The Athenian scenes frame the scenes of erotic mayhem in the wood, which are internally framed in turn by the casting scene for Quince and company that precedes them and the reunion of Bottom with his troupe that concludes them. This double frame throws into relief the fact that Bottom's dalliance with Titania in Act III is the centrepiece of the comedy. The play's scenic structure is symmetrically designed to converge on the moment when a common working man is wooed by a queen and transformed into a 'gentleman' (III.i.156) who takes her adoration in his stride, while a queen is reduced to a tradesman's concubine and her royal spouse is cuckolded, albeit with his own consent, by a clothmaker: 'Who would give a bird the lie,' asks Bottom, just before Titania addresses him, 'though he cry "Cuckoo" never so?' (III.i.128–9).

The significance of this incongruous coupling is magnified by its strategic placement at the pivotal point of the comedy. A comparable effect is achieved by the order in which the scenes are arranged. The long central sequence that begins in Act II, Scene ii, when Titania lies down to sleep, and closes with Bottom's awakening at the end of Act IV, Scene i, constitutes a virtually continuous action on stage. That this movement culminates in Bottom's waking up to muse on his 'most rare vision' (IV.i.202), rather than in a waking of Titania by Oberon or the waking of the lovers by Theseus, speaks volumes about the devious architecture of the play. By reversing the expected order of the scenes and crowning the sequence with 'Bottom's Dream', Shakespeare covertly inverts the hierarchy that prevails in the workaday world, just as he does by handing Act V over to the mechanicals and by making Bottom's liaison with royalty the highpoint of the whole comedy. The ruler of fairyland may despise the star of 'Pyramus and Thisbe' as a 'hateful fool' (IV.i.48), and the ruler of Athens may scoff at the 'tedious brief scene' (V.i.56) the craftsmen lay on 'To ease the anguish of a torturing hour' (V.i.37). But the formal orchestration of the play holds 'sweet bully Bottom' (IV.ii.18) and the 'palpable-gross play' (V.i.360) performed by his 'crew of patches' (III.ii.9) in higher esteem.

If that seems to credit dramatic form with a more profound impact on the play's vision than it deserves, corroboration lies ready to hand in the *Dream*'s production history. Between the Restoration revival Pepys derided and Frederick Reynolds's adaptation in 1816, the stage history of *A Midsummer Night's Dream* is a tale of unremitting dismemberment, truncation and reconstruction. Nothing demonstrates more graphically the egalitarian thrust of the play's original design than the zest with which subsequent productions set about splitting its threefold narrative into separate stories and restoring decorum to the sequence of the scenes. *The Merry Conceited Humours of Bottom the Weaver* (1661), for example, lopped off everything unrelated to the plebeian cast of 'Pyramus and Thisbe'. In *The Fairies* (1755), David Garrick's first adaptation of the play, it was the mechanicals' turn to be cut completely, along with three-quarters of Shakespeare's text, to focus attention exclusively on the lovers and the court; and in his second adaptation, *The Fairy Tale* (1763), Garrick ditched the lovers and the court to concentrate entirely on the fairies.

Even productions prepared to tolerate the mingling of all three groups within the play lost no time excising the other things that troubled them about it. The unknown adapter of *The Fairy Queen* (1692) not only cut the text by half to accommodate Henry Purcell's glorious contribution, but also purged the final sequence of the working men and their play; all we see of 'Pyramus and Thisbe' is the fragment rehearsed in the wood and, after his reunion with his fellow thespians, Bottom disappears from the play. A century later, in Reynolds's version, Shakespeare's play underwent similar radical surgery: Theseus watched the mechanicals rehearse in the wood, and that was the last spectators saw of 'young Pyramus / And his love Thisbe' (V.i.56–7), for the final act belonged no longer to Bottom, Quince, Starveling, Flute and Snug, but to a spectacular military parade featuring '*A Grand Pageant, commemorative of the Triumphs of* Theseus'.

Although most of Shakespeare's script was restored to performance in the course of the nineteenth century, productions kept on rejigging the running order of the scenes to fit class-bound notions of precedence and propriety. In particular, the sequence of awakenings in Act IV, Scene i, which moves from the fairies to the aristocrats and climaxes with Bottom, could clearly not be countenanced as it stood. From Madame Vestris's acclaimed production at Covent Garden (1840) onwards, it

therefore became *de rigueur* to play Bottom's awakening and reunion
with the troupe immediately after Titania's awakening, so that the
scene could culminate in Theseus's discovery and arousal of the sleeping lovers.

   This stage history of dissection and reconstruction underscores the
transgressive disposition of *A Midsummer Night's Dream* as Shakespeare
composed it. What the theatrical taste of the Restoration, Augustan and
Victorian eras clearly found unpalatable was the unseemly cohabitation of
high and low within the same dramatic sphere and the double displacement of the aristocratic characters by the fairy world of folklore and by
Bottom and his band of horny-handed thespians. Directors and adapters
knew instinctively that to have the latter not just rubbing shoulders with
their betters – whether mortal or immortal – but dethroning and upstag-
ing them, was to play havoc with the iron laws of class distinction. They
knew instinctively, in other words, that the mechanicals and the fairies are
united by their secret consanguinity, and that, as a result of their inclusion
in the comedy alongside its noble protagonists, 'the kinship of blood
stretches out to include the courtly ones', as Murry puts it.

   Analysis of the points at which the three groups of *dramatis personae*
appear makes it quite conceivable, moreover, that the *Dream* was originally designed to allow the actors playing the mechanicals to double as
Titania's fairy retinue, and the actors playing Theseus and Hippolyta to
double as Titania and Oberon. Indeed, modern productions have frequently exploited these possibilities, sometimes to striking effect, and
the result is invariably to reinforce the play's confounding of the
boundaries between the groups and its tacit assertion of their latent
identity and capacity for communion. At its best, the doubling of parts
in *A Midsummer Night's Dream* enables an audience to see the potential confraternity of the characters made flesh, in flagrant contradiction
of the official protocol that requires their segregation at the surface
level of the story.

'The forms of things unknown'

No critic has come nearer to grasping the comedy's utopian vision of
virtual community, and grasping it as a product of articulate form, than
G. K. Chesterton, from whose wonderful essay on the play I briefly
quoted earlier. The first paragraph of Chesterton's essay deserves to be
quoted in full, not least because of its heretical contention that
Shakespeare's genius may have found its fullest expression in the genre

to which he turned most often rather than in the tragic masterpieces for which he is most revered:

> The greatest of Shakespeare's comedies is also, from a certain point of view, the greatest of his plays. No one would maintain that it occupied this position in the matter of psychological study, if by psychological study we mean the study of individual characters in a play. No one would maintain that Puck was a character in the sense that Falstaff is a character, or that the critic stood awed before the psychology of Peaseblossom. But there is a sense in which the play is perhaps a greater triumph of psychology than *Hamlet* itself. It may well be questioned whether in any other literary work in the world is so vividly rendered a social and spiritual atmosphere. There is an atmosphere in *Hamlet*, for instance, a somewhat murky and even melodramatic one, but it is subordinate to the great character, and morally inferior to him; the darkness is only a background for the isolated star of intellect. But *A Midsummer Night's Dream* is a psychological study, not of a solitary man, but of a spirit that unites mankind. The six men may sit talking in an inn; they may not know each other's names or see each other's faces before or after, but night or wine or great stories, or some rich and branching discussion may make them all at one, if not absolutely with each other, at least with that invisible seventh man who is the harmony of all of them. That seventh man is the hero of *A Midsummer Night's Dream*.

This idea of the comedy creating through its multivocal imagination a personality more profound than any individual character possesses is richly suggestive, not only for our understanding of *A Midsummer Night's Dream*, but also for our understanding of Shakespearean comedy in general, which is always more fascinated with the fate of the constellation than with the destiny of a single star. Chesterton perceives that the way the *Dream* is shaped and worded implies far more than the most faithful synopsis of what is said and done by its cast could ever hope to convey. His 'seventh man' is the invisible incarnation of the concerted vision the play invites us to adopt: the harmonious 'social and spiritual atmosphere' it creates by the way it correlates its discordant elements. Consequently, although 'In pure poetry and the intoxication of words, Shakespeare never rose higher than he rises in this play', for Chesterton 'the supreme literary merit of *A Midsummer Night's Dream* is a merit of design', a design that displays not only 'amazing symmetry', but also 'amazing artistic and moral beauty'.

What Chesterton calls 'the mental hospitality and the thoughtless wisdom of Shakespeare' find expression in *A Midsummer Night's Dream* not so much in the form of statements as in the statements of form – in the structural acts of inclusion and displacement intrinsic to the architecture of the play. The concinnity of the comedy is indivisible from its 'moral beauty', its configuration of speech and action insepara-ble from its prefiguration of true community. The play itself muses on these matters in the speech Shakespeare gives Theseus at the start of Act V to disparage the 'tricks' of 'strong imagination' that his fiancée con-siders more credible:

HIPPOLYTA.	'Tis strange, my Theseus, that these lovers speak of.
THESEUS.	More strange than true. I never may believe
	These antique fables, nor these fairy toys.
	Lovers and madmen have such seething brains,
	Such shaping fantasies, that apprehend
	More than cool reason ever comprehends.
	The lunatic, the lover, and the poet
	Are of imagination all compact.
	One sees more devils than vast hell can hold:
	That is the madman. The lover, all as frantic,
	Sees Helen's beauty in a brow of Egypt.
	The poet's eye, in a fine frenzy rolling,
	Doth glance from heaven to earth, from earth to heaven,
	And as imagination bodies forth
	The forms of things unknown, the poet's pen
	Turns them to shapes, and gives to airy nothing
	A local habitation and a name.
	Such tricks hath strong imagination
	That if it would but apprehend some joy
	It comprehends some bringer of that joy;
	Or in the night, imagining some fear,
	How easy is a bush supposed a bear!
HIPPOLYTA.	But all the story of the night told over,
	And all their minds transfigured so together,
	More witnesseth than fancy's images,
	And grows to something of great constancy;
	But howsoever, strange and admirable.

(V.i.1–27)

Because of what we and Bottom have witnessed with our own eyes, Theseus's rational incredulity is discredited before he opens his mouth. Considered in the light of the first four acts and Hippolyta's pensive demurral, his urbane mockery of the mind's gift for deluding itself mutates into an apology for poetry, an eloquent defence of the art of Shakespearean comedy.

The authority of Theseus's argument is undermined at the outset by the fact that he is a creation of 'antique fables' himself, and therefore hardly in a position to discount the veracity of 'fairy toys'. He begins the argument by proposing that lovers and madmen have the same 'seething brains', the same mental derangement that leads them to perceive things that are not there or to misperceive things that are. He then turns this duo driven by 'shaping fantasies' and bereft of 'cool reason' into a trio: 'The lunatic, the lover, and the poet / Are of imagination all compact.' At this point, for a moment, Shakespeare's own profession is tarred by the same presumption of insanity. But within three lines the poet's dementia has turned into 'a fine frenzy', and the tone shifts from derogatory to laudatory as Shakespeare glorifies the awesome creative power of 'the poet's pen':

> The poet's eye, in a fine frenzy rolling,
> Doth glance from heaven to earth, from earth to heaven,
> And as imagination bodies forth
> The forms of things unknown, the poet's pen
> Turns them to shapes, and gives to airy nothing
> A local habitation and a name.

On the simplest, most immediate level, this passage accounts for the dramatic poet's ability not merely to imagine mythical beings like Theseus or supernatural creatures like the fairies, but to bring them to embodied life through language and performance on the stage, and in that sense invest 'things unknown' with form, endowing 'airy nothing' with the solid specificity of 'A local habitation and a name'. But with Chesterton's stress on the virtuosity of the play's design in mind, and the key role of that design in creating the 'invisible seventh man' who haunts it, the phrase 'The forms of things unknown' acquires a deeper resonance. It points to the idea of form as a medium of proleptic thought – of Shakespeare's 'thoughtless wisdom' – in its own right. The shaping fantasy of the poetic imagination at work in dramatic form enables things that are *not yet* known, that have *not yet* been experienced, to materialize and be grasped by the audience.

The utopian bent of the proleptic imagination in *A Midsummer Night's Dream*, indeed the utopian logic of Shakespearean comedy at large, is captured precisely in the next three lines:

> Such tricks hath strong imagination
> That if it would but apprehend some joy
> It comprehends some bringer of that joy;

To satisfy our deep-seated desire that 'Jack shall have Jill, / Naught shall go ill, / the man shall have his mare again, and all shall be well', Shakespeare's 'strong imagination' in *A Midsummer Night's Dream* devises the means of deliverance in the shape of Oberon and Puck, the bringers of the joy that we would apprehend. But it does more than effect a benign resolution of the conflicts and confusions that have beset the characters. As Shakespeare's contemporary, Francis Bacon, observed: 'Neither is the Imagination simply and only a messenger; but is invested with or at least usurpeth no small authority in itself, besides the duty of the message.' Shakespeare's shaping fantasy conscripts the rhetorical power of poetry and the structural art of implication to envision the way things are from the perspective of the way they should be.

Shakespeare's fellow poet John Donne understood exactly the kind of power they had at their command: 'How empty a thing is Rhetorique?' he wrote in one of his sermons, '(and yet Rhetorique will make absent and remote things present to your understanding). How weak a thing is Poetry? (and yet Poetry is a counterfeit Creation, and makes things that are not, as though they were).' The dramatic design and poetic discourse of Shakespeare's 'counterfeit Creation' in *A Midsummer Night's Dream* allow us to apprehend a dispensation that is 'absent and remote' as if it were actually present and in place, to perceive 'things that are not, as though they were'. The final vision of the comedy, like 'the story of the night' produced by 'minds transfigured so together', is coherent and consistent, yet its full significance remains elusive. In Hippolyta's words, it 'grows to something of great constancy', but what that 'something' is defies abstraction and definition, because it's a proposition constituted by the play as a whole, a proposition whose strangeness is truly 'admirable', a constant source of wonder.

'a most rare vision'

To cast the whole 'strange and admirable' vision of the comedy as a dream was Shakespeare's *coup de maître*. No other governing conceit could have coped so perfectly with such diverse demands. By using it, Shakespeare commandeered for his comedy both the special liberties and the vatic privileges conferred on this mysterious breach of consciousness since time immemorial. What better ploy for disclaiming serious intent, while inviting divination and disclosing hidden depths, than to present your play as nothing more than the dream of a midsummer night, and end it with the calculated equivocation of Puck's farewell to the audience?

> If we shadows have offended,
> Think but this, and all is mended:
> That you have but slumbered here,
> While these visions did appear;
> And this weak and idle theme,
> No more yielding but a dream [. . .]
> (Epil. 1–6)

Throughout the play Shakespeare keeps not only the idea of dreaming dancing in our minds through constant allusions, but also the state of sleep that gives rise to dreams, the state that Puck suggests may have seized us for the duration of the performance. Slumber as a fugue state, which interrupts and suspends the flow of waking awareness, is repeatedly embodied on the stage: at one point in Act IV no less than six characters are shown fast asleep. What makes watching a play like falling asleep and having a dream is that it requires a similar suspension of ordinary activity and awareness, and a similar surrender of the conscious control required of the mind beyond the enclave of the theatre. *A Midsummer Night's Dream* frees Shakespeare to do what a dream can do with impunity: unhinge hierarchy and confound decorum by shuffling ranks and species; unleash desire from propriety and language from accepted usage; and obliquely vent truths and premonitions that could not be voiced in quotidian speech or routine written discourse.

That the play deserves to be treated as an instance of *oneiros*, as a true predictive or prophetic dream that repays interpretation, we are left in no doubt by Bottom, the sole sojourner in the wood to enjoy a wholly marvellous and blissful vision. His fleeting affair with Titania is the most extreme example of social inversion and misrule in the entire Shakespearean canon, which may explain the fascination it has held for painters seeking to epitomize both the play and its author's art. When the fairy queen's dream-boat comes round from his 'exposition of sleep' (IV.i.38) and wonders aloud what has hit him, the direct bearing of his topsy-turvy speech on the comedy that contains it is immediately apparent:

> I have had a most rare vision. I have had a dream past the wit of man to say what dream it was. Man is but an ass if he go about t'expound this dream. Methought I was – there is no man can tell what. Methought I was, and methought I had – but man is but a patched fool if he will offer to say what methought I had. The eye of man hath not heard, the ear of man hath not seen, man's hand is not able to taste, his tongue to conceive, nor his heart to report what my dream was. I will get Peter Quince to write a ballad of this dream. It shall be called 'Bottom's Dream', because it hath no bottom [. . .]
>
> (IV.i.202–13)

The riddling idiom simultaneously solicits and resists unravelling. Bottom's resonant nonsense teases us with the prospect of revelation, prompting us to decipher its hidden message, even as it places it beyond reach, leaving interpretation baffled. The effect is to arouse in us as we watch the play the expectation of an ulterior import that can be apprehended but not expounded.

That effect is clinched by Bottom's garbling of I Corinthians 2: 9: 'Eye hath not seen, nor ear heard, neither have entered into the heart of man, the things which God hath prepared for them that love him.' The weaver's synaesthetic scrambling of the New Testament text appropriates the oracular authority of the original, endowing Bottom with the *docta ignorantia*, the witless wisdom, of the holy fool. But it appropriates it to intimate that Bottom's 'most rare vision' has been a prevision of the celestial delight denied to his sort in this world, but glimpsed by him alone by grace of *A Midsummer Night's Dream*. If we return the passage Bottom echoes to its biblical context and read on, its utopian subtext is unmistakable:

> the parts of the body which seem to be weaker are indispensable, and those parts of the body we invest with greater honour, and our unpresentable parts are treated with greater modesty, which our more presentable parts do not require. But God has so adjusted the body, giving the greater honour to the inferior part, that there may be no discord in the body, but that the members may have the same care for one another.
>
> (I Corinthians 12: 14–15)

The secular scripture of Shakespeare's *Dream* likewise exalts the humble, 'giving the greater honour to the inferior part' by granting Bottom the privilege it denies its aristocratic protagonists. The exaltation of Bottom implies, too, that the conversion of subjection into community depends on collapsing the distinction between ruler and ruled. Once again, it's a question of the play *implying* – in this case by riddling, paradox and allusion – far more than synopsis or paraphrase can capture, and exploiting the infinite latitude of dreams to do so.

Taking things at face value just won't wash with *A Midsummer Night's Dream* – or any Shakespearean comedy for that matter – because the play, like a real dream, is always saying one thing and meaning another. It's a striking feature of dreams, observes Chesterton, that they display 'an utter discordance of incident combined with a curious unity of mood', and '*A Midsummer Night's Dream* has in a most singular degree effected this difficult, this almost desperate subtlety' by producing an impact on us wholly at odds with the objective import of what we see and hear:

> The events in the wandering wood are in themselves, and regarded as in broad daylight, not merely melancholy but bitterly cruel and ignominious. But yet by the spreading of an atmosphere as magic as the fog of Puck, Shakespeare contrives to make the whole matter mysteriously hilarious while it is palpably tragic, and mysteriously charitable, while it is in itself cynical. He contrives somehow to rob tragedy and treachery of their full sharpness, just as a toothache or a deadly danger from a tiger, or a precipice, is robbed of its sharpness in a pleasant dream. The creation of a brooding sentiment like this, a sentiment not merely independent of but actually opposed to the events, is a much greater triumph of art than the creation of the character of Othello.

Cruel, ignominious, melancholy and 'palpably tragic' the events of the play most certainly are, when viewed in the disenchanted light of day, or through the eyes of critics so keen to indict the comedy for complicity with the patriarchal, class-divided culture from which it sprang that they blind themselves to its 'desperate subtlety'. An irrational, barbaric threat, endorsed and delivered by Theseus at her father's request, hangs over Hermia throughout the first four acts: 'Either to die the death, or to abjure / For ever the society of men' (I.i.65–6). In the *selva oscura* to which the lovers flee to escape 'the sharp Athenian law' (I.i.162), indiscriminate male desire – with a little help from the juice of 'love-in-idleness' (II.i.168) – runs riot, turning the men's pledges of undying devotion to 'deepest loathing' (II.ii.144) in a trice, and inciting both the men and the women to verbal abuse and physical violence. The marriage of Theseus to Hippolyta that frames the action had its origin, by Theseus's own admission, in violence as well. Once all three couples are wed, moreover, only Hippolyta, presumably in deference to her rank, is allowed the odd mild quip at the mechanicals' expense; from her fellow brides, Hermia and Helena, we hear not a single word from the end of Act IV onwards.

Not that there's much to recommend what passes for married life in the fairy kingdom either. Having become 'passing fell and wroth' because Titania 'as her attendant, hath / A lovely boy stol'n from an Indian king' (II.i.20–2) and refuses to give the boy to him, 'jealous Oberon' (II.i.24) resolves to 'torment [her] for this injury' (II.i.147) by making her so 'full of hateful fantasies' (II.i.258) that she becomes besotted with 'some vile thing' (II.ii.40). Only when Titania has yielded up 'her changeling child' (IV.i.58) does Oberon 'undo / This hateful imperfection of her eyes' (IV.i.61–2) and, his revenge exacted and his authority reasserted, declare himself and his queen to be 'new in amity' (IV.i.86). And when the 'vile thing' on which Titania doted is transformed once more into Pyramus in the final act, he becomes, along with his fellow performers, the butt of wisecracks that emphatically divide the plebeian actors from their aristocratic audience, leaving hierarchy as intact among humankind as it is among the good folk of fairyland.

All this is undeniably true. At the end of the play, the coercive structures of social and sexual inequality that fostered the conflicts the comedy must resolve are still in place for mortal and immortal characters alike. Indeed, the resolution can plausibly be seen as achieved, in one way or another, at the cost of the women, the working men, and even the stolen, nameless Indian boy, whose bond with Titania is sacrificed to Oberon's *amour propre*. But to reduce the whole comedy to its 'palpably tragic' and 'cynical' tenor by ignoring what makes it 'mysteriously hilarious' and 'mysteriously charitable' at the same time is to distort Shakespeare's *Dream* beyond recognition. Shakespeare doesn't disguise for a moment the harsh facts of division and subjection that disfigure relationships within the play. What he does is persuade us to perceive those realities from a standpoint that robs them of their force by foreshadowing their transformation. The play's formal strategies of polyphony, dislocation and ironic detachment release the *audience* from the force-field that locks the *characters* into their world. It's by these means that Shakespeare creates in *A Midsummer Night's Dream* 'a sentiment not merely independent of but actually opposed to the events', enabling *us* to perceive the 'seventh man' the characters cannot see.

Another way of putting this would be to say that in *A Midsummer Night's Dream* Shakespearean comedy launches a full-scale, frontal assault on realism, the mentality cultivated by the status quo to forestall its transformation. This brazen violation of the realist code of representation was the chief source of Wittgenstein's notorious aversion to Shakespeare. In his notebooks, the doyen of logical positivism and scourge of metaphysics shrewdly linked this quality of Shakespeare's plays with the surreal logic of dreams:

Shakespeare and dreams. A dream is all wrong, absurd, composite, and yet at the same time it is completely right: put together in *this* strange way it makes an impression. Why? I don't know. And if Shakespeare is great, as he is said to be, then it must be possible to say of him: it's all wrong, things *aren't like that* – and yet at the same time it's quite right according to a law of its own [. . . Shakespeare] is completely unrealistic. (Like a dream.)

Although Wittgenstein didn't have *A Midsummer Night's Dream* specifically in mind, his description of Shakespeare as 'completely unrealistic', as somehow being, just like a dream, 'all wrong' and yet 'completely right', goes to the heart of the play that epitomizes Shakespearean comedy. The 'composite', anachronistic universe in which Elizabethan tradesmen consort with ancient Athenian aristocrats and fairies, who owe as much to classical as to native pagan mythology, is manifestly 'absurd'. Equally preposterous are the magical transmutations of personality and appearance inflicted on the lovers and on Bottom by the 'liquor' from 'a little western flower' (II.i.166, 178) and a mischievous hobgoblin. The resort to the same supernatural sorcery to provide a solution which human beings alone could not contrive places the comedy entirely beyond the bounds of credibility. But, as Wittgenstein is obliged to concede, that's precisely the point. Things indeed '*aren't like that*' and don't turn out that way according to the laws of likelihood. Yet because the play has been 'put together in *this* strange way', because of its singular configuration of language and form, 'at the same time it's quite right according to a law of its own'. Under this law the rational realism espoused by the ruler, Theseus, the guardian of the status quo, is deposed by a revelation that renders the improbable plausible: the revelation of utopian possibilities within seemingly intractable realities.

'All for your delight / We are not here'

The dramatic duplicity that makes this revelation possible is replicated in
the play within the play. '*The Most Lamentable Comedy and Most Cruel
Death of Pyramus and Thisbe*' (I.ii.11–12), like the comedy it concludes,
is 'very tragical mirth' or, as Theseus puts it, 'hot ice and wondrous
strange black snow', and 'the concord of this discord' (V.i.57, 59, 60) is
to be found in the total experience of *A Midsummer Night's Dream*.
Through the play the mechanicals perform to kill time for their ruler,
Shakespeare furnishes a self-conscious critique of his own art's relationship to power, and makes clear how much is at stake when drama conspires to recreate the world 'according to a law of its own'.

   The buffoonery of Bottom and his stage-struck fellow craftsmen is
first and foremost an affectionate study in theatrical naivety and ineptitude, which serves as a foil for the astonishing sophistication of *A
Midsummer Night's Dream* itself. A measure of self-mockery on
Shakespeare's part may also be involved, insofar as the laughter the
tradesmen attract rubs off on the enterprise in which the dramatist and
his company are engaged. The latter, after all, sprang from the same
class as 'these lads [. . .] these hearts' (IV.ii.23), and in the person of
Peter Quince the carpenter, the troupe's long-suffering writer and
director, we may well behold an ironic self-portrait of the glover's lad
from Stratford at work. But the idea of the mechanicals as a cartoon
version of Shakespeare and the Lord Chamberlain's Men is double-
edged, because their ridiculous incompetence also serves as a smokescreen to conceal more serious concerns and less innocuous objectives.

   The mechanicals' play betrays Shakespeare's awareness of the subversive potential of *A Midsummer Night's Dream* and his anxiety about
creating comedy that calls the current social order into question. The
outmoded idiom and ham-fisted delivery of the ludicrous script may
muffle its antagonistic import, but they can't repress it completely.
Indeed, they may be the most effective way of smuggling it through
unchallenged. The sight of 'Hard-handed men that work' performing
their own adaptation of a classical Ovidian tale is without precedent in
English theatrical history: Quince's company are trespassing on the
preserve of educated amateurs and authors. The ominous topic of the
play they present as a wedding entertainment for the three noble couples is true love tragically obstructed by circumstance and destroyed by
death. The plebeian players show the lovers, in a comically cushioned
form, the fatal course their passion might have taken, had the violence
latent in their relationships been given full vent. They also provide a

reminder of the tragic course it might yet take in a world where, all too often, 'The jaws of darkness do devour it up' and 'quick bright things come to confusion' (I.i.148–9).

Moreover, by re-enacting the lovers' plight in a style that makes it risible, 'Pyramus and Thisbe' reinforces the *Dream*'s disenchantment with the tyrannical delusions of romantic love and the pernicious poetic discourse that feeds them. That disenchantment can be seen deepening throughout the previous comedies, and in *A Midsummer Night's Dream* Shakespeare gives us two couples incarcerated in romantic clichés and terrorized by ruthless, predatory attachments that drive them to distraction. The madness in the palace wood only intensifies the torment that this travesty of love inflicts on the lovers long before they arrive there. As Hermia laments:

Before the time I did Lysander see
Seemed Athens as a paradise to me.
O then, what graces in my love do dwell,
That he hath turned a heaven unto a hell?
(I.i.204–7)

'Pyramus and Thisbe' completes the comedy's disengagement from this crippling emotional affliction sanctified by Shakespeare's culture and underscores its alignment with Bottom's view of the matter: 'And yet, to say the truth, reason and love keep little company together nowadays – the more the pity that some honest neighbours will not make them friends' (III.i.136–9).

Nor does Shakespeare's alienation from the ethos personified by Theseus and the lovers end there. The first hint that more may be at issue in the comedy than meets the eye occurs in the second scene, when the mechanicals harp on about their fear that, if they were to 'fright the Duchess and the ladies that they would shriek [. . .] that were enough to hang us all' (I.ii.70-2). The fear of alarming the ladies recurs at their first rehearsal, leading Starveling to say, 'I believe we must leave the killing out' (III.i.13). Before the command performance itself, Theseus reviews the alternative entertainments on offer: 'The battle with the centaurs, to be sung / By an Athenian eunuch to the harp' (V.i.44–5); 'The riot of the tipsy bacchanals / Tearing the Thracian singer in their rage' (V.i.48–9); and 'The thrice-three muses mourning for the death / Of learning, late deceased in beggary' (V.i.52–3). The theme of the first, involving carnage at a wedding feast, and the theme of the second, in which ritual revelry turns homicidal, are singularly unpropitious subjects, 'Not sorting with a nuptial ceremony' (V.i.55), as Theseus points out; while all three themes betray subliminal anxieties about the vulnerability of poets and performers, evoking images of emasculation, dismemberment and impoverished oblivion, which are equally incongruous with the ostensibly carefree nature of the occasion.

When Shakespeare's counterpart, Quince, steps forward at last to deliver the prologue to the play 'preferred' (IV.ii.34) by Theseus, the grounds for such anxieties become increasingly apparent:

> If we offend, it is with our good will.
>   That you should think: we come not to offend,
> But with good will. To show our simple skill,
>   That is the true beginning of our end.
> Consider then we come but in despite.
>   We do not come as minding to content you,
> Our true intent is. All for your delight
>   We are not here. That you should here repent you,
> The actors are at hand, and by their show
> You shall know all that you are like to know.
>   (V.i.108–17)

This strikes me as an extraordinary moment in the comedy. We have been subconsciously cued by Theseus to see a nervous actor 'Make periods in the midst of sentences' (V.i.96). But nothing has prepared us for the sheer nerve Shakespeare shows in giving his surrogate these lines. In the guise of a bungling amateur, the actor playing Quince exploits the pretext of mispunctuation to tell the noble onstage audience that the actors' intention is not to delight them, but to offend them and make them repent, although he seems to cast doubt, in the cryptic last line, on their capacity to comprehend the full significance of 'their show'. The prologue is a paradigm of the technique Shakespeare employs in *A Midsummer Night's Dream* as a whole: it takes a discourse whose import is compliant and conventional, and by repunctuating it – that is, by manipulating its *form* – transforms that import, making it communicate the converse of what it would otherwise signify.

Confirmation that the tables have been discreetly turned, and that more than Quince's speech is 'not in government' and 'all disordered' (V.i.122, 125), emerges once the play proper is under way. During the performance of 'Pyramus and Thisbe' the mechanicals speak verse, which is normally the preserve of the aristocratic characters, while the latter speak the prose generally reserved for the mechanicals. This arsy-versy transposition is perfectly in tune with an 'interlude' (V.i.154) intent on turning Ovid's poignant tale of love supreme into cues for obscene innuendos. The coarse stage-business demanded by such double entendres as 'My cherry lips have often kissed thy stones' (V.i.189), where 'stones' is also slang for testicles, and 'I kiss the wall's hole, not your lips at all' (V.i.200), leave little to the imagination and not a shred of the tale's heroism, pathos or dignity intact.

No such effect is intended by the mechanicals, of course, and their quip-cracking, upper-crust audience are anything but offended by the unwitting demolition of ideals they hold so dear. But the contempt for the powerful and their culture that simmers beneath the surface of the play within the play is not entirely defused by clowning or deflected by ridicule. So much is clear from the echoes of apprehension that persist to the very end of the play. Theseus assures Bottom that no epilogue is required, 'for your play needs no excuse. Never excuse; for when the players are all dead there need none to be blamed. Marry, if he that writ it had played Pyramus and hanged himself in Thisbe's garter it would have been a fine tragedy' (V.i.349–53). But Shakespeare plainly thinks otherwise, at least as far as *A Midsummer Night's Dream* is concerned, and he makes a point of giving Puck an epilogue expressly designed to excuse unintended offence, avert 'the serpent's tongue' and promise to 'make amends ere long' (Epil.11, 12) for whatever defects the comedy has displayed.

'spirits of another sort'

'Pyramus and Thisbe' reveals Shakespeare's anxiety about the liberties he's taking, and that anxiety is one index of the distance his imagination has travelled beyond his world and time. The other is his creation of the fairies as the magical means by which human tragedy is transmuted into human happiness, and it's apt that these mysterious beings are granted the final word. In one sense, they can be construed as a metaphor for the 'strong imagination' of the poet that 'comprehends some bringer of that joy' which it would apprehend. As personified projections of human fears, desires and fantasies, who inhabit a parallel world that so transparently apes our own, they possess a reassuring familiarity, especially if one recalls Murry's remark that they are 'accidents of the same substance' as the mechanicals. Yet they are also inscrutably alien creatures, 'spirits of another sort' (III.ii.389), whose exact origin, nature and aims are unfathomable, and whose attitude to 'human mortals'

(II.i.101) is aloof bemusement at the behaviour of an inferior species: 'Lord, what fools these mortals be!' (III.ii.115). The upshot of their invisible intercourse with our kind is on this occasion benign, but they have the capacity to create mayhem on a personal and a cosmic scale. Both Oberon and Puck exhibit an appetite for malice, and before the fairies confer their blessing on the newly-weds, Puck reminds us that they are creatures of the night, at home in regions from which human beings recoil in horror:

> Now the hungry lion roars,
>   And the wolf behowls the moon,
> Whilst the heavy ploughman snores,
>   All with weary task fordone.
> Now the wasted brands do glow
>   Whilst the screech-owl, screeching loud,
> Puts the wretch that lies in woe
>   In remembrance of a shroud.
> Now it is the time of night
>   That the graves, all gaping wide,
> Every one lets forth his sprite
>   In the churchway paths to glide;
> And we fairies that do run
>   By the triple Hecate's team,
> From the presence of the sun,
>   Following darkness like a dream,
> Now are frolic.
>
>   (V.ii.1–17)

Although they wear human faces, the sinister, non-human aspect of these supernatural beings should be borne in mind, not least in light of Shakespeare's invitation to us to share their Olympian perspective. In Act IV the comedy begins to resound with evocations of harmonious difference and disparity in unity – 'musical confusion' (IV.i.109), 'one mutual cry' (IV.i.116), 'So musical a discord, such sweet thunder' (IV.i.117) – and Theseus asks in wonder:

> How comes this gentle concord in the world,
> That hatred is so far from jealousy
> To sleep by hate, and fear no enmity?
>
>   (IV.i.142–4)

Neither Theseus nor the lovers know the answer to this question; 'I wot not by what power', says the bewildered Demetrius, 'but by some power it is' (IV.i.163–4). But *we* know by what power it is, because we alone, along with Bottom, have been privileged to behold the alien beings responsible for the resolution, and we alone are placed in a position to understand the process by which this state of 'gentle concord' has come into the world. Shakespeare makes visible and explicable to the audience what remains invisible and inexplicable to the human *dramatis personae*. In so doing he estranges the audience from that human world, propelling them beyond the orbit of human experience and understanding in his time to a point from which they can look back down upon our kind as if they were away with the fairies and no longer belonged to it.

Our special bond with the spirits of *A Midsummer Night's Dream* is sealed by our close encounter with them in the epilogue, when Puck addresses us directly and offers us their friendship. Insofar as they are 'shadows' (Epil. 1) in the figurative sense of 'actors', they assure us that the utopian denouement they have engineered lies within the reach of human powers; but insofar as the word 'shadows' insists on their discarnate, spectral nature and radical difference from us, it suggests that something more may be required to turn the world as we still know it upside down, something 'more strange than true' that lies beyond the reach of humanity as we understand it. When that 'one touch is added which makes the play colossal', and Shakespeare's 'spirits of another sort' steal on to the stage as the 'human mortals' vanish, they bring with them, and we breathe with them, that 'luft von anderem planeten' evoked by the German poet Stefan George: the air of another planet, which releases us, if only for a moment, from the gravity of this one.

6

'The deed of kind': *The Merchant of Venice*

'a wonder of ingenuity and art'

'Omit Antonio and Shylock, and the play becomes a romantic fairy tale like *A Midsummer Night's Dream*', wrote W. H. Auden in his essay on *The Merchant of Venice* in *The Dyer's Hand*. Even with the eponymous protagonist and his implacable antagonist omitted, however, the play might still struggle to pass itself off as cast in the same mould as Shakespeare's first great comedy. One can see, of course, what Auden was driving at. Uncoupled from the Venetian flesh-bond plot and confined to the enchanted realm of Belmont, the story of the handsome, impecunious suitor, who wins the hand of the beautiful heiress by solving the riddle of the caskets devised by her father, would be far less prone to provoke disquiet than it is in the play as Shakespeare wrote it. Shakespeare's decision to fuse the casket-plot with the flesh-bond plot, to implicate the love-story of Portia and Bassanio in the tale of Shylock's revenge on Antonio, dashed whatever chance *The Merchant* had of becoming the kind of comedy the *Dream* became.

At first glance, to be sure, the broad generic resemblance of the plays is unmistakable. Like *A Midsummer Night's Dream*, *The Merchant of Venice* enlists the extraordinary powers of a figure sprung from folklore to avert the catastrophe looming over the lovers and to forge, in blithe contempt of probability, a resolution filled with moonlight and the promise of marital harmony. In this respect, a utopian trajectory can be traced in the arc of the later play's narrative too. But the parallels between Portia and Oberon, and between the plights of the imperilled protagonists in both plays, cannot survive closer scrutiny and, notwithstanding *The Merchant*'s allusion to the theme of the mechanicals' play –

> In such a night
> Did Thisbe fearfully o'ertrip the dew
> And saw the lion's shadow ere himself,
> And ran dismayed away.
>   (V.i.6–9)

– a very different sort of game is clearly afoot in the comedy Schlegel hailed as 'one of Shakespeare's most perfect works' and 'a wonder of ingenuity and art for the reflecting critic'.

Although few critics, past or present, would be prepared to share Schlegel's view of the play's perfection, most have felt compelled to reflect on its artful ingenuity. *The Merchant of Venice* plainly has a palpable design on the minds and emotions of its audience, but the precise nature of that design has been the cause of violent controversy for centuries. The nub of the trouble, needless to say, is Shakespeare's characterization of Shylock, and how we are meant to respond to his merciless insistence on his bloodthirsty bond and his crushing defeat by the Christians in court. Our response to Shylock will determine in turn whether we regard the play as a comedy or as something else altogether.

As far back as 1709 Nicholas Rowe, one of Shakespeare's first editors, can be found worrying about what he was up to in *The Merchant of Venice*, which Rowe nonetheless ranked, like Schlegel after him, as 'one of the most finish'd' of all Shakespeare's plays:

> Tho' we have seen that Play Receiv'd and Acted as a Comedy, and the Part of the *Jew* perform'd by an Excellent Comedian, yet I cannot but think it was design'd Tragically by the Author. There appears in it such a deadly Spirit of Revenge, such a savage Fierceness and Fellness, and such a bloody designation of Cruelty and Mischief, as cannot agree with the Stile or Characters of Comedy.

Writing a century later, Heinrich Heine, himself a Jew, drew much the same conclusion, prompted by a performance of *The Merchant* in Drury Lane, during which 'a pale British beauty' in the audience 'at the end of the fourth Act, wept passionately, and many times cried out, "The poor man is wronged!"':

> When I think of those tears I must include the *Merchant of Venice* among the tragedies, although the frame of the work is a

composition of laughing masks and sunny faces, satyr forms and amorets, as though the poet meant to make a comedy.

More than a century on from Heine, however, Auden spoke for many modern critics when he decided that the play defied definition as either a comedy or a tragedy, and that consequently, '*The Merchant of Venice* is, among other things, as much a "problem" play as one by Ibsen or Shaw'. A powerful case can unquestionably be made for viewing *The Merchant* as Shakespeare's first stab at the deliberately disconcerting drama to which he was to return with a vengeance in *All's Well That Ends Well* and *Measure for Measure*.

These deep-seated doubts about the play's generic identity can be tracked all the way back to its earliest appearances in print. The First Folio of 1623 had no qualms about placing it in the 'Comedies' section of the volume under the simple title *The Merchant of Venice*. But if we return to the play's first known mention, an entry on 22 July 1598 in the Stationer's Register of books authorized for publication, we find it billed as 'a book of the Merchant of Venice, or Otherwise Called the Jew of Venice', which suggests that Shakespeare's contemporaries may have been as confused about the referent of the title and the identity of the play's real main protagonist as audiences and students have been ever since. Two years later, the first Quarto edition of the play was published with the following rubric on the title-page:

> The most excellent Historie of the *Merchant of Venice*. With the extreame crueltie of *Shylocke* the Iewe towards the sayd Merchant, in cutting a iust pound of his flesh: and the obtaining of *Portia* by the choyse of three chests.

Although it would be unwise to read too much into the wording of an anonymous blurb, it's noteworthy that this descriptive title opts for the term 'Historie' rather than comedy to advertise the play, and that a hint as to why that term seemed more apt may be contained in the phrase 'a iust pound of his flesh', which pinpoints the legal impasse on which Shylock impales his adversaries, and on which the would-be comedy arguably founders. By 'Historie' the title means simply a story, tale or narrative rather than a historical chronicle or a history play like *Richard II*. But, given the inherently ambivalent nature of the term, it's tempting to perceive in the use of 'Historie' a reflection of the play's anchorage in hard realities that resist the wiles of romantic comedy, such as the fact that Shylock's barbaric bond is upheld as just by Venetian law.

The Quarto's uncertainty about the status of *The Merchant* is compounded by the title it provides on the first page of the text and in the running heads at the top of the pages: 'The comicall History of the Merchant of Venice'. This calls to mind Shakespeare's curious definition of comedy in *The Taming of the Shrew* as 'a kind of history' (Ind.2.136), and suggests that, at the very least, a more elastic expectation of Shakespearean comedy may be required to accommodate the conflicting imperatives of *The Merchant of Venice*.

The play's capacity to polarize perceptions of its intent is most vividly demonstrated by its stage history, and especially by the ways actors have chosen to interpret the part of Shylock. How Shakespeare's company, the Lord Chamberlain's Men, portrayed the Jew, and what sort of slant they put on their 'comicall History', is unknown. It's entirely possible that Antonio's arch enemy was originally played, either by Richard Burbage or possibly by the company's chief clown, Will Kemp, as a grotesque comic villain, complete with red wig and huge prosthetic nose, the staple accoutrements of the Elizabethan stage Jew. When the play was revived in 1701 in the mangled form of George Granville's adaptation, *The Jew of Venice*, it was certainly the comic stereotype that prevailed, the role of Shylock being assigned to the celebrated clown Thomas Doggett, the 'Excellent Comedian' whom Rowe saw in the part.

The Jew of Venice was the only version of Shakespeare's play performed on the London stage for the next 40 years, and the tradition of playing Shylock as a buffoon was broken only when Charles Macklin took over the part in a version much closer to Shakespeare's original text. Macklin still played Shylock as a villain, but a fearsome rather than a funny one, in whose malevolence there was, according to the contemporary critic Francis Gentleman, 'a forcible and terrifying ferocity'. Macklin's Shylock held the stage until the end of the eighteenth century and remained the accepted way of playing the role until Edmund Kean revolutionized the conception of the character in 1814. Defying stage tradition by appearing in a black wig, loose gaberdine and Venetian slippers, Kean transformed Shakespeare's Jew through his subtle, impassioned portrayal into a tragic martyr, a man who was, like Lear, 'no less sinned against than sinning', as Kean's performance compelled Hazlitt to conclude. It was Kean's Shylock who drew tears of compassion from Heine's 'pale British beauty' and convinced the poet that Shakespeare had created a tragedy in spite of himself.

Shylock's potential to display dignity and evoke pathos continued to be exploited by Victorian actors, but by none more consummately than

Henry Irving, whose legendary renderings of the role began in 1879. Irving regarded Shylock as 'the type of a persecuted race; almost the only gentleman in the play, and most ill-used', and he played him accordingly as an elderly, Oriental Jew whose humanity in his suffering redeemed his ruthlessness in revenge, and who retained his self-control and dignified demeanour at the moment of defeat. This tragic interpretation of both Shylock and the play was vigorously challenged at the turn of the twentieth century by the director William Poel, who satirized it in his sarcastic parody of the first Quarto's title page: 'The tragical history of the Jew of Venice, with the extreme injustice of Portia towards the said Jew in denying him the right to cut a just pound of the Merchant's flesh, together with the obtaining of the rich heiress by the prodigal Bassanio.' In his 1898 production for the Elizabethan Stage Society, Poel set out to revive the simple, swifter style of staging and acting that the play's first audiences would have enjoyed. He boldly reverted to playing Shylock as the villainous comic Jew, tricked out with the obligatory big nose and red wig, who exits at the end of the trial scene not as a broken victim of Christian injustice, but as a cunning scoundrel furious at being outwitted.

Poel's production was far from the last iconoclastic riposte to the conception of Shylock and *The Merchant* entrenched in theatrical culture by Kean and Irving. Theodore Komisarjevsky's landmark production at Stratford in 1932 was particularly notable for the panache with which it swept the old pieties aside by turning the comedy into a zany carnival and Shylock into a Jewish music-hall comedian. The clowning of Komisarjevsky's Jew did not, however, obscure the fact that he was the victim of racial prejudice: the Shylock of Kean and Irving cast a long shadow, and has continued to exert a powerful influence, both in the theatre and in criticism, to this day. In post-war British theatre, in the wake of the Holocaust and the recent history of the Middle East, it still sets the agenda for actors and productions, compelling them to ratify or resist its sympathetic reading of the character and its tragic inflection of the comedy. From Laurence Olivier's compassionate portrayal of Shylock in Jonathan Miller's 1970 National Theatre production to the murderous alien created by Antony Sher under Bill Alexander's direction at the RSC in 1987, and in every major production ever since, views of Shylock, and thus views of *The Merchant of Venice*, have shuttled just like critical accounts of the play between the same two predictable poles.

In doing so, however, they have missed the whole point of the play, which is no more interested in justifying and exalting Shylock than it is in colluding with the Christians in his vilification. The vision of

The Merchant of Venice drives beyond the simplistic dichotomies of such sentimental moralism, which prevents us from confronting the unpalatable truths the play is designed to reveal. As long as critics and directors remain fixated on the question of which party deserves the condemnation and which the absolution, with readings and productions switching their sympathies back and forth between the Christian Venetians and their Jewish foe, the deeper, more disturbing questions posed by *The Merchant of Venice* can be kept safely at bay. The point of the play is not to vindicate the Jew at the expense of the Christians, or the Christians at the expense of the Jew. Nor will it do to find both parties equally culpable and neither sympathetic, because that still leaves us immured in the mentality that blames the moral delinquency of individuals for a predicament forged by cultural forces beyond the individual's control. So does the glib liberal conclusion that *The Merchant of Venice* is ambivalent about its main characters, and contrives to leave us in two minds about them. Like the moralistic concentration on character, the critical resort to ambiguity is another ruse for repressing the revelation dramatized by the play as a whole.

The Lesson of Laban's Sheep

To cut to the core of that revelation means confronting afresh the problem of Shylock and the significance of his revenge. It means refusing to rest content with the polarized judgements that critics and productions habitually settle for, and thinking the implications of Shylock's vengeance all the way through. The best place to start is still Hazlitt, though even he stops short of where his own sharpest insights are pointing, blinded by his intellectual empathy with the Jew and his moral contempt for his abusers, from which not even Portia is exempt. 'Shylock is *a good hater*', contends Hazlitt. 'If he carries his revenge too far, yet he has strong grounds for "the lodged hate he bears Anthonio", which he explains with equal force of eloquence and reason', having 'a strong, quick, and deep sense of justice mixed up with the gall and bitterness of his resentment'. In Shylock, Hazlitt continues,

> The desire of revenge is almost inseparable from the sense of wrong; and we can hardly help sympathising with the proud spirit, hid beneath his 'Jewish gaberdine', stung to madness by repeated undeserved provocations, and labouring to throw off the load of obloquy and oppression heaped upon him and all his tribe by one desperate

act of 'lawful' revenge, till the ferociousness of the means by which
he is to execute his purpose, and the pertinacity with which he
adheres to it, turn us against him; but even at last, when disappointed of the sanguinary revenge with which he had glutted his
hopes, and exposed to beggary and contempt by the letter of the law
on which he had insisted with so little remorse, we pity him, and
think him hardly dealt with by his judges. In all his answers and
retorts upon his adversaries, he has the best not only of the argument
but of the question, reasoning on their own principles and practice.

As for those adversaries, Hazlitt concludes, given the shameless intransigence of Antonio's loathing for Shylock, 'the appeal to the Jew's
mercy, as if there were any common principle of right and wrong
between them, is the rankest hypocrisy, or the blindest prejudice'.
Indeed the fundamental difference between them and Shylock is that
'He is honest in his vices; they are hypocrites in their virtues.'

Hazlitt's analysis of Shylock's behaviour and the conflicting emotions it excites in us would be hard to better as far as it goes, but it does-
n't go anywhere near far enough to do justice to what matters in *The
Merchant of Venice*. His most acute insight into Shylock is that 'In all his
answers and retorts upon his adversaries, he has the best not only of the
argument but of the question, reasoning on their own principles and
practice' and thus 'taking them on their own ground'. Here Hazlitt
comes closest to unravelling the lethal logic of Shylock's attempt to
exact retribution from his bitterest enemy.

From Shylock's first scene, in which he strikes his fateful bargain
with Antonio, Shakespeare makes no secret of what the moneylender
has in mind. His opening exchange with Bassanio (I.iii.1–30) about the
proposed terms of the loan is already fraught with ominous undertones.
Shylock's trademark tic of repetition as he echoes each term ('Three
thousand ducats', 'For three months', 'Antonio shall become bound')
and weighs it with a phatic 'Well' betrays his engrossment in private
reflections, which the parroted phrases adroitly screen off. It also
underscores, right at the outset of his encounter with his adversaries, his
reflexive trick of mirroring them, which is about to go far beyond the
mere duplication of their diction. Shylock's dwelling on the idea of
'Antonio bound' resonates in retrospect as the point where the seeds of
the flesh-bond are sown in his mind. But, even at this stage, his pon-
dering of the phrase ignites the suspicion that it may be loaded, especially when it's immediately followed by the seeming *non sequitur*,
'Antonio is a good man'. This naturally prompts Bassanio to demand,

'Have you heard any imputation to the contrary?', to which Shylock replies, with a vocal show of genial reassurance, 'Ho, no, no, no, no! My meaning in saying he is a good man is to have you understand me that he is sufficient' – in other words, financially solvent. Moments before Antonio himself enters, Shylock slyly puts his moral calibre into question by converting it into a question of cash.

Shylock greets Antonio's entrance with an aside (I.iii.39–50), which leaves the audience in no doubt that his hatred for the latter as a Christian and a saboteur of the usurer's trade is the spawn of Antonio's hatred of 'our sacred nation', as Shylock puts it, and his public railing 'On me, my bargains, and my well-won thrift – / Which he calls interest'. Nor does Shylock disguise the fact that contriving Antonio's comeuppance is uppermost in his thoughts: 'If I can catch him once upon the hip', he says, taking us into his confidence and inviting our complicity, 'I will feed fat the ancient grudge I bear him.' The memory of that feeding metaphor lingers long enough to activate the sinister connotations of the figure of speech with which Shylock finally addresses Antonio: 'Rest you fair, good signor. / Your worship was the last man in our mouths' (I.iii.57–8).

The irony of Antonio's being forced to 'break a custom' and 'borrow / Upon advantage' in order 'to supply the ripe wants of my friend' (I.iii.61–2, 68–9) is not lost on Shylock. On the contrary, he exploits the merchant's *volte-face* to increase his discomfiture by playing on his affinity with the usurious Jew he detests. Shylock's response to Antonio's insistence that – with the exception of the present occasion – he will 'neither lend nor borrow / By taking nor by giving of excess' (I.iii.59–60), is to recount the Old Testament tale of how Jacob made a profit from his uncle Laban's sheep. 'And what of him? Did he take interest?' asks Antonio, interrupting Shylock, whom he rightly suspects of having something up his sleeve besides the justification of usury. 'No, not take interest,' replies Shylock, laying deliberate stress on the point, 'not, as you would say, / Directly int'rest' (I.iii.75–6). Shakespeare's phrasing is at pains to emphasize the exquisite sarcasm of the word 'Directly', which adverts to the indirect means by which Antonio goes about exactly the same business as Shylock, the business of turning a huge profit without lifting a finger. A few dozen lines later in the scene, Antonio reassures Bassanio that he has nothing to fear from sealing to Shylock's flesh-bond, because within two months 'I do expect return / Of thrice three times the values of this bond' (I.iii.157–8).

The tale of Laban's sheep is primed to needle Antonio by underlining the affinity that he's so anxious to disavow. Jacob dupes Laban into giving him the lion's share of the sheep by using his ingenuity and tricking the ewes into conceiving parti-coloured lambs 'in the doing of the deed of kind' (I.iii.84). The phrase 'the deed of kind' refers, of course, to the act of mating, whose aim is reproduction, the cloning of more of the same 'kind', or species, of creature. But the word 'kind' doesn't only connote sameness and generic identity; it also animates the affective connotations of the term used as an adjective, which will shortly breed as fast as Shylock's gold and silver, as his dialogue with Antonio develops. For the moment, though, Shylock's chief concern is to charge their exchange with the insinuation of kinship, on the grounds that they both employ the same duplicitous 'way to thrive' (I.iii.88).

That Shylock succeeds in nettling Antonio is confirmed by Antonio's reaction to the tale, which is to reject its validity as a biblical warrant for usury: 'This was a venture, sir, that Jacob served for – / A thing not in his power to bring to pass' (I.iii.90–1). But his choice of the word 'venture' to reassert the difference he perceives between his way of thriving and Shylock's only clinches the latter's case for their being two of a kind. For 'venture' is the term Antonio applies to his own mercantile enterprise, as he does in the first scene when he assures Salerio that his 'ventures are not in one bottom trusted' (I.i.42). By claiming Jacob's profiteering ploy as an example of venturing rather than a blueprint for usury, he unthinkingly concedes the congruence of his commercial activity with Shylock's. The fact that he follows this contention with the question, 'Was this inserted to make interest good, / Or is your gold and silver ewes and rams?' (I.iii.93–4), shows that Antonio remains disconcerted by Shylock's biblical analogy, whose ulterior import he senses, but cannot quite grasp. Antonio's attempt to erect an insuperable moral barrier between the Jew's trade and his own has backfired on him, and his sanctimonious conclusion that 'The devil can cite Scripture for his purpose' rebounds upon him, stirring doubts about the identity of the 'evil soul producing holy witness', when one considers 'what a goodly outside falsehood hath' (I.iii. 97–8, 101).

This opening skirmish between moneylender and merchant moves up a gear as Shylock capitalizes on Antonio's need for his money to vent his resentment at the way the latter has treated him. Hitherto, Antonio has openly treated Shylock as subhuman: 'You call me misbeliever, cutthroat, dog, / And spit upon my Jewish gaberdine' (I.iii.110–11). But now Shylock is expected to behave as if he has never been kicked aside by Antonio like 'a stranger cur', and never had to wipe Antonio's 'rheum' from his beard (I.iii.116–17). The bind in which Antonio finds himself cries out to be savagely satirized, and Shylock seizes his chance with both hands:

> What should I say to you? Should I not say
> 'Hath a dog money? Is it possible
> A cur can lend three thousand ducats?' Or
> Shall I bend low, and in a bondman's key,
> With bated breath and whisp'ring humbleness
> Say this: 'Fair sir, you spat on me on Wednesday last;
> You spurned me such a day; another time
> You called me dog; and for these courtesies
> I'll lend you thus much moneys'?
>
> (I.iii.119–27)

Taking things literally in order to reflect the Christians' behaviour back to them and expose its inhumanity is a strategy Shylock will push to the extreme, when he insists on his pound of flesh in the trial scene. But at this point the exposure of his callous inconsistency leaves Antonio unrepentant and his venomous hatred of Shylock undiminished: 'I am as like to call thee so again, / To spit on thee again, to spurn thee too' (I.iii.128–9). This is the man of whom Salerio will later say, 'A kinder gentleman treads not the earth' (II.viii.35).

It's to that keyword 'kind', which cropped up first in the phrase 'the deed of kind', that the initial confrontation between Shylock and Antonio returns compulsively in its final movement. If you're going to lend me the money, says Antonio, then lend it to me not as your friend but as your enemy, so that if I default you may 'with better face / Exact the penalty' (I.iii.134–5). But Shylock insists, 'I would be friends with you, and have your love' (I.iii.136), to prove which he offers to lend Antonio the money without interest – in other words, on Antonio's own 'Christian' terms. 'This is kind I offer', says Shylock, to which Bassanio replies, 'This were kindness', which prompts Shylock to promise, in a line brimming with ambiguity, 'This kindness will I show' (I.iii.140–2).

By harping on the word, Shakespeare calls its more complex implications to our attention and alerts us to Shylock's equivocal usage. Bassanio and Antonio take and use the word in its straightforward sense of 'generous'. But, bearing in mind 'the deed of kind' and Shylock's undoing of the difference between merchant and moneylender, the kindness he intends to show will be the kindness that proves them to be the same, in more ways than one. The 'merry bond' (I.iii.172) that Shylock proposes, eschewing usury in favour of a penalty for failure to repay, is designed to demonstrate that the mutual resemblance of debtor and creditor goes deeper than their pursuit of exorbitant profits. Shylock specifies that the forfeit for defaulting on the loan be 'an equal pound / Of your fair flesh to be cut off and taken / In what part of your body pleaseth me' (I.iii.148–50). The word 'equal' means 'exact', but it also transmits the idea of equality encapsulated in the pound of flesh. Shylock stipulates repayment in the currency that defines their kind: the flesh that constitutes the physical proof that they belong to the same species, the human race.

The specification of a *pound* of flesh, however, secretes a sardonic comment on the commodification of humanity, to which both parties to the bond are prey in the money-driven, merchant-capitalist culture of Venice. As Shylock observes a few lines later, spelling out the subtext of his penalty plainly, this is a world in which

> A pound of man's flesh taken from a man
> Is not so estimable, profitable neither,
> As flesh of muttons, beeves, or goats.
> (I.iii.164–6)

The terms of the bond pose the question 'What is a human being worth?' in such a world, where commodities count for more than kindness and human values are at the mercy of monetary calculation. In the same satirical spirit Shylock will later nominate the heart as the part of the merchant's body from which the pound of flesh must be taken. 'I will have the heart of him if he forfeit' (III.i.117–18), he swears to Tubal in the wake of Jessica's treacherous elopement; and in the court scene Portia concedes his legal right to 'A pound of flesh, to be by him cut off / Nearest the merchant's heart' (IV.i.229–30). Shylock's objective is to make manifest the figurative heartlessness of Venice, a city where the human heart is a quantifiable lump of meat, by making its epitome literally heartless.

The Jew's logic is the monstrous, symmetrical logic of the terrorist: to inflict on the foe the mirror-image of their own malignity, dramatizing the consequences of the cruelty they hypocritically disown. That logic underlies Shylock's ostensibly innocuous, but inwardly ironic response to Bassanio's fear that the bond will place Antonio in jeopardy: 'O father Abram, what these Christians are, / Whose own hard dealings teaches them suspect / The thoughts of others!' (I.iii.159–61). What Shylock seeks is punitive poetic justice: to pay his Christian tormentors back in kind, with interest. In doing so, however, he becomes the advocate of the very values he repudiates through his pitiless 'exaction of the forfeiture' (I.iii.163). When Antonio agrees to the bond with the wry remark, 'there is much kindness in the Jew' (I.iii.152), and repeats the gibe as Shylock exits ('The Hebrew will turn Christian; he grows kind' (I.iii.177)), the word on which the play pivots resounds with an irony too profound for either Shylock or Antonio to grasp. For through its violation of human kindness, Shylock's revenge reveals the basis of the obligation to be kind in the physical constitution shared by Christian and Jew alike. In this respect the revenge turns out to be itself 'a deed of kind' in a quite different sense, which makes this dark, relentless play a 'comicall history' after all.

'The villainy you teach me'

It's worth dwelling in such detail on Act I, Scene iii, because everything else unfolds from it; it's the key that unlocks not just the Shylock plot, but the rest of the play as well. Two acts later, devastated by Jessica's flight with Lorenzo and galled by the gloating of Solanio and Salerio over her desertion, Shylock sets the machinery of revenge in motion by making it clear that he was in deadly earnest when he proposed his 'merry bond'. The cue for Shylock's most celebrated speech is provided by Solanio's and Salerio's quibbling with his description of his daughter as 'My own flesh and blood' (III.i.32), a phrase which evokes both the terms of the bond and the issue they were framed to bring into focus. 'There is more difference between thy flesh and hers than between jet and ivory', protests Salerio, 'more between your bloods than there is between red wine and Rhenish' (III.i.35–7). Salerio's allusion in his next breath to Antonio's losses goads Shylock into denouncing the latter as 'A bankrupt, a prodigal' and 'a beggar', and repeating thrice the baleful injunction: 'Let him look to his bond' (III.i.40–3). 'Why, I am sure if he forfeit thou wilt not take his flesh. What's that good for?' demands Salerio, his anxiety aroused by the obsessive repetition. 'To bait fish withal', replies Shylock, reminding us of his earlier caustic estimate of the value of human flesh in Venice:

> If it will feed nothing else it will feed my revenge. He hath disgraced me, and hindered me half a million; laughed at my losses, mocked at my gains, scorned my nation, thwarted my bargains, cooled my friends, heated mine enemies, and what's his reason? – I am a Jew. Hath not a Jew eyes? Hath not a Jew hands, organs, dimensions,

senses, affections, passions; fed with the same food, hurt with the same weapons, subject to the same diseases, healed by the same means, warmed and cooled by the same winter and summer as a Christian is? If you prick us do we not bleed? If you tickle us do we not laugh? If you poison us do we not die? And if you wrong us shall we not revenge? If we are like you in the rest, we will resemble you in that. If a Jew wrong a Christian, what is his humility? Revenge. If a Christian wrong a Jew, what should his sufferance be by Christian example? Why, revenge. The villainy you teach me I will execute, and it shall go hard but I will better the instruction.

(III.i.47–68)

In this stunning speech Shylock makes completely explicit what was largely implicit in Act I, Scene iii. He rebukes the Jew-baiting Christians on the grounds that they share the same physiology, faculties, feelings and needs, which render them equally vulnerable, equally mortal and equally disposed to avenge the wrongs done to them. His arraignment of their anti-Semitism invokes a concept of fundamental human equality that indicts every form of inhuman discrimination, making this speech one of the most eloquent and trenchant protests against prejudice ever penned. The bitter irony is that Shylock is determined to vindicate the compassionate egalitarian principles to which he appeals by violating them through revenge. His objective is to demonstrate his human identity with his persecutors by replicating their rejection of that identity and his attendant right to be treated with equal regard. The last line of Shylock's speech makes no bones about his intention of teaching them a lesson by mirroring their treatment of him, by aping their inhumanity: 'The villainy you teach me I will execute, and it shall go hard but I will better the instruction.' Unfortunately for Shylock, it does go hard in the trial scene, where he learns to his cost that 'If a Jew wrong a Christian', the Christian's response will indeed be revenge rather than 'humility'. Nonetheless, by provoking the Christians to take revenge on him in turn, Shylock completes his Pyrrhic victory over them by piercing their hypocritical façade and proving his view of them to be true.

Shakespeare's demystification of the cultivated world of Christian Venice reaches its climax in the trial scene. By mimicking Antonio's disavowed villainy, Shylock turns his antagonist into his victimized twin, making him feel what it's like to be the isolated object of irrational animosity. Before Shylock's entrance the Duke describes him to Antonio as 'A stony adversary, an inhuman wretch / Uncapable of pity, void and empty / From any dram of mercy' (IV.i.3–5). By the time Shylock has left the stage, crushed by the remorseless mercy of the Venetian court, there should be no doubt about how well that description fits Antonio himself. Shakespeare draws our attention to their doubling of each other in the startling question he gives Portia to ask, when she enters the court in the guise of the lawyer, Balthasar: 'Which is the merchant here, and which the Jew?' (IV.i.171). The difficulty Portia has in telling the merchant and the moneylender apart duplicates the ambiguity inscribed in the play's earliest Elizabethan title, 'a book of the Merchant of Venice, or Otherwise Called the Jew of Venice'. By exposing the frailty of the distinction on which the antagonism of the two men is founded, Portia's question foregrounds the dissolution of difference upon which the trial scene is bent.

From his opening speech in the scene, Shylock is cast as the nemesis not merely of Antonio, but of the heartless, hypocritical ethos Antonio personifies. He answers the Duke's plea that he be 'touched with human gentleness and love' (IV.i.24) by demanding that 'the due and forfeit' (IV.i.36) of his bond be paid in full. What is at stake, Shylock reminds the Duke, is nothing less than the judicial integrity and political liberty of the Venetian state: 'If you deny it, let the danger light / Upon your charter and your city's freedom' (IV.i.37–8). As for why he should 'rather choose to have / A weight of carrion flesh than to receive / Three thousand ducats' (IV.i.39–41), it's a question of sheer caprice, says Shylock, as arbitrary and inexplicable as a phobic aversion to pigs, cats or bagpipes:

> So can I give no reason, nor I will not,
> More than a lodged hate and a certain loathing
> I bear Antonio, that I follow thus
> A losing suit against him.
>
> (IV.i.58–61)

The Duke, Antonio and the court remain oblivious to Shylock's mordant burlesque of the equally arbitrary and inexplicable 'lodged hate' and 'certain loathing' they bear him because he is a Jew. The thrust of the unanswerable argument he mounts in response to the Duke's renewed plea for clemency is likewise lost on them, but by this point it should not be lost on us. 'How shalt thou hope for mercy, rend'ring none?' asks the Duke, to which Shylock replies:

> What judgment shall I dread, doing no wrong?
> You have among you many a purchased slave

Which, like your asses and your dogs and mules,
You use in abject and in slavish parts
Because you bought them. Shall I say to you
'Let them be free, marry them to your heirs.
Why sweat they under burdens? Let their beds
Be made as soft as yours, and let their palates
Be seasoned with such viands.' You will answer
'The slaves are ours.' So do I answer you.
The pound of flesh which I demand of him
Is dearly bought. 'Tis mine, and I will have it.
If you deny me, fie upon your law:
There is no force in the decrees of Venice.
I stand for judgment. Answer: shall I have it?
                              (IV.i.88–102)

Even the most astute accounts of the play have flinched from unpacking the full import of Shylock's 'instruction' of Venice by its own example. The 'harsh Jew' cursed by Graziano as a 'damned, inexorable dog', whose 'currish spirit / Governed a wolf' (IV.i.122, 127, 132–3) demonstrates irrefutably that his 'wolvish, bloody, starved, and ravenous' conduct (IV.i.137) is the very foundation of Venetian society, whose institutionalized inhumanity is ratified as 'justice' (IV.i.200) by its laws. Shylock's legal entitlement to his pound of human flesh is repeatedly acknowledged by Portia: 'the Venetian law / Cannot impugn you as you do proceed' (IV.i.175–6); 'lawfully by this the Jew may claim / A pound of flesh' (IV.i.228–9). How could it be otherwise in a world whose citizens enjoy the same legal right to purchase and possess pounds of human flesh in the form of slaves? When you forgo *that* right, Shylock argues in effect, when you treat your slaves with kindness as free, fellow human beings like yourselves rather than as commodities to trade and animals to abuse, then I shall be happy to forgo my right to my pound of Antonio's flesh.

In condemning Shylock, in short, the Christians condemn themselves. That's not to say, however, that the play seeks to exculpate Shylock by turning its moral sympathy over to him. On the contrary, Shakespeare keeps sympathy for the vindictive, avaricious Jew, whose vengeance is far in excess of his injury, systematically at bay, just as he prevents our taking the Christians' sanguine view of themselves at face value by undermining it through Shylock. As John Middleton Murry observes: 'It is the morality of a whole society, to which Antonio and his friends belong no less than Shylock, which Shylock challenges here, and by anticipation blunts the edge of Portia's great plea for mercy.' Through the revenge plot and the trial scene, through the ironies and contradictions they lay bare, *The Merchant of Venice* unmasks a supposedly civilized society as in fact based on barbarism, on the ruthless priority of economic values over human values, of the rights of property over the innate human rights of individuals, regardless of their race or creed.

'The deeds of mercy'

The last twist in the tale of Shylock's revenge is its demystification of mercy. Taken out of context, Portia's eulogy of the quality that 'droppeth as the gentle rain from heaven' and 'blesseth him that gives, and him that takes' (IV.i.182, 184) is rhetorically sublime and utterly compelling. She concludes it with the solemn words: 'We do pray for mercy, / And that same prayer doth teach us all to render / The deeds of mercy' (IV.i.197–9). But it soon transpires that she and her fellow Christians are as disinclined to learn the lesson of mercy as they are to be instructed by Shylock's vicious mimicry of their mores. (As Portia confesses on her first appearance in the play: 'It is a good divine that follows his own instructions. I can easier teach twenty what were good to be done than to be one of the twenty to follow mine own teaching' (I.ii.14–17).) The flagrant contradiction between what the Christians preach and what they practise reveals Portia's paean to mercy to be grandiloquent cant. When Shylock refuses to fall for it, the mask of magnanimity drops and mercy, having failed as a euphemism for Shylock's compliance, becomes a smokescreen for retaliation. Shylock's sarcastic catechizing of his tormentors returns to haunt him as a prophecy of his fate: 'If a Jew wrong a Christian, what is his humility? Revenge' (III.i.63–4). Christian humility and clemency are the last things on Portia's mind as she turns Shylock's winning suit into 'A losing suit' (IV.i.61) he had not foreseen by turning the tables on him. She defeats him by matching his inflexible literalism in the application of the law – 'This bond doth give thee here no jot of blood' (IV.i.303) – and paying him back in kind, in the currency that attests, ironically, to their human consanguinity, which the Christians deny.

Shylock's 'The villainy you teach me I will execute, and it shall go hard but I will better the instruction' is answered exactly by Portia's 'For as thou urgest justice, be assured / Thou shalt have justice more than thou desir'st' (IV.i.313–14). The sardonic quotation marks

ound the word 'justice' are as audible as those that flank the word
'mercy' when it comes from Portia's mouth. Not content with thwarting the Jew's plot by the same legalistic means, she proceeds with feline
ferocity to humiliate and destroy him. She rejects the opportunity to
resolve the matter and show true mercy when she rejects Bassanio's
offer to 'Pay the bond thrice' (IV.i.316) as Shylock proposes, and again
when she refuses to let Bassanio repay merely the original loan, for
which Shylock is prepared to settle (IV.i.333–5). The Jew isn't even
allowed to leave the court empty-handed, as he attempts to, but is
trapped on a trumped-up charge of attempted murder that places his
life at the mercy of the Duke and his wealth at the mercy of Antonio.
When Portia orders Shylock to drop to his knees, saying 'Down, therefore, and beg mercy of the Duke' (IV.i.360), the hollowness of her contention that 'The quality of mercy is not strained' (IV.i.181) stands fully
revealed.

Invited by Portia to display the same Christian mercy as the Duke,
Antonio twists the knife by requesting the court 'To quit the fine for
one half of [Shylock's] goods', provided that

> he will let me have
> The other half in use, to render it
> Upon his death unto the gentleman
> That lately stole his daughter.
> (IV.i.379–82)

When he twists it again by demanding 'that for this favour / He
presently become a Christian' and upon his death leave everything
'Unto his son, Lorenzo, and his daughter' (IV.i.387), the demystification of mercy is complete. Of this fact the Christian characters are, of
course, quite unconscious. The irony of the Duke's assuring Shylock
'thou shalt see the difference of our spirit' (IV.i.365) escapes them. As
Murry remarks, 'They do not realize any more than did the average
decent man of Shakespeare's day, that their morality is essentially no
finer than Shylock's, or rather that Shylock's is the logical consequence
of their own.' But the concerted evidence of the play as a whole conspires to make *us* conscious that under the guise of Christian clemency
the Jew has been robbed of his daughter and his religion, and robbed
of the wealth that has financed Bassanio's wooing of Portia and
Lorenzo's elopement with Jessica, secured the prosperity of the latter's
marriage, and thus bankrolled the festive conclusion of the comedy in
marital badinage.

The final irony of the trial scene is that Antonio's malicious act of remission only confirms the kinship he is so desperate to deny by vilifying Shylock. His proposal to take half of Shylock's money 'in use' – as an investment, in other words, for Lorenzo and Jessica – implicates him in the detested financial practice of his adversary; while the upshot of his stipulation that the Jew convert to Christianity is to make them the same by erasing the difference of faith that divides them. The differences that fuel hostility and discrimination are dissolved in the reciprocity of retaliation, which paradoxically attests to the latent identity and parity of the antagonists.

None of this, needless to say, is apparent to Antonio, but once it becomes apparent to the audience, the reason for his loathing of Shylock and keenness to crush him in court is as clear as the source of his unfathomable sadness. In the miserly usurer, flagrantly bent upon the naked pursuit of exorbitant profit, the merchant of Venice catches the unflattering reflection of himself, stripped of his genteel façade and the armour of self-deception. In fact, insofar as Antonio personifies the merchant-capitalist mode of production that propelled early modern culture, both the citizens of Venice on stage and the citizens of Shakespeare's London in the audience confront in Shylock the unpalatable reality round which their world revolves. It's therefore imperative that the Jew be disowned, demonized and ostracized in order to keep such intolerable self-knowledge at bay. It's because Shylock is so brazenly the same as them that he must be transmuted into something totally different and destroyed. But the form taken by Shylock's abortive revenge, and by the revenge his enemies take on him, exposes the true ulterior motive of Antonio and his Christian allies. Few people attract hatred more intense than the hatred reserved for those on whom we can project the qualities we most despise in ourselves. Shylock is thus perfectly cast as the scapegoat for the Christians' secret self-loathing. The animosity they provoke in him supplies the pretext to gratify their guilty hatred of themselves by vilifying that side of themselves they see epitomized in him. Shylock's direct assault on Antonio's life licenses them to give their self-disgust full rein, to satisfy their psychological need to punish themselves by proxy. That need is only sharpened by *le secret de tous connu*: the knowledge that Shylock has done nothing to deserve his demonization. Consequently, the mere sight of him constitutes a moral rebuke for those in whose stead he has been made to suffer for the sin of being the same. In his consignment to internal exile within their community Shylock incarnates the Christians' alienation from their own humanity.

The Melancholy Merchant and the Sad Chatelaine

Antonio is the play's supreme instance of the impact of such alienation upon the soul. The reward for his successful pursuit of mercantile wealth and the kudos that accompanies it is a pervasive, obscure sadness, the motiveless melancholy that Freud defined as grief without an object.

> In sooth, I know not why I am so sad.
> It wearies me, you say it wearies you,
> But how I caught it, found it, or came by it,
> What stuff 'tis made of, whereof it is born,
> I am to learn;
> And such a want-wit sadness makes of me
> That I have much ado to know myself.
>   (I.i.1–7)

In what may well be the most enigmatic opening scene in Shakespeare, the friends of the play's eponymous protagonist strive in vain to solve the mystery of his misery by assigning it a cause. Their contention that Antonio's mind 'is tossing on the ocean', consumed with anxiety for the fate of his 'argosies' (I.i.8–9), is dismissed as roundly by Antonio as their resort to the theory that he must be 'in love' (I.i.46), leaving them no alternative but to give up: 'Then let us say you are sad / Because you are not merry' (I.i.47–8).

In retrospect, Antonio's dismissal of both explanations seems more than somewhat disingenuous, since neither turns out to be without foundation. The affection that binds him to Bassanio as his closest male friend betrays at knife-point a passionate excess that even Elizabethan convention might struggle to accommodate: 'Give me your hand, Bassanio; fare you well. / Grieve not that I am fall'n to this for you' (IV.i.262–3). Likewise, when he learns from Portia at the end of the play that 'three of [his] argosies / Are richly come to harbour suddenly' (V.i.276–7), his response is anything but impassive: 'Sweet lady, you have given me life and living' (V.i.286). One need only recall Shylock's plea to the court as it divests him of his wealth – 'you take my life / When you do take the means whereby I live' (IV.i.373–4) – to realize that Antonio's very being is as deeply invested in acquisition as his antagonist's. Nevertheless, Shakespeare deliberately discounts both reasons for the merchant's melancholy in order to suggest that the real reason lies beyond the reach of Antonio's understanding.

The malaise that grips the merchant of Venice is the endemic effect of inhabiting a world where self-interest severs individuals from themselves and from their kind, profit takes precedence over kindness, and 'a pound of man's flesh' costs less than a pound of beef or mutton. Well may the baffled Antonio lament, 'I have much ado to know myself', for like all the principal characters in the play, his life and love have been converted into commodities with an exchange value and so no longer belong to him. The ducats and jewels Jessica loots from her father are the price-tag attached to Lorenzo's love. For Shylock, his child and his chattels, his money and the meaning of life are synonymous: 'I would my daughter were dead at my foot and the jewels in her ear' (III.i.82–3). In Portia, Bassanio woos 'a lady richly left' (I.i.161) in order, as he puts it, 'to get clear of all the debts I owe' (I.i.134). When Bassanio chooses the lead casket in which the lady is 'locked' (III.ii.40), Portia declares: 'Myself and what is mine to you and yours / Is now converted' (III.ii.166–7). The cost of their marriage is the cash Antonio must borrow from Shylock, with his life as collateral, to finance Bassanio's venture, thereby proving his love for the man who owes him 'the most in money and in love' (I.i.131) by placing a price on it.

The true root cause of Antonio's sadness is his grief for the death of himself – the self usurped by the merchant of Venice – and his contempt for that usurper finds displaced expression in his contempt for his alter ego: when he spits upon Shylock's Jewish gaberdine, he spits upon the spitting image of himself. In this light, the strange terms in which he couches his resignation to his fate at Shylock's hands appear all too intelligible:

> I am a tainted wether of the flock,
> Meetest for death. The weakest kind of fruit
> Drops earliest to the ground; and so let me.
> (IV.i.113–15)

These lines do more than voice the despair of one whose life is blighted at the core. The opening echo of his first exchange with Shylock about the tale of Laban's sheep suggests that something else is at stake in Antonio's keenness for the court to execute the sentence and terminate his plight. The phrase 'Meetest for death' entails not only the idea that he is fittest for death, but also the recognition that his death at the hands of Shylock is somehow deserved. Who better, after all, to dispatch Antonio than his demonic double, the malign

mirror-image of the self he despises, and the man he has unjustly persecuted? The prospect harbours for him a terrible poetic justice, which
explains his eagerness to embrace it and his beseeching of the court to
brook no more delay: 'Let me have judgement and the Jew his will'
(IV.i.82).

In the dejected figure of the merchant of Venice, in thrall to a hopeless lassitude he cannot fathom, Shakespeare diagnoses the dismay of a
whole culture at its estrangement from the ideal of human community
it has betrayed. That's why the play takes its name from him, not from
Shylock, and why it commences with the conundrum of his pathologi-
cal sadness, which strikes the keynote of the comedy. The nominal hero
of *The Merchant of Venice* remains to the end a dramatically inert, passive presence, the absent centre round which the action revolves. But,
as Murry remarks,

> it is not the function of Antonio to be primarily a dramatic 'charac-
> ter'. In that capacity, he is negative; he is a shadow beside Shylock
> and Portia, and unsubstantial even in comparison with his Venetian
> entourage. But as the vehicle of an atmosphere, he is one of the most
> important elements in the play. He provides, for the beginning of
> the play, what the lyrical antiphony of Lorenzo and Jessica supplies
> for the end of it – a kind of musical overtone which sets the spiritual
> proportions of the drama.

Antonio's true significance lies in his embodiment of the void at the
heart of Venice. By entitling the play *The Merchant of Venice*,
Shakespeare creates the expectation that the character who occupies
that role, the character on whom the spotlight falls in the opening
scene, will be the hero with whom we instinctively identify, because the
positive values endorsed by the comedy are invested in him. By deliberately frustrating that expectation, by refusing to cast Antonio as the
hero of the play that takes its name from him, Shakespeare provides the
measure of the play's disenchantment with the early modern capitalist
culture Antonio personifies.

For proof that Antonio's malaise is not peculiar to him one need
look no further than Portia. As Antonio exits at the end of the
first scene, the chatelaine of Belmont enters and begins the second
by disclosing that she suffers from an affliction of the spirit that
clearly rhymes with his. Unlike Salerio and Solanio, however, who confess themselves stumped by the riddle of Antonio's *tristesse*, Portia's

lady-in-waiting, Nerissa, pinpoints the cause of her mistress's complaint immediately:

> PORTIA. By my troth, Nerissa, my little body is aweary of this great world.
> NERISSA. You would be, sweet madam, if your miseries were in the same abundance as your good fortunes are; and yet, for aught I see, they are as sick that surfeit with too much as they that starve with nothing.
>
> (I.ii.1–6)

The accuracy of Nerissa's diagnosis cannot save Portia from being dogged by her dispiriting ennui to the end of the play. Despite her triumph over Shylock in the court, and her deliverance of her husband's dearest friend from death, Portia returns home to Belmont *in propria persona* in a mood polluted by the same nameless gloom that possessed her at the start:

> This night, methinks, is but the daylight sick.
> It looks a little paler. 'Tis a day
> Such as the day is when the sun is hid.
>
> (V.i.124–6)

Disappointment at Bassanio's failure of the ring-test is not enough to account for such despondency, whose effect on the tone of the comedy's denouement is corrosive. Portia is manifestly as divided from herself by her inherited wealth as Antonio is by the riches he has amassed through mercantile trade.

Nor is this the sole respect in which they resemble each other more closely than might at first appear. On the face of it, the merchant of Venice and the heiress of Belmont dwell in diametrically opposed worlds, an opposition underscored by their unspoken but patent rivalry for Bassanio's affections. Belmont belongs to the enchanted realm of fairy tale, a realm remote from the cut-throat rapacity of Venetian commerce. In Portia's universe it makes perfect sense for a brave, bright prince to free his princess from the lead casket in which she is locked by solving the riddle posed by her father; on the Rialto, where unblinkered realism and rationality hold sway, such things are inconceivable. For this reason, Belmont, as its glamorous romance name suggests, is clearly meant to be the counterpart of the wood in *A Midsummer*

Night's Dream, the Forest of Arden in *As You Like It*, or Illyria in *Twelfth Night*: a country of the mind rather than a place on the map, in which the harsh laws of probability have been temporarily suspended. In *The Merchant of Venice*, however, the idyllic *locus amoenus* is not a transient state the characters pass through before re-entering the reality it released them from; it's the final moonlit destination, the place of grace, bounty and forgiveness at which the three married couples arrive, leaving the unredeemed reality of Venice behind them. It's thus all the more devastating to realize, as the play proceeds, that Belmont is not the ideal, alternative world it claims to be, but a cosmetically enhanced version of Venice, to whose values it tacitly subscribes.

The most blatant proof that Belmont is in cahoots with Venice is the disguised Portia's defence of Antonio and merciless defeat of Shylock. The calculated malice with which she confutes and undoes the Jew should come as no surprise, however, from the woman appalled by the idea of marrying a suitor who has 'the complexion of a devil' (I.ii.127). At his first encounter with Portia, the Prince of Morocco begins by saying, 'Mislike me not for my complexion, / The shadowed livery of the burnished sun', and inviting her to bring him 'the fairest creature northward born', so that they may 'make incision for [her] love / To prove whose blood is reddest' (II.i.1–2, 4, 6–7). Their second encounter ends, after Morocco's failure to choose the right casket, with the brusque scorn of Portia's closing couplet: 'A gentle riddance. Draw the curtains, go. / Let all of his complexion choose me so' (II.vii.78–9). Portia's first meeting with Morocco follows straight on from the crucial scene in which Antonio strikes his fateful bargain with the Jew. The concept of 'kindness', symbolized by the pound of human flesh that mocks the distinction between Hebrew and Christian, is immediately juxtaposed with the image of the red human blood that flows through the veins of black and white human beings alike. The juxtaposition highlights the fact that sickness of heart and the plague of prejudice go hand in hand in both Portia and Antonio.

Wives and Daughters

Considered as a wealthy aristocrat and mistress of Belmont, Portia reveals herself in these respects to be cut from the same cloth as the Venetian merchant, despite the fact that his world is so alien to her that she must change her identity to enter it. But considered as a *woman*, in a patriarchal culture where fathers and husbands call the tune, Portia's predicament displays striking parallels with that of Shylock as a Jew subject to Christian constraint. The sexual injustice Portia must endure as the object of men's vision, choice and possession is the counterpart of the racial injustice Shylock is obliged to suffer, nor is it a coincidence that the same kind of society breeds both kinds of oppression.

'O me, the word "choose"!' exclaims Portia within seconds of her first entrance. 'I may neither choose who I would nor refuse who I dislike; so is the will of a living daughter curbed by the will of a dead father' (I.ii.21–4). But having her marital fate dictated posthumously by a father who has imprisoned her as her image in a coffin-like casket is not the least of her problems. For the man of her dreams, Bassanio, Portia is first and foremost the means to clear his debts at a stroke; if she were not, the appeal of her beauty and virtue alone would clearly not suffice to make him embark for Belmont. When Bassanio at last opens the lead casket to find 'Fair Portia's counterfeit' (III.ii.115), it's the 'counterfeit' on which his gaze and thoughts dwell rather than Portia herself, and the sinister, sepulchral connotations of her image that transfix him:

> Here in her hairs
> The painter plays the spider, and hath woven
> A golden mesh t'entrap the hearts of men
> Faster than gnats in cobwebs.
> (III.ii.120–3)

Portia's reaction is complete capitulation as she surrenders herself, her property and her power lock, stock and barrel to the suitor who sees life through her father's eyes:

> But now I was the lord
> Of this fair mansion, master of my servants,
> Queen o'er myself; and even now, but now,
> This house, these servants, and this same myself
> Are yours, my lord's.
> (III.ii.167–71)

The cost of Portia's surrender of sovereignty over herself is thrown into sharp relief by the freedom of thought, speech and behaviour she enjoys while alone with Nerissa, with whom she mocks the posturing of men – 'I have within my mind / A thousand raw tricks of these bragging Jacks / Which I will practise' (III.iv.76–8) – and while cloaked in male apparel as the lawyer Balthasar.

The forensic ingenuity and eloquence she commands in court may save Antonio, but they can't save Portia from doubts about the quality of Bassanio's love, and thus from a romantic finale fraught with ominous insinuations about the future of their marriage. The seeds of doubt are sown when Bassanio assures Antonio that 'life itself, my wife, and all the world / Are not with me esteemed above thy life', to which the disguised Portia retorts aside, 'Your wife would give you little thanks for that / If she were by to hear you make the offer' (IV.i.281–2, 285–6). The doubt deepens when, under duress, Bassanio bestows on 'Balthasar' the ring which, Portia had warned him, 'when you part from, lose, or give away, / Let it presage the ruin of your love, / And be my vantage to exclaim on you' (III.ii.172–4). And exclaim on him she does, when she meets him again as herself in the final scene of the comedy and baits him about the worth of his words when he swore: 'But when this ring / Parts from this finger, then parts life from hence. / O, then be bold to say Bassanio's dead' (III.ii.183–5). That Nerissa has the same grounds for grievance with Graziano – 'You swore to me when I did give it you / That you would wear it till your hour of death' (V.i.152–3) – confirms that the position in which Portia finds herself is not unique to her, but one that she shares with her sex.

The closing scene of the comedy is cushioned against disaster by our knowledge that both husbands unwittingly returned their rings to their wives in the guise of men. Thanks to the comedic device of cross-dressing, a potentially explosive crisis is defused, but that doesn't dispose of the recriminations in which Portia and Nerissa persist for a third of the last act. This disquieting note of marital discord is amplified by the women's teasing threats of infidelity in revenge for their husbands' inconstancy: 'Lie not a night from home', warns Portia, 'Watch me like Argus' (V.i.230). The play closes uncomfortably, moreover, on a double entendre designed to muffle Graziano's expression of male sexual anxiety: 'Well, while I live I'll fear no other thing / So sore as keeping safe Nerissa's ring' (V.i.306–7).

The discordant atmosphere that clouds the couples' reunion is foreshadowed at the start of Act V by the rapturous duet of Lorenzo and Jessica, whose hymn of love is infected by a rash of allusions to treacherous or tragically doomed lovers: Troilus and Cressida, Pyramus and Thisbe, Dido and Aeneas, Jason and Medea (V.i.1–14). The duet concludes with an antiphonal exchange of accusations, whose playfulness barely veils the home truths and justified fears they contain:

LORENZO.   In such a night
    Did Jessica steal from the wealthy Jew,

And with an unthrift love did run from Venice
As far as Belmont.
JESSICA.   In such a night
Did young Lorenzo swear he loved her well,
Stealing her soul with many vows of faith,
And ne'er a true one.

(V.i.14–20)

The subplot of Jessica's elopement with Lorenzo, for whose sake she 'steals from' her father in both senses and forsakes her religion, foreshadows Shylock's traumatic experience of expropriation and conversion at the end of Act IV. But when Jessica sneaks out of her father's house at night, tossing the loot down to Lorenzo with the words 'Here, catch this casket. It is worth the pains' (II.vi.33), the pointed use of the word 'casket' connects the episode with the casket plot too, inviting a comparison between this couple and their more glamorous counterparts in Belmont which is less than flattering to the latter. For the comparison recasts Lorenzo and Jessica as a cynical caricature of Bassanio and Portia, whose fairy-tale romance boils down to a fortune-hunter hooking 'a lady richly left' and making a fool of her father. To pursue the comparison is to recognize that Portia as a woman and a daughter may have more in common with the Jewess who breaks her father's heart than a resort to cross-dressing. The fact that Lorenzo and Jessica elope in Bassanio's wake to Belmont, where Portia appoints them to govern in the absence of herself and her husband, and where they are destined to remain as one of the resident trio of couples, keeps us conscious of these telling parallels right to the end of the play.

The link between Portia's situation as wife and daughter, and the situation of both Jessica and her father as Jews, is underlined by Shylock in the trial scene. When Bassanio and Graziano protest in turn that they would gladly sacrifice their wives in order to save the life of Antonio, the disguised Portia and Nerissa deliver their acid comments on their husbands' callous gallantry as asides to the audience, on whose shared outrage they can count. The second aside by Nerissa is immediately followed, however, by a third, conclusive aside from Shylock, which aligns his standpoint with that of the women and solicits the same empathy and approval:

These be the Christian husbands. I have a daughter.
Would any of the stock of Barabbas
Had been her husband rather than a Christian.

(IV.i.292–4)

Framed as an aside, uttered in confidence to the audience out of earshot of the court, the remark acquires a choric authority, which reinforces its recognition of the point where racial injustice and sexual injustice converge.

By far the most disturbing instance of this recognition occurs in the dying moments of the play, when Antonio undertakes to heal the breach between Portia and Bassanio by offering himself once again as collateral for his friend:

> I once did lend my body for his wealth
> Which, but for him that had your husband's ring,
> Had quite miscarried. I dare be bound again,
> My soul upon the forfeit, that your lord
> Will never more break faith advisedly.
>
> (V.i.249–53)

The speech duplicates in the domain of love the triangular financial bond that brought the comedy to the brink of tragedy, but with Portia now placed in the position of creditor previously occupied by Shylock. The conscious echo calls attention to the symmetry of their plights, which confirms the structural identity of Portia's subjugation under patriarchy with the anti-Semitic discrimination to which Shylock is forced to submit.

'The seeming truth which cunning times put on'

The harder one looks at *The Merchant of Venice*, the harder it becomes to tell its protagonists apart. Characters who at first seemed to be the complete antithesis of each other turn out on closer inspection to be identical twins, which plays havoc with the apparent objectives of the comedy and the values it ostensibly seeks to underwrite. Conventional, clear-cut moral distinctions collapse under the pressure of dramatic scrutiny, throwing entrenched allegiances into question and standing accepted attitudes on their heads.

If this view of the play seems unconvincing, the result of reading it against the grain of its intention, it's worth pointing out that Shakespeare goes out of his way to foster it. The foremost strategy he employs to this end is built into the casket plot, which does more than test the moral fibre and intelligence of Portia's suitors. It schools our expectations in the logic of inversion that runs throughout the play, exposing the disparity between the visible and the veiled nature of people and things, between supposed worth and actual value:

> So may the outward shows be least themselves.
> The world is still deceived with ornament.
> In law, what plea so tainted and corrupt
> But, being seasoned with a gracious voice,
> Obscures the show of evil?
>
> (III.ii.73–7)

The bearing of these lines on the trial scene and Portia's plea for mercy scarcely needs spelling out. But the long speech from which they come, the speech delivered by Bassanio as he contemplates the gold, silver and lead caskets, goes far beyond a pre-emptive critique of what transpires in court in the following act. Its primary purpose is to demonstrate Bassanio's perspicacity and wisdom, and hence his worthiness of Portia, but in the process it exceeds the character's remit, and winds up drawing conclusions that cut the ground from under everything he and his class stand for. In this respect, it serves as a paradigm of the way the whole play works, which is by subverting and transforming its vision as it proceeds. Indeed, the entire point of *The Merchant of Venice* might be seen as an assault on what Bassanio calls 'The seeming truth which cunning times put on / To entrap the wisest' (III.ii.100–1).

The most intriguing device the play employs to expose the trap set for the wisest by the seeming truth takes the form of the clown, Lancelot Gobbo. Like his near-namesake and fellow servant Launce in *The Two Gentlemen of Verona*, and like the fully-fledged professional fools Touchstone and Feste, who perform a similar function in *As You Like It* and *Twelfth Night* respectively, Gobbo has privileged access to what's preying on the play's mind, and a gift for voicing it in a manner that's all the more compelling for being distorted or absurd. 'How every fool can play upon the word!' (III.v.41) exclaims an exasperated Lorenzo after Gobbo has confounded him with quibbles:

> The fool hath planted in his memory
> An army of good words, and I do know
> A many fools that stand in better place,
> Garnished like him, that for a tricksy word
> Defy the matter.
>
> (III.v.61–5)

Using words in a 'tricksy' way to 'defy the matter' – that is, to sabotage
the plain meaning of the matter in hand by derailing it and switching it
on to another track altogether – is the speciality of Gobbo's trade. And
nowhere does he ply his trade more profitably for us than in the scene
in which he makes his first appearance.

In a grotesquely vivid comic monologue, which parodies the plight
of the soul in the old morality plays, Gobbo depicts himself as torn
between his conscience's demand that he remain in the service of
Shylock and the devil's insistence that he abandon him:

> well, my conscience says, 'Lancelot, budge not'; 'Budge!' says the
> fiend; 'Budge not', says my conscience. 'Conscience,' say I, 'you
> counsel well'; 'Fiend,' say I, 'you counsel well.' To be ruled by my
> conscience I should stay with the Jew my master who, God bless the
> mark, is a kind of devil; and to run away from the Jew I should be
> ruled by the fiend who, saving your reverence, is the devil himself.
> Certainly the Jew is the very devil incarnation; and in my conscience,
> my conscience is but a kind of hard conscience to offer to counsel me
> to stay with the Jew. The fiend gives the more friendly counsel. I will
> run, fiend. My heels are at your commandment. I will run.
>
> (II.ii.17–29)

That lame term 'comic relief' can't begin to do justice to this
remarkable speech, which dramatizes the crisis of conscience and alle-
giance Shylock provokes in the audience and simultaneously deflates it
by turning it into a pantomime. Gobbo's decision to desert the Jew is
unequivocally defined as a decision to heed the counsel of the fiend,
which directly contradicts the attitude to Shylock his characterization
encourages us to adopt. Conversely, to stand by the Jew in spite of his
portrayal as 'the very devil incarnation' is commended as the course
that conscience dictates. In his own inimitable, teasing fashion, Gobbo
makes it clear where the play's conscience lies and the consequences of
following the fiend's friendly counsel and taking the Jew at the
Christians' estimate. The wise fool of the comedy cautions us against
accepting its 'seeming truth' unquestioningly, and counsels us instead to
be prepared to find the reverse of what convention endorses to be the
case. At the same time, his jocular perspective on the grim dilemma at
the centre of the play allows us to enjoy a moment of ironic detachment
from the bitter antagonisms in which the protagonists are embroiled.

The same fleeting sense of emancipation from the conflicts in which
the characters are trapped is created when Gobbo twits his father at

length about his own paternity ('It is a wise father that knows his own child' (II.ii.72–3)) and when he greets Jessica's declaration, 'I shall be saved by my husband. He hath made me a Christian', with the riposte:

> Truly, the more to blame he! We were Christians enough before, e'en as many as could well live one by another. This making of Christians will raise the price of hogs. If we grow all to be pork-eaters we shall not shortly have a rasher on the coals for money.
>
> (III.v.17–24)

In the first case, the facetious taunting of Old Gobbo makes a joke of the predicament in which Jessica and Portia find themselves thanks to their fathers. In the second, with its allusion to Jessica's conversion and foreshadowing of Shylock's, the crux of the whole comedy, the deadly antipathy between Christian and Jew, is reduced to the farcical consequence of arbitrary distinctions and customs. Through Gobbo we catch a glimpse of the wider point of view from which *The Merchant of Venice* is written. It's a point of view that lies beyond the grasp of either Antonio or Portia or Shylock, because it's committed to the common human cause of 'kindness', which the principal characters – including Shylock, who brings the cause to light – are fated to betray. When the depth of the comedy's commitment to that cause is fully recognized, Schlegel's judgement that it is 'one of Shakespeare's most perfect works' may come to seem less eccentric.

7
'Pribbles and prabbles': *The Merry Wives of Windsor*

'let's hear Verdi'

It's tempting to take the standard critical line on *The Merry Wives of Windsor* and write it off as a lightweight, knockabout farce, whose popularity down through the centuries and all over the world is a testament to its lack of profundity and eagerness to please rather than to its possession of the controversial or visionary qualities that have kept Shakespeare's critically acclaimed comedies alive and kicking.

The play's first significant critic, John Dryden, praised it in 1679 for 'the mechanic beauties of the plot, which are the observation of the three Unities, Time, Place, and Action'. But Dryden's commendation did the comedy no more favours in the long run than Nicholas Rowe's conclusion 30 years later that 'the whole play is admirable; the humours are various and well oppos'd; the main design, which is to cure *Ford* of his unreasonable jealousie, is extremely well conducted', because both men were congratulating it for complying with the rules of the craft as they conceived them, and thus endorsing through its design the principles of moral decorum they espoused. From this unintended damnation by faint praise Dr Johnson saw no comparable grounds for redeeming *The Merry Wives of Windsor*. Commenting on the play in 1773, he drew a conclusion diametrically opposed to Dryden's and Rowe's: 'The conduct of this drama is deficient; the action begins and ends often before the conclusion and the different parts might change places without inconvenience.' So much for 'the mechanic beauties of the plot'. Characteristically, however, given the dialectical cast of his mind, Johnson cut the ground from beneath his disparagement of the play in the very next sentence: 'but its general power, that power by which all works of genius shall finally be tried, is such that perhaps it never yet had reader or spectator who did not think it too soon at an end'. Johnson's honesty obliged him to acknowledge, in other words, that *The Merry Wives of Windsor* demonstrated a capacity to delight that scrutiny of its formal execution alone could not account for.

Johnson's shrewd hunch that there was more to *Merry Wives* than met the eye, even if criticism was so far at a loss to explain the source of 'its general power', was never followed up. Hazlitt, while conceding that '*The Merry Wives of Windsor* is no doubt a very amusing play, with a great deal of humour, character, and nature in it', grumbled that it would have been a much better play if its hero had not been Falstaff, whose 'unconscious indignities' and 'sensible mortifications' at the hands of Mistress Ford and Mistress Page betrayed the indomitable character he cut in *Henry IV* and thus crippled the whole comedy. Coleridge found nothing of note to say about the play, and even the Lambs were unable to discern in the stratagems devised for the fat knight's comeuppance and in the courtship of Anne Page sufficient amusement or instruction to warrant the comedy's inclusion in their *Tales from Shakespeare* (1807). The play received equally short shrift from George Bernard Shaw, for whom its sole claim to fame was as the inspiration for Verdi's last opera, *Falstaff* (1893). W. H. Auden was of exactly the same mind as Shaw half a century later. In 1946–7 Auden delivered a series of brilliant public lectures in New York, in which he covered all of Shakespeare's plays except *Titus Andronicus*; when he came to *The Merry Wives of Windsor*, however, all he had to say was:

> *The Merry Wives of Windsor* is a very dull play indeed. We can be grateful for its having been written, because it provided the occasion of Verdi's *Falstaff*, a very great operatic masterpiece. Mr Page, Shallow, Slender, and the Host disappear. I have nothing to say about Shakespeare's play, so let's hear Verdi.

Nor did *The Merry Wives of Windsor* fare much better with academic critics in the second half of the twentieth century, which witnessed an exponential boom in Shakespeare studies that has shown no signs of subsiding in the twenty-first. This period saw the publication of what remain two of the most influential modern studies of Shakespearean comedy, C. L. Barber's *Shakespeare's Festive Comedy* (1959) and Northrop Frye's *A Natural Perspective* (1965). Frye's formulation of the generic laws of Shakespearean comedy and romance owes next to nothing to *The Merry Wives of Windsor*, in which he finds only an eccentric corroboration of his thesis. Barber excludes the play from consideration altogether, despite

the ease with which he might have accommodated it within the sub-
genre of festive comedy he set out to define. Since Barber, most books
about Shakespeare's comedies have continued to cold-shoulder *Merry
Wives* or grant it at best a passing nod as a poor relation of *Twelfth Night*
and *As You Like It*. The very few recent critics who have accorded it more
than a glance have invariably done so to demonstrate its value as a docu-
ment of the age in which it's anchored rather than as a unique work of
verbal and dramatic art, which can't be accounted for in terms of historical context alone. Not even Harold Bloom, the most bardolatrous critic
of modern times, for whom Falstaff is Shakespeare's supreme creation,
can find a kind word to say for the comedy. On the contrary, in
Shakespeare: The Invention of the Human (1999) Bloom denounces the
comedy's principal character as a travesty of the presiding genius of
Henry IV, 'a nameless impostor masquerading as the great Sir John
Falstaff', and dismisses the entire play in four pages, convinced that '*The
Merry Wives of Windsor* is Shakespeare's only play that he himself seems
to hold in contempt'.

The belief Bloom shares with Hazlitt that the Falstaff of *Merry Wives*
is a fraud because, in Hazlitt's words, 'His wit and eloquence have left
him', and because 'Instead of making a butt of others, he is made a butt
of by them', is hard to square with the facts of the play when it's set
alongside the two parts of *Henry IV*. The repeated discomfiture of the
obese rogue in *Merry Wives* by its eponymous heroines merely continues
the regimen of comic retribution imposed on him in the history plays.
Falstaff is hoodwinked by Hal during the Gadshill robbery in *Henry IV
Part 1*, and unmasked as a liar and coward both then and later on the
battlefield, when he steals the credit for killing Hotspur; while *Part II*
notoriously culminates in his brutal rejection by the newly crowned
Henry V – 'I know thee not, old man. Fall to thy prayers' (V.v.47) –
which disabuses Falstaff not only of his faith in Hal's friendship, but also
of his dreams of licensed plunder, and thus shows him more compre-
hensively and cruelly duped than he could ever have been by the merry
wives of Windsor. Indeed, no sooner have the latter finished teaching
the old 'bag of flax' (V.v.150) his third and final lesson than Mistress
Page invites him home with all the rest to 'laugh this sport o'er by a
country fire' (V.v.234) – a genial act of generosity which confirms the
high regard in which the comedy holds its star, and which gives the lie
to Bloom's view that it leaves Falstaff crushed and emasculated, the victim of a perverse masochistic impulse on Shakespeare's part.

The charge that the 'puffed man' (V.v.151) has been robbed of his
wit and eloquence in *The Merry Wives of Windsor* seems equally hard to

substantiate. The snappy ripostes with which he dispatches Shallow's allegations in their opening exchange suggest that his capacity for quick-fire repartee is undiminished:

> SHALLOW. Knight, you have beaten my men, killed my deer, and broke open my lodge.
> FALSTAFF. But not kissed your keeper's daughter?
> SHALLOW. Tut, a pin. This shall be answered.
> FALSTAFF. I will answer it straight: I have done all this. That is now answered.
>
> (I.i.104–9)

As for Sir John's rhetorical and poetic powers, even Shaw couldn't withhold his admiration from Falstaff's *résumé* of his confinement in the foul-smelling buck-basket and his subsequent ducking in the Thames:

> I suffered the pangs of three several deaths. First, an intolerable fright, to be detected with a jealous rotten bell-wether. Next, to be compassed like a good bilbo in the circumference of a peck, hilt to point, heel to head. And then, to be stopped in, like a strong distillation, with stinking clothes that fretted in their own grease. Think of that – a man of my kidney – think of that – that am as subject to heat as butter, a man of continual dissolution and thaw. It was a miracle to scape suffocation. And in the height of this bath, when I was more than half stewed in grease like a Dutch dish, to be thrown into the Thames and cooled, glowing-hot, in that surge, like a horseshoe. Think of that – hissing hot – think of that, Master Brooke!
>
> (III.v.99–113)

The superb command of surreal simile and climactic hyperbole exhibited here proves that Falstaff's eloquence, far from having deserted him upon his arrival in Windsor, remains the means by which he transforms physical humiliation and moral reproof into verbal victory, making nonsense of Hazlitt's notion that he 'is not the man he was in the two parts of *Henry IV*' and Bloom's contemptuous dismissal of him as 'a horned, chained pseudo-Falstaff, victim of sadomasochistic farce'.

Such views rest, moreover, on the highly questionable assumption that the composition of *The Merry Wives of Windsor* postdates the writing of both parts of *Henry IV*. The most recent Arden edition by Giorgio Melchiori (2000) endorses this assumption by dating the play

1599 and placing it probably just before, but possibly just after, *Henry V*, whose composition may confidently be assigned to that year. Most scholars, however, would beg to disagree with this controversial hypothesis, deeming it more plausible that the earliest version of *Merry Wives* was written between 1597 and 1598 – in other words, after *Henry IV Part 1* and either before, or about the same time as, *Henry IV Part 2*. In fact, some have suggested that Shakespeare interrupted the composition of *Henry IV Part 2* in order to write *The Merry Wives of Windsor*, a conjecture lent credence by the high proportion of distinctive words shared by these two plays alone, as well as by their equally distinctive shared concern with the texture of life in provincial English milieux. Although this contention, too, must remain a matter of speculation, there are strong grounds for rejecting the idea that the protagonist of *The Merry Wives of Windsor* is a pale shadow of the comic colossus created in two earlier plays, and sound reasons for believing that he and the merry wives who outwit him were forged in the same crucible as the history plays he inhabits. If this *is* the case, and if there's consequently no essential difference between the Falstaff of *Merry Wives* and the Falstaff of *1* and *2 Henry IV*, then it may be that the real explanation for critics' dissatisfaction with the former lies elsewhere.

What really irks them, I suspect, is not any change in Falstaff's characterization, but his transplantation from the royal domain of momentous historical events, in which the fate of the entire English nation is at stake, to the confines of a citizen comedy set in a market town, where middle-class morality prevails, family affairs and household duties take priority, and the attainment of prosperity and respectability through marriage is the chief ambition and source of conflict. From this point of view, it's Falstaff's relocation from history play to farce that belittles him rather than any intrinsic diminution or distortion of his character. His outrageous transgressions and delinquencies matter far less in the domestic realm of Windsor than they do on the grand stage of English history, where he consorts with the crown prince and his cynical creed of self-gratification calls the avowed ideals of the monarchy into question. For the critics who relish Falstaff's insubordination in the presence of royalty and in the thick of civil war, it's understandably galling to see him outflanked by a couple of housewives instead of by Prince Hal; whereas the same critics wouldn't have turned a hair if the heir to throne had played exactly the same practical jokes on Sir Jack, and made him look just as big a fool, in the metropolitan milieu of Eastcheap. The real beef critics like Hazlitt and Bloom have with *The Merry Wives of Windsor* is with the kind of comedy it is rather than with the way it portrays Falstaff or the nature of the indignities it subjects him to.

Shakespeare's Black Sheep

So what kind and calibre of comedy is it, and how does it measure up to the comedies of Shakespeare that preceded and succeeded it? Refuting the charge that the play is botched because it betrays the ruling spirit of *Henry IV* is one thing, but it doesn't dispose of the broader charge that, quite apart from the question of Falstaff, *The Merry Wives of Windsor* – however hilarious in performance it may be – is ultimately second-rate stuff, an Elizabethan sit-com as slight as the witless Slender and as shallow as the prattling Justice of the Peace who has the misfortune to be his kin. If one brings these expectations to the play, it's undeniably not difficult to have them fulfilled. They doubtless have their origin in the legend, hatched by John Dennis and Nicholas Rowe in the early eighteenth century, that the comedy was dashed off in a fortnight at the express command of Queen Elizabeth, who was so smitten with the rotund reprobate in the two parts of *Henry IV* that she demanded another play designed to portray him in the throes of love. This apocryphal but irresistible account of the comedy's conception dovetails with the more credible scholarly conjecture that Shakespeare broke off from drafting *2 Henry IV* to write it, and with the widespread assumption that the celebration of the Order of the Garter it features in Act V proves it to have been at some point, at least in part, a *pièce de circonstance* for an exclusive audience as well as a commercial entertainment for the popular stage. These theories about the play's genesis, whether believable or baseless, have combined to cement its reputation as a mere bagatelle, a specially commissioned spin-off from artistic endeavours of much greater moment. The fact that *Merry Wives* is its author's sole foray into citizen comedy of the kind made famous by Thomas Dekker in *The Shoemaker's Holiday*, and which most major dramatists of the day had a crack at, has also conspired to set the play apart as a stray offshoot from the comedy branch of the Shakespearean canon.

As a result, even the play's stoutest allies have been content to leave it stranded by itself in a cul-de-sac, an exception to the rule of Shakespearean comedy, whose normal rationale it throws into relief, and a curious precursor of the Restoration comedy of marital manners and sexual intrigue, from which the screwball comedies of early twentieth-century Hollywood in turn trace their descent. No sooner has this routine view of *Merry Wives* been registered, however, than objections to its isolation of the play as anomalous crowd round it. All sorts of analogies link it back to Shakespeare's previous Elizabethan comedies and forward to *Much Ado*, *As You Like It* and *Twelfth Night*, making it seem less like the black sheep and more like a bona fide member of the family of Shakespearean comedy.

Connubial slapstick and duplicity already abound in *The Comedy of Errors* (Adriana and Antipholus of Ephesus), *The Taming of the Shrew* (Kate and Petruchio), *A Midsummer Night's Dream* (Oberon, Titania and Bottom) and *The Merchant of Venice* (the ring-trick played by Portia and Nerissa on their husbands). The competition between Slender, Dr Caius and Fenton for the hand of Anne Page is basically an action replay of the courtship of Bianca by Hortensio, Gremio and Lucentio, and a dying echo of Bassanio's triumph over Morocco and Aragon in Shakespeare's preceding comedy. The linguistic quirks and vagaries of Caius, Evans, Pistol and Nim have their counterparts in the ludicrous parlance of Armado, Nathaniel and Holofernes in *Love's Labour's Lost*, while the unwitting gaffes and obscenities of Mistress Quickly hark back to the malapropisms of Launce, Costard and Bottom and look ahead to the howlers perpetrated by Dogberry and Verges in *Much Ado*. Slender resurfaces in *Twelfth Night* as Olivia's equally ectomorphic and brainless suitor, Sir Andrew Aguecheek; the bibulous freeloader Sir John Falstaff morphs into the bibulous freeloader Sir Toby Belch to fleece Sir Andrew and defy the killjoy Malvolio; and in Portia and Nerissa, who not only outsmart the devious alien menacing their community, but also put one over on their husbands in the process, can be seen the progenitors of the merry wives themselves, who bring both the predatory Falstaff and the pathologically jealous Ford to book.

The connections between *Merry Wives* and the other comedies aren't restricted, however, to correspondences between characters and plots. Precedents for the play's bourgeois setting and preoccupations lie ready to hand in the mercantile worlds of Ephesus and Venice, while its domestic ambience and concern with household matters are mirrored in parts of *The Comedy of Errors* and *The Taming of the Shrew*, as well as in the focal locations of *Much Ado About Nothing* and *Twelfth Night*. Like *Love's Labour's Lost* and *A Midsummer Night's Dream*, moreover, *The Merry Wives of Windsor* culminates in a fifth-act play within the play, in which low comic characters masquerade as highborn or superhuman mythical figures for the delectation of on-stage observers. The climax of this phantasmagorical masque, which takes place 'in Windsor Forest' (IV.iv.28) and 'In deep of night' (IV.iv.39), sees Falstaff, 'Disguised like

Herne, with huge horns on his head' (IV.iv.42), baited and pinched by fairies at the behest of their Queen, abetted by 'a Satyr' and by 'Hobgoblin', alias Puck or Robin Goodfellow. The parallels between *Merry Wives* and *A Midsummer Night's Dream* at this point are too close to be unconscious, and it's possible to perceive in the transmogrification and tormenting of Falstaff a warped reflection of Bottom's metamorphosis and the pampering he enjoys in the arms of the lovestruck Titania. On the strength of this final scene of *Merry Wives* alone the play was routinely coupled with *A Midsummer Night's Dream* throughout the eighteenth and nineteenth centuries as the epitome of Shakespearean comedy at its most fanciful.

But the recognition of its kinship with the other comedies is scarcely sufficient in itself to rescue *The Merry Wives of Windsor* from being underrated. On the contrary, the play is just as liable to suffer from the comparison with Shakespeare's more admired ventures in the same vein as to be flattered by it. Closer scrutiny of the final scene in Windsor Forest, for example, reveals what a gulf divides its imaginative vision from that of *A Midsummer Night's Dream*. In the latter the fairies are real supernatural creatures and the wood outside Athens is a place of genuine enchantment, in which conventional boundaries and constraints no longer hold and human beings are physically and emotionally transfigured by their encounter with forces beyond their ken. No such mysterious magic is at work in the royal park of Windsor, whose transformations are as real and convincing as Falstaff's detachable antlers. Conflicts are resolved, attitudes are adjusted and relationships reconfigured, but no one is transported beyond themselves or changed, which is no more than one would expect in a disenchanted forest, where the fairies are just the local children in fancy dress and the Fairy Queen, the Satyr and Hobgoblin are merely Mistress Quickly, Parson Evans and Pistol in disguise. From this perspective, the fact that *The Merry Wives of Windsor* shares so much material with its fellow Shakespearean comedies is unlikely to sway anyone convinced that it remains a genial *jeu d'esprit*, devoid of any deeper resonance.

Pointing the Moral: Falstaff, Ford and Fenton

The blatant thrust of both the play's plots would certainly seem to back up that conviction. In Fenton and Falstaff the good citizens of Windsor confront what they perceive as impecunious intruders from the upper classes, hell-bent on purloining their hard-earned wealth by poaching their daughters and wives. In both cases their fears are well-founded. Falstaff hobbles his plan to ensnare Mistress Ford and Mistress Page before it's up and running by overestimating his aristocratic allure, underestimating their intelligence and probity, and sending them identically worded *billets-doux*. The instinctive distrust any prosperous, middle-class community would feel, when faced with a rootless, patrician intruder from the murkier depths of the metropolis, proves completely justified at their first encounter. But George Page has every reason to mistrust the motives of Fenton, too, and forbid him to court his nubile daughter, Anne. Fenton is, after all, a prodigal, a prototype of the *jeune premier* of countless Jacobean city comedies, who doesn't deny the 'riots past' and 'wild societies' (III.iv.8) he enjoyed as one of Prince Hal's hangers-on, or the fact that he has squandered his estate through self-indulgence and needs to replenish his coffers. That Page objects to him not simply as 'too great of birth' for Anne, but as a feckless toff who could never love her 'but as a property' (III.iv.4, 10) is perfectly understandable. Fenton himself confesses, while protesting his genuine love for Anne, that his initial intentions were mercenary:

> Albeit I will confess thy father's wealth
> Was the first motive that I wooed thee, Anne,
> Yet, wooing thee, I found thee of more value
> Than stamps in gold or sums in sealèd bags;
> And 'tis the very riches of thyself
> That now I aim at.
>   (III.iv.13–18)

As it turns out, however, the integrity of Fenton's feelings for Anne are vindicated and her father's view of him proved groundless, as a result of which the young prodigal reaps a reward for his labours that is the reverse of the fate visited upon his fellow interloper, Falstaff.

Falstaff's motives, unlike Fenton's, remain purely pecuniary from first to last: 'She is a region in Guiana, all gold and bounty', he declares of Mistress Page. 'I will be cheaters to them both, and they shall be exchequers to me. They shall be my East and West Indies, and I will trade to them both' (I.iii.61–5). His brazen concupiscence is simply a smokescreen for his craving for cash. Outraged by Falstaff's misconstruction of their mirth as wantonness, and appalled by his presumption that both his knighthood and his manhood must be irresistible to a couple of middle-aged housewives, Mistress Ford and Mistress Page resolve to take their revenge on him. Their aim is to hit him hardest where he most deserves to be hurt, by puncturing his sexual pride and impoverishing him. To that end they propose to 'entertain him with hope, till the wicked fire of lust have melted him in his own grease' (II.i.63–5), and 'lead him on with a fine baited delay till he hath pawned his horses to mine Host of the Garter' (II.i.91–2).

The improvised means they employ to humiliate and chasten Falstaff – each more ignominious than the last – are equally apt, given the domestic nature of the realm they rule and Sir John's ambition to make cuckolds of their husbands. What punishment more condign for a lubricious knight, who thinks a mere housewife easy prey, than to be dumped in the Thames in a basket of malodorous laundry to cool his lust? How better to repay a shameless misogynist, who treats women with cavalier contempt as instruments of male gratification, than to force him to don full drag as 'the old woman of Brentford' (IV.ii.77) and be beaten black and blue for being 'A witch, a quean, an old, cozening quean!' (IV.ii.158) by the husband he'd hoped to cuckold? And, for the grand finale, few things could be more fitting than to con the would-be cuckolder into fixing 'great ragg'd horns' (IV.iv.30) on his own head and turn this travesty of 'Herne the hunter' (IV.iv.27) into the prey of fairies, who sing as they torment him:

> Fie on sinful fantasy!
> Fie on lust and luxury!
> Lust is but a bloody fire,
> Kindled with unchaste desire,
> Fed in heart, whose flames aspire,
> As thoughts do blow them, higher and higher.
> Pinch him, fairies, mutually.
> Pinch him for his villainy.
> Pinch him, and burn him, and turn him about,
> Till candles and starlight and moonshine be out.
> (V.v.92–101)

The phrasing of the fairies' castigation might seem a mite severe, especially as loot rather than lust was what Falstaff chiefly had in mind. But it points the moral for prowling adulterers plainly enough, as the threat to the marital security and moral stability of Windsor is ritually mocked, denounced and ostracized by the community. (The scene may once have served as an antimasque in an entertainment devised to celebrate the Order of the Garter, in which case Falstaff's role would have been to exemplify the vices a virtuous Knight of the Garter was expected to shun.) Once he twigs that the merry wives and their spouses have 'made an ass' (V.v.118) of him, Falstaff completes the process of reproof by acknowledging the 'guiltiness of [his] mind' (V.v.122) and underlining the lesson he has learned: 'See now how wit may be made a Jack-a-Lent when 'tis upon ill employment!' (V.v.125–7). The moral of the play that matters most to the wives, though, is the one Mistress Page spells out earlier, in the midst of the old woman of Brentford jape, enlisting couplets to lend her exit lines epigrammatic force:

> We'll leave a proof by that which we will do,
> Wives may be merry, and yet honest, too.
> We do not act that often jest and laugh.
> 'Tis old but true: 'Still swine eats all the draff'.
>   (IV.ii.94–7)

The lines are aimed not only at Falstaff, but also at Ford, whom the wives are also engaged in gulling for a second time – though in Ford's case the objective is to purge him of paranoid jealousy rather than lecherous avarice. Blinded by their egotistical *idées fixes*, both men fail to see and value the women as they are, preferring to project upon them their own self-serving fantasies. That's why making a fool of Ford is just as important to them as making a fool of Falstaff: 'I know not which pleases me better', muses Mistress Ford in the wake of the buck-basket episode, 'that my husband is deceived, or Sir John' (III.iii.168–9). Falstaff and Ford must be deceived in order to cure them of their delusions about the wives. Furthermore, in order 'to scrape the figures out of [her] husband's brains' (IV.ii.201–2) as well as Sir John's, Mistress Ford must conspire with Mistress Page to have both him and 'the poor, unvirtuous, fat knight', as she puts it, 'publicly shamed' (IV.ii.203, 208). The public exposure and acknowledgement of their folly, in the theatrical equivalent of a charivari or skimmington ride, are crucial to the restoration of the wives' authority and self-esteem. Ford is made a laughing-stock before his friends and neighbours, in whose presence he begs Mistress Ford's forgiveness:

> Pardon me, wife. Henceforth do what thou wilt.
> I rather will suspect the sun with cold
> Than thee with wantonness. Now doth thy honour stand,
> In him that was of late an heretic,
> As firm as faith.
>   (IV.iv.5–9)

And at the end of Falstaff's ordeal as Herne the hunter, as both women and their husbands step forward to make it clear that the game is up, Mistress Page makes sure Falstaff knows who to thank for his plight, and how wide of the mark his judgement has been from the start: 'Now, good Sir John, how like you Windsor wives?' (V.v.105).

The moral of the dramatized fabliau that revolves around Falstaff is underscored by the romantic parallel plot, which is propelled by Fenton's courtship of Anne. Fenton's victory offsets Falstaff's defeat by the crafty burghers of Windsor. If Falstaff confirms the latter's worst suspicions of his class, Fenton redeems the reputation of the upper crust by demonstrating that he is far from thinking of Anne 'but as a property' (III.iv.10) – in marked contrast to her own father and mother, who are vying to marry her profitably off against her will to suitors they deem more suitable: the well-heeled idiot, Slender, and the well-connected French physician and certified crackpot, Dr Caius. At the point where the two plots intersect in the final scene, after turning the tables both on Anne's parents and on his rivals for her hand, Fenton upbraids the Pages and defends his subterfuge by appealing to principles which the comedy clearly applauds:

> Hear the truth of it.
> You would have married her, most shamefully,
> Where there was no proportion held in love.
> The truth is, she and I, long since contracted,
> Are now so sure that nothing can dissolve us.
> Th'offence is holy that she hath committed,
> And this deceit loses the name of craft,
> Of disobedience, or unduteous title,
> Since therein she doth evitate and shun
> A thousand irreligious cursèd hours
> Which forcèd marriage would have brought upon her.
> (V.v.212–22)

This enlightened sentiment complements the tenor of the tricks played on Falstaff and Ford by the merry wives; for in commending the ideal of a freely chosen, companionate marriage, founded on mutual regard rather than on money, it reinforces the wives' rejection of the proprietary attitude to women as chattels that Ford and Falstaff share with Mistress Page and her husband. The play's approval of Fenton's high-minded homily is unqualified, as Page's immediate, affable acceptance of the *fait accompli* attests: 'Well, what remedy? Fenton, heaven give thee joy! / What cannot be eschewed must be embraced' (V.v.228–9). The reformed rake Fenton can thus be incorporated into the Windsor community through wedlock, whereas the unregenerate *roué* routed by the wives cannot, notwithstanding the indulgence with which he's treated at the close.

'cozenage, mere cozenage!'

The comedy goes out of its way, however, to ensure that Falstaff's not the only character whose bright idea backfires and who winds up looking a fool. At the eleventh hour Fenton pulls a fast one on both the Pages, and thereby on Dr Caius and Slender too, leaving all four bewildered by the failure of their ruses. Mistress Page may have got the better of Falstaff, but she and her husband are easily outfoxed by their future son-in-law, and they are riding for a fall when they and Ford take their gloating over Falstaff's defeat too far for the comedy's liking:

> MISTRESS PAGE.   Why, Sir John, do you think, though we would have thrust virtue out of our hearts by the head and shoulders, and have given ourselves without scruple to hell, that ever the devil could have made you our delight?
>
> FORD.   What, a hodge-pudding, a bag of flax?
>
> MISTRESS PAGE.   A puffed man?
>
> PAGE.   Old, cold, withered, and of intolerable entrails?
>
> FORD.   And one that is as slanderous as Satan?
>
> PAGE.   And as poor as Job?
>
>   (V.v.145–54)

Falstaff is left with no option but to cave in completely: 'Well, I am your theme; you have the start of me. I am dejected. I am not able to answer the Welsh flannel. Ignorance itself is a plummet o'er me. Use me as you will' (V.v.159–62).

But the last laugh is reserved for the 'hodge-pudding', who has the pleasure of seeing Page and his merry wife hoist by their own petard. No sooner has Page announced that Slender has just married his daughter, thereby foiling his wife's little scheme, than Slender rushes in to reveal that his blushing bride turned out to be 'a great lubberly boy' (V.v.181) at the altar. And hardly has Mistress Page finished begging her husband's forgiveness for double-crossing him, when an apoplectic

Caius storms onto the stage, exclaiming: 'Ver is Mistress Page? By Gar, I am cozened! I ha' married *un garçon*, a boy, *un paysan*, by Gar. A boy! It is not Anne Page, by Gar. I am cozened' (V.v.200–2). When Fenton and Anne enter to clear up the confusion and explain how her parents have been cozened too, no one could begrudge Falstaff his barbed remark to his tormentors: 'I am glad, though you have ta'en a special stand to strike at me, that your arrow hath glanced' (V.v.226–7).

In a sense, Falstaff gets pretty much what he wished for earlier, in the aftermath of the old woman of Brentford fiasco: 'I would all the world might be cozened, for I have been cozened, and beaten too' (IV.v.87–8). His remark is prompted by understandable *Schadenfreude* at the hoaxing of the Host by Caius and Evans, who have just relieved him of three horses with the connivance of Bardolph and three fictitious 'German devils, three Doctor Faustuses' (IV.5.65) or, as the inimitable Evans puts it, 'three cozen Garmombles that has cozened all the hosts of Reading, of Maidenhead, of Colnbrook, of horses and money' (IV.v.71–4). The hoax is in reprisal, of course, for the Host's duping of the doctor and the parson during their abortive duel; the result of his making them 'his vlouting-stog' (laughing-stock), however, is to drive them into an alliance 'to be revenge on this same scall, scurvy, cogging companion, the Host of the Garter' (III.i.109, 111–12). The Host may take comfort, nevertheless, from the fact that most of the play's principal characters find out what it means to have one's best-laid plans boomerang, and to suffer the unintended consequences of making a mug of someone else.

The word 'cozen' and its derivatives occur ten times in *The Merry Wives of Windsor*, more often by far than in any other play by Shakespeare. Just before Bardolph barges into the Garter to deliver the punch-line of the horse-stealing hoax, crying 'O Lord, sir, cozenage, mere cozenage!' (IV.v.60), there's a curious little exchange between Falstaff and Slender's aptly named servant, Simple. Asked by Simple on his master's behalf 'whether one Nim, sir, that beguiled him of a chain, had the chain or no' (IV.v.29–31), Falstaff replies on behalf of 'the wise woman of Brentford' (IV.v.24–5) with a vacuous, evasive tautology, which the wise woman herself could not have bettered: 'Marry, she says that the very same man that beguiled Master Slender of his chain cozened him of it' (IV.v.34–5). So widespread is the practice of cozening that allusions to it creep into every corner of the comedy. Indeed, a chain of mutual cozenage links practically everyone in both the main plots and the subsidiary plots, as becomes clear when it's disentangled in the final act.

The pervasiveness of this preoccupation with biters being bit, with those who think they are wilier winding up beguiled, betrays a deeper

moral logic at work in the play than that which drives the harrowing of
Falstaff and the curing of Ford by the merry wives, or Fenton's scolding of the Pages for their venal view of marriage. The rationale for these
acts of retribution is self-evidently sound as far as it goes and is strongly
underwritten by the way they are dramatized. Nowhere is the play's
sympathy with the decent bourgeois values the wives espouse more
apparent than in the way it warps the characters of Pistol and Nim, who
refuse to carry letters to Mistress Page and Mistress Ford because it
offends their sense of propriety. 'Shall I Sir Pandarus of Troy become,'
protests Pistol, 'And by my side wear steel? Then Lucifer take all!' Nim
is equally adamant: 'I will run no base humour. Here, take the humour-
letter. I will keep the haviour of reputation' (I.iii.69–73). To see these
two inveterate scoundrels strike such a principled posture is to realize
how quickly they have been contaminated by the moral tone of middle-
class Windsor.

The same predisposition can be detected in Shakespeare's deviations
from the putative source of the episodes featuring Falstaff, Ford and the
buck-basket. In Ser Giovanni Fiorentino's *Il pecorone*, on which
Shakespeare certainly drew in devising *The Merchant of Venice*, a young
student cuckolds his old master and escapes scot-free thanks to the wife's
ploy of hiding him under a pile of washing when her husband turns up
to catch him. In *The Merry Wives of Windsor*, however, Falstaff's adulterous ambitions are not fulfilled and Ford's horns remain figments of
his imagination. Ford, moreover, is much younger than his corpulent
rival for his wife's favours, who is not only well past his prime, but also
the prime target of the tricks played upon him. And, unlike her counterpart in Ser Giovanni's story, Mistress Ford is no young thing wedded to
an elderly husband against her will, but a happily married matron, who
by her own admission is no longer 'in the holiday time of [her] beauty'
(II.i.1–2), and who greets Falstaff's overtures with derision.

These reversals of the clichés of his Italian template are a further
measure of Shakespeare's decision to load the dice in favour of the merry
wives and the ethos they embody. It would be a mistake, nonetheless, to
reduce the comedy to a ratification of that ethos, because, as Mistress
Page discovers, the arbiters of the community's mores at one moment
can find themselves in the dock at the next. When the Pages prove as
vulnerable to duplicity as Falstaff, it's clear that no one is immune to the
law of cozenage that operates in the world of this play, no matter how
safe from deception they believe themselves to be. As Pistol observes,
with the notorious trickery of gamblers in mind, 'high and low beguiles
the rich and poor' (I.iii.81). The comedy's commitment to the precepts

implicit in the gulling of Falstaff, Ford and the Pages is eclipsed by its subscription to a more comprehensive code that governs human relationships. That code is no respecter of the respectable, who are no less subject to its jurisdiction than the unscrupulous. Its workings, furthermore, are beyond the command of the characters, whose purposes it's as likely to frustrate as to fulfil. As Falstaff observes in his last speech in the play: 'When night-dogs run, all sorts of deer are chased' (V.v.230).

'Sir John and all'

The audience alone, with their omniscient overview of events, are privy to this ironic perspective and thus attuned to the egalitarian ethic it implies. Falstaff, Ford and the Pages are seen to get their just deserts for their transgressions, but a superior form of poetic justice dictates the speed with which retribution turns into reconciliation. Page is quick to comfort the crestfallen Falstaff with a more convivial prospect: 'Yet be cheerful, knight. Thou shalt eat a posset tonight at my house, where I will desire thee to laugh at my wife that now laughs at thee' (V.v.168-70). Moreover, as we've seen, he's just as quick to forgive Fenton for giving Falstaff equally good grounds for laughing at him. But it's Mistress Page's final speech that captures the true spirit of the comedy, which generously embraces everyone, including Falstaff, within the festive community it has forged at the close:

> Well, I will muse no further. Master Fenton,
> Heaven give you many, many merry days!
> Good husband, let us every one go home,
> And laugh this sport o'er by a country fire,
> Sir John and all.
> (V.v.231–5)

'Sir John and all': in the end, despite a brave stab at casting him as the scapegoat in a pseudo-pagan rite, *The Merry Wives of Windsor* cannot banish plump Jack after all. Indeed, the play grants him the last word by proxy through Ford's stage-clearing couplet, which concedes Falstaff's figurative victory:

> Let it be so, Sir John.
> To Master Brooke you yet shall hold your word,
> For he tonight shall lie with Mistress Ford.   *Exeunt*
> (V.v.235–7)

That Falstaff should have his way, if only by dint of a double entendre, at the conclusion of the play is only right, since it was his intrusive advent that sparked Windsor's carnival of cozenage. It's not by chance that the comedy kicks off with Justice Shallow's fury at the liberties taken by Falstaff, who runs rings round his accuser and gets clean away with grievous bodily harm, breaking and entering, and theft. Right from the start, the embodiment of illicit desire and festive recklessness acts as a catalyst in the community he has invaded, menacing its propriety and stability, but also inaugurating a reign of innocuous mischief that reveals and intensifies its vitality.

As the comedy's self-appointed Lord of Misrule, Falstaff authorizes an outbreak of bawdiness which infects the phrasing of most of the cast, and from which the merry wives themselves are far from exempt. The receipt of Falstaff's duplicate love-letter prompts Mistress Page to doubt the modesty of her demeanour, and triggers a bout of lewd repartee between her and Mistress Ford:

> MISTRESS PAGE. Nay, I know not. It makes me almost ready to wrangle with mine own honesty. I'll entertain myself like one that I am not acquainted withal; for, sure, unless he know some strain in me that I know not myself, he would never have boarded me in this fury.
> MISTRESS FORD. 'Boarding' call you it? I'll be sure to keep him above deck.
> MISTRESS PAGE. So will I. If he come under my hatches, I'll never to sea again.
>
> (II.i.81–9)

As she shrewdly suspects, Falstaff's advance has elicited a 'strain' in Mistress Page that she knew not herself, and, just as punning permits the wives to indulge in indecency under the cover of metaphor, so the duping of Falstaff and Ford gives them the gratification of cuckolding their husbands without the opprobrium that actual adultery would incur.

Above all, however, Falstaff presides over a feast of contagious fooling to which all the principals end up invited, and at which anyone could find themselves a guest. Verdi and his librettist, Boito, caught this quality of the comedy's conclusion perfectly by bringing the whole cast of *Falstaff* together in a final fugal chorus that celebrates the ubiquity of human folly and the liability of everyone to wind up being laughed at. It's this crowning affirmation of expansive hospitality, which can house the indigenous and the alien alike, that makes *The Merry Wives of Windsor* much more than a middle-class morality play tricked out as a preposterous romp.

'Lèse majesté'

If the comedy is reconsidered in this light, the clues to its true scope become apparent from the opening scene onwards. The title itself alerts us to crucial respects in which this play will depart from the course on which Shakespeare's previous comedies had been set. *The Merry Wives of Windsor* – the title under which the play appeared in the First Folio, and which it has retained ever since – is the only title of a Shakespearean comedy (leaving aside the problem play *Troilus and Cressida*) to foreground female characters, in marked contrast to *The Two Gentlemen of Verona* and *The Merchant of Venice*. The eponymous heroines, moreover, are 'wives' rather than unmarried women, which precludes their being the protagonists of the kind of romantic comedy Shakespeare had written hitherto. At the same time, the fact that they are 'merry' wives makes it clear that they will be the hub round which the humour of the comedy revolves. The term 'wives' also locates the comedy in the social sphere of the middling sort, as distinct from the world of the aristocracy and gentry in which *Two Gentlemen*, *Love's Labour's Lost* and *A Midsummer Night's Dream* are set. The alliterative coupling of the wives with Windsor reinforces this implication by planting the play very specifically in the Berkshire market town well west of the metropolis, and thus bypassing the London locations favoured by Elizabethan and Jacobean 'city' comedy and by Shakespeare himself in the Eastcheap scenes of *Henry IV*. But Windsor is also best known as the seat of majesty, so by placing his merry middle-class wives there, Shakespeare creates an ironic tension in his title between the royal connotations of the play's setting and its far from regal protagonists. Promoting the play's location to the title, furthermore, accords it the same importance as the wives: like Venice, Windsor assumes the status of a protagonist in its own right, whose collective identity is as significant as its individual citizens. And the inclusion of Windsor in the title highlights the much more remarkable fact that *The Merry Wives of Windsor* is Shakespeare's only comedy set entirely in England.

A great deal may be gleaned from the title about the ground-breaking qualities that set Shakespeare's English comedy apart as a singular achievement rather than a minor amusement, a brief detour from the high road leading to *Much Ado, As You Like It* and *Twelfth Night*. The decision to hand the command of the comedy over to a pair of middle-aged, bourgeois housewives instead of a pair of nubile young noble-women in the mould of Portia or the ladies of *Love's Labour's Lost* was a bold one. Having them defy the stereotypes of medieval fabliaux and Italian novellas by being not only clever and resourceful, but also faith-ful and respectable – without being any less funny and admirable – gives the principal plot a further ingenious twist. The stock romantic comedy of Fenton's winning of Anne is upstaged by the tale of how two amiable but unglamorous matrons get the upper hand of a marauding knight and bring a demented husband to book. One of the most appealing things about *The Merry Wives of Windsor* is its admiration for the ordi-nary townswomen of Shakespeare's own class, and its consequent col-lusion with his heroines in what Mistress Page calls 'the putting down of men' (II.i.27).

The slant of the play's sexual politics is also apparent in the power it accords Mistress Quickly, Dr Caius's garrulous housekeeper. As the indis-pensable 'she-mercury' (II.ii.78–9) of *Merry Wives*, Quickly has a grasp of the machinery of both plots which no other character possesses, and which makes her the unlikely counterpart of Oberon in *A Midsummer Night's Dream*. Her role as the instrument of the merry wives' will places Falstaff at her mercy as the victim of deception, completely reversing their relationship in *Henry IV*, when she was the 'hostess of a tavern' in Eastcheap. Nor does her elevation end there. The last scene sees the apotheosis of 'that foolish carrion Mistress Quickly' (III.iii.183–4) as the Queen of Fairies, in which august guise she oversees the final humiliation of Falstaff. But nothing in the comedy encapsulates its commitment to 'the putting down of men' more perfectly than the iconic image of Sir John *en travesti*: the only adult male in the whole of Shakespeare forced to dress up as a woman. When the play was first published in a Quarto edition in 1602, its title gave Falstaff top billing: 'A Most pleasaunt and excellent conceited Comedie, of *Syr Iohn Falstaffe*, and the merrie Wiues of *Windsor*.' His total eclipse by his co-stars in the title by which the play has been known since 1623 bears witness to the enduring consensus that the heart of the comedy is in their keeping.

That said, it's worth noting that the full title of the 1602 Quarto reads: 'A Most pleasant and excellent conceited Comedie, of *Syr Iohn Falstaffe*, and the merrie Wiues of *Windsor*. // Entermixed with sundrie variable and pleasing humours, of Syr *Hugh* the Welch Knight, Iustice *Shallow*, and his wise Cousin M. *Slender*. // With the swaggering vaine of Auncient *Pistoll*, and Corporal *Nym*.' Apart from turning Parson

Evans into a knight and the pea-brained Slender into a wise man, the extended title is instructive. It suggests that the play's appeal to Elizabethan audiences, just like its appeal to subsequent audiences, was inseparable from its being an ensemble piece, whose supporting characters are in no way overshadowed by the principal *dramatis personae*. Indeed, Shakespeare animates the comedy's gallery of batty eccentrics and blinkered obsessives with such gusto that at times they threaten to steal the show. The Quarto title draws attention to the play's congregation of 'sundrie variable' characters, who constitute the stage community of Windsor. It's hard to think of another play by Shakespeare which spans such a diverse social spectrum, which includes so many different sorts of people and such a range of ages, ranks and professions, providing an extraordinary panorama of small-town life in early modern England. In this respect, *The Merry Wives of Windsor* is manifestly possessed by the same impartial, democratic spirit as its master of revels, Falstaff, who 'woos both high and low, both rich and poor, / Both young and old, one with another' and 'loves the gallimaufry' (II.i.108–10).

That democratic inclusiveness is most strikingly confirmed by the comedy's exclusion of the one class one would expect to encounter in a play set in Windsor: royalty. The absence of the monarch is made all the more glaring by the presence of Falstaff, the former boon companion of the once 'wild Prince' (III.ii.66) King Henry V, to whom he makes not a single allusion. Not the least arresting aspect of *The Merry Wives of Windsor* is its decision to write royalty out of its own domain and the entire court and aristocracy (Sir John apart) along with it. At the core of the comedy lurks a deftly disguised act of *lèse majesté*, which exiles the sovereign and his blue-blooded entourage to the wings and moves the run-of-the mill townsfolk and the riff-raff of Windsor to the centre of the stage. Dynastic ambitions, political intrigue and the throes of civil war are displaced by petty scoundrels on the make, marital machinations and squabbles about poaching.

In the densely populated world of Shakespeare's Windsor, housewives rule the roost and the parson, the doctor, the innkeeper and the post-boy count more than any courtier. Household chores and humdrum activities – laundering, birding, a schoolboy's lessons – are given the same weight and prominence they would have in the lives of Shakespeare's audience. It's their own daily round that he's conjuring up, not the remote affairs of some exotic realm, when he has Mistress Quickly say, 'I wash, wring, brew, bake, scour, dress meat and drink, make the beds, and do all myself' (II.i.91–3). The delight Shakespeare takes in bringing alive on stage the sights, sounds, smells and feel of the domestic life he knew so well from his Stratford days is palpable. The language is thronged with allusions to sea-coal fires, possets, paring-knives, bleaching, mufflers, pepperboxes, butcher's offal, turnips, kerchiefs, sawpits, kiln-holes, thrummed hats and salt-butter. As a result, the prosaic commoner's kingdom of Windsor is invested with a sensuous immediacy and tactile familiarity which the audience is invited to savour along with the dramatist.

This effect is intensified by the play's fastidious use of local topography to anchor events in the vicinity of Windsor. The characters' speech is peppered with references to Old Windsor, Datchet Mead, Datchet Lane, Frogmore and Eton, as well as to Windsor Forest, the Thames and the outlying towns and villages of Maidenhead, Reading, Colebrook and Brentford. Like the demotic idiom in which the characters for the most part converse, these references are designed to make the play's Elizabethan audience feel completely at home in its emphatically English universe. The originality of *The Merry Wives of Windsor* in this regard cannot be overstated. Unlike many of his theatrical rivals, Shakespeare had a predilection for dramatizing tales set in real or imaginary foreign climes and cultures. Those that he did set in his native land dealt almost invariably with the historical matter of Britain, whether factual or fabulous, and thus were distanced in time from the world in which he wrote. The fears, delights and dreams of his own world and time were always his true subject, of course. The Englishness and the actuality of his drama's concerns habitually obtrude in the most unlikely locations to remind us of this – as when Bottom and his 'crew of patches' (*MND*, III.ii.9) are transported through time and space from early modern England to ancient Athens with their Elizabethan locutions and allusions intact. Nevertheless, it says much about Shakespeare, both as a man and as a dramatist, that he preferred to confront the reality of the present in the guise of other times and places, as if his intellect and imagination could set to work on his world only after it had been transposed to some parallel universe.

To this deeply ingrained habit of mind *The Merry Wives of Windsor* is a startling exception. It's not just that it's set wholly in England, unlike all Shakespeare's other comedies; it's also arguably the only entire play by Shakespeare that's set, or that certainly feels as though it's set, in contemporary Elizabethan England. Ostensibly, the presence of Falstaff, Mistress Quickly and the 'Irregular Humorists' (as the Folio calls them) of the *Henry IV* plays, plus the mention of 'the wild Prince and Poins' (III.ii.66–7), push the action back into the early fifteenth century. But the absence of the royal and noble figures that would have locked the action into the past unshackles the characters from the context of the history plays and frees them to frolic in a space and time continuous with that of Shakespeare's audience. The comedy's radical anachronism is confirmed, and all pretence of retrospection discarded, when the masque in the final act pays homage not to a king but to 'Our radiant Queen' (V.v.45).

This contemporary quality of *The Merry Wives of Windsor* brings its vision to bear on the experience of its original audience in a manner unparalleled in the rest of the comedies or, for that matter, in any play by Shakespeare. What other play of Shakespeare's strives to create the continuous illusion that its characters are living and breathing, here and now, in the same England its first spectators inhabited? It's this vivid, concrete vitality to which Friedrich Engels was responding when he wrote in a letter to Karl Marx: 'The first act of the *Merry Wives* alone contains more life and reality than all German literature.' That a comedy habitually discounted as Shakespeare Lite should appeal so powerfully to the authors of the *Communist Manifesto* might seem bizarre, but it makes perfect sense once one grasps the play's vitality as inseparable from the nascent vision of community that suffuses it.

'Non sans droict'

That vision finds expression at the start of the play in Shakespeare's jocular mockery of Shallow's pomposity, as he preens himself, with the aid of the unctuous Slender, on being a Justice of the Peace 'and a gentleman born' (I.i.7). Slender's garbled brag that as a gentleman his esteemed relative 'writes himself "Armigero"' (i.e., 'Esquire'), which means he has the right to a coat of arms, is the cue for what John Middleton Murry calls the 'obscure armorial jokes at the beginning of *The Merry Wives*'. Shakespeare latches on to the boast that for the past three centuries, the Shallow family have displayed 'the dozen white luces [i.e., pikes] in their coat' (I.i.14), and he enlists Evans's Welsh accent to turn the twelve luces into 'The dozen white louses' infesting 'an old coad' (I.i.16) – with a bonus quibble on 'coat' and 'cod' to keep the fish gags going. Some scholars have believed this to be a private dig at Sir Thomas Lucy, whose coat of arms sported three silver luces, because according to legend Lucy had accused the young Shakespeare of stealing his deer, and had forced him to leave Stratford as a consequence. The explanation is tenuous at best, though extremely attractive, not least because it fits so snugly with the way Falstaff confounds Shallow by brazenly admitting stealing his deer. But, whether they are fuelled by autobiographical fact or not, the personal animus invested in these satirical gibes at pretensions to rank are undeniable. Shakespeare may or may not have Sir Thomas Lucy in his sights, but he's certainly gunning for those who flatter themselves that they are gentlemen born, unlike Shakespeare, who had just acquired a coat of arms himself, emblazoned with the motto '*Non sans droict*' ('Not without right'). As Murry observes, when at last the arms were granted in 1596, only a year or so before he wrote *The Merry Wives of Windsor*, 'Shakespeare could write himself *Armigero*. And who could forbear the thought that the motto: *Non sans droict*, was Shakespeare's subtle-simple assertion of the right of genius to the privilege of blood?'

While it would be misguided to dub *Merry Wives* a revenge comedy sparked by *ressentiment* on the strength of this exchange, it would be equally misguided to ignore the broad hint it drops about the play's social stance from the outset. The comedy begins in a derisive mood of irreverence, which is sustained until the end, dictating the erasure of royalty, the triumph of the wives, the ubiquity of cozenage, and Falstaff's assimilation by a festive community intent on laughter at itself. This insubordinate attitude inflects the structure, form and style of the play in less obtrusive, but no less potent, ways as well. For a start, the normal relationship between main plot and subplot in Shakespearean comedy is stood on its head. As a rule, it's the high romantic plot of thwarted young love winning through in the end that calls the tune, while the low comic subplot, with its crude gags and clowning, is condemned to play second fiddle, as *Two Gentlemen*, *Love's Labour's Lost* and *A Midsummer Night's Dream* attest. But in *The Merry Wives of Windsor* it's the vulgar, physical farce of thwarted adultery that hogs the limelight, while the edifying tale of true romance is reduced to a sideshow, whose chief function is to trigger the reversals of the denouement.

The mechanism that unlocks the denouement is the masque of Herne the hunter. At the climax of the play, where the confusion is compounded and then unravelled, a theatrical form exclusively tailored for the royal court is appropriated by a cast of commoners for their own plebeian ends. The part of Hobgoblin goes to that loud-mouthed rapscallion, Pistol, the Satyr is played by the Welsh windbag, Evans, and the plum role of Queen of Fairies seems to have been snatched at the last minute from Anne Page ('My Nan shall be the Queen of all the Fairies, / Finely attirèd in a robe of white' (IV.iv.70–1)) by Mistress Quickly. Quickly's usurpation of the pivotal regal part in the show is especially piquant. The masque in *Merry Wives* is almost certainly an adaptation of a previous court masque intended as a homage to 'Our radiant Queen' (V.v.45), who was traditionally represented – most famously in Edmund Spenser's epic poem – by the allegorical figure of the Fairy Queen. One can't help wondering what the reaction of her royal highness would have been to seeing herself impersonated by 'that foolish carrion, Mistress Quickly' (III.iii.183–4), when the comedy was 'Acted by the right Honorable my Lord Chamberlaines seruants [. . .] before her Maiestie', as the title-page of the Quarto assures us it was. (The impropriety of casting Quickly as the Fairy Queen obviously struck Boito, who restored some semblance of decorum by reassigning the role to Nannetta, the counterpart of Anne Page, in his libretto for *Falstaff*.)

This impertinent masterstroke of miscasting is perfectly consistent with a play which has elbowed royalty aside on its own patch. It's no surprise, therefore, to find that the comedy has the effrontery to hijack the elevated, lyrical verse of the court masque to voice the feeling of unanimity that comes over the characters at the close. Pistol, Evans and Quickly undergo a miraculous linguistic metamorphosis as the cacophony of their prose idiolects is transformed into a single, harmonious discourse, couched in couplets and voicing sentiments of which none of them could be the author:

> Fairies black, grey, green, and white,
> You moonshine revellers, and shades of night,
> You orphan heirs of fixèd destiny,
> Attend your office and your quality.
>
> (V.v.36–9)

The contrast with the plays put on by the comical characters in *Love's Labour's Lost* and *A Midsummer Night's Dream* could scarcely be starker. In the Pageant of the Nine Worthies and 'Pyramus and Thisbe', humour is generated at the actors' expense by the incongruity between them and their heroic or tragic roles, which exposes them to the gibes of their social superiors in the onstage audience. But in the baiting of Herne the hunter the plebeian cast commandeers the aristocratic form of the masque, and by annexing its discourse and vanishing into their roles, become immune to ridicule.

The Triumph of Prose

Shakespeare's resort to verse for the masque throws into relief yet another respect in which *The Merry Wives of Windsor* marks a fundamental break with his normal practice in earlier comedies: the play is composed almost entirely in prose. In fact, nearly 90 per cent of the comedy consists of prose, making *Merry Wives* the play with by far the highest proportion of prose speech in the Shakespearean canon. To appreciate how dramatically *Merry Wives* differs from its predecessors in this regard, it's worth noting that the prose count in Shakespeare's previous comedy, *The Merchant of Venice*, is a mere 21 per cent and that of *A Midsummer Night's Dream* only 19 per cent, while the highest percentage of prose in any Shakespearean comedy prior to *Merry Wives* is the 36 per cent to be found in *Love's Labour's Lost*. Equally telling is the fact that the second-highest percentage for any play written by Shakespeare after *Merry Wives* is just over 70 per cent for his next comedy, *Much Ado About Nothing*, followed by *Twelfth Night* with 62 per cent and *As You Like It* with 52 per cent – all three of these comedies having been written within a few years of *Merry Wives*. The prose count continues to drop in the 'problem' comedies *All's Well That Ends Well* (48 per cent) and *Measure for Measure* (39 per cent), but it nevertheless remains higher than in any comedy before *Merry Wives*. In short, as far as the use of prose is concerned, *The Merry Wives of Windsor* unquestionably signals a sea-change in Shakespearean comedy.

The significance of that change hardly needs spelling out. Prose is normally reserved in Shakespeare for middle- and lower-class characters in order to demarcate their discursive domain and distinguish it from that of the gentry, aristocracy and royalty, whose usual theatrical dialect is blank verse or rhyming couplets. The distinction proves far from hard and fast in dramatic practice, of course, and ruling-class characters can be found exploiting the more informal and flexible resources of prose in any number of plays of quite different kinds by Shakespeare. But whenever they do, they cross the discursive class-divide by displaying their affinity with those reaches of society in which the vernacular prevails on stage. Spoken prose can sometimes be highly ornate and artificial, especially when used for formal or parodic purposes, but the closer it comes to the diction, syntax and sound of colloquial speech, irrespective of the speaker's rank, the more pronounced its surreptitious levelling effect will be.

In *The Merry Wives of Windsor* the shift in the social centre of gravity entails a corresponding shift in the linguistic centre of gravity. The displacement of the realm of the rulers by the realm of the ruled is reflected not only in the subordination of romance plot to farce, but also in the surrender of verse to the sway of the richest colloquial prose in Shakespearean comedy. The use of verse in *Merry Wives* is confined almost completely to the aristocratic masque, or dialogue directly connected to it, and to scenes involving the high-born Fenton, which signals their concern with the more serious, refined dilemmas of romantic courtship. At the same time, not only Anne but also Mistress Page, Mistress Ford and the Host have no trouble switching to blank verse when engaged in conversation with Fenton; Ford slides as effortlessly into blank verse when announcing his reformation in Act IV, Scene iv as Page does in replying to him; and Mistress Quickly, Pistol and Evans declaim the courtly couplets assigned them in the masque as to the manner born. Not content with the colonization of practically the whole play by prose, Shakespeare widens the levelling impact of its language by showing bourgeois and plebeian characters as much at home in the verbal preserve of their betters as Sir John Falstaff clearly is in theirs.

If the uniqueness of its citizen setting in contemporary England and the fact that – buck-basket scene apart – its plot has no direct source are not enough to confirm the originality of *The Merry Wives of Windsor* and its importance in the evolution of Shakespearean comedy, then its wholesale recasting of comedy in colloquial prose, and the profound implications of that shift, should put the matter beyond dispute.

To do justice to the amazing diversity of the play's prose would require another chapter. No other play, including *Love's Labour's Lost*, whose linguistic exuberance and eccentricity it plainly echoes, numbers so many characters, each with their own quirk of speech, their own unique discursive signature, among its cast. The epic syntactical crescendos and extravagant comparisons employed by Falstaff to transmute emasculation into rhetorical might have already been noted. Mistress Quickly's speciality is malapropism, the unwitting equivocation that twists 'direction' into 'erection' (III.v.38), 'genitive case' into 'Jenny's case' (IV.i.53, 56) – 'case' being a euphemism for 'cunt' – and the 'virtuous' Mistress Ford into the 'fartuous' (II.ii.96) Mistress Ford. Pistol's speech is imprisoned in the bombastic diction and outmoded metre of an obsolete form of drama: 'O base Hungarian wight, wilt thou the spigot wield?' (I.iii.19). Nym's monomaniacal mind is in thrall to the word 'humour', which he uses indiscriminately as noun or verb to mean whatever he likes, however cryptic the consequences: 'The Humour rises; it is good. Humour me the angels!' (I.iii.50). The hallmark of Evans's defective dialect, on the other hand, is the way his Welsh accent warps the native English sound of words, substituting 't' for 'd', 'p' for 'b' and 'f' for 'v' ('Fery goot. I will make a prief of it in my notebook' (I.i.132)), dropping initial consonants ('But can you affection the 'oman?' (I.i.210)), and pluralizing singular nouns ('Why, it

is affectations!' (I.i.138)). Like Nym, Evans is also a dab hand at forc-
ing nouns to serve as verbs and adjectives, whether they like it or not:
'Master Slender, I will description the matter to you, if you be capacity
of it' (I.i.198–9). And he's just as adept as Quickly at mangling words
and phrases through malapropism, although in his case the result is less
often unconscious innuendo and more often the mutation of ordinary
parlance into fully intelligible gobbledygook: when Evans says to
Shallow, 'Take your 'visaments in that' (I.i.34–5), or tells Slender 'you
must speak positable' (I.i.218–19), in the context of the dialogue we
know exactly what he means.

The same goes for the inspired gibberish spouted by Dr Caius, who
is prone to desert his ineffable Franglais in exasperation for his mother
tongue, turning his speech into a macaronic *mélange* of both languages:
'Vat is you sing? I do not like dese toys. Pray you go and vetch me in my
closet *un boîtier vert* – a box, a green-a box. Do intend vat I speak? A
green-a box' (I.iv.41–3). It would be disingenuous to deny that such
humour battens on the linguistic incompetence of the character in
question, which confirms the audience's proficiency in standard
English by deviating from it so absurdly. But the delight Shakespeare
takes in concocting these travesties of his tongue, and the delight every
audience takes in hearing them (actors in the coveted role of Caius regularly steal the show from Falstaff), transcend the satisfactions of mere
satire. Much of the pleasure that springs from such aberrant elocution
lies in the licence it grants to indulge in indecent wordplay:

> EVANS. If there is one, I shall make two in the company.
> CAIUS. If there be one or two, I shall make-a the turd.
> (III.iii.224–5)

By keeping the primal facts and functions of the body in view, the
bawdy subtext forged by these means contributes to the carnivalization
of life in the world of the play. It creates a powerful semantic undertow,
which pulls the *dramatis personae* together and towards the point at
which their differences disappear.

Making Fritters of English

The rich rewards of setting language loose to traffic in obscenities can't
quite explain, however, the special virtue of the verbal mayhem this
comedy causes. The key to the explanation can be found in the scene in

which Evans puts Master William Page through his grammatical paces, while being heckled by Mistress Quickly. Whether the lad's Christian name is a wry allusion to Shakespeare's own experience of being catechized in this fashion as a boy must remain a moot point, though the fact that Evans harps on the name, employing it 11 times, certainly lends weight to the conjecture. What undoubtedly *is* deliberate is the setting of the scene on a 'playing day' (IV.i.9), which establishes the tacit mood of holiday licence the dialogue is about to exploit. Despite there being 'no school today' (IV.i.10), William's mother requests Evans to 'ask him some questions in his accidence' (IV.i.14–15), and the parson proceeds to take the boy through part of the drill that would have been horribly familiar to Shakespeare and to generations of schoolboys obliged to learn by rote whole swathes of *A Shorte Introduction of Grammar [. . .] for the bryngynge up of all those that entende to atteyne the knowledge of the Latine tongue.* This textbook, the work of William Lilly and John Colet, had been a cornerstone of the curriculum ever since its publication in 1549, when Edward VI decreed that it be used in schools throughout the kingdom. The Latin lesson in *The Merry Wives of Windsor* is Shakespeare's revenge on Lilly and Colet: a loud raspberry blown not only at the mindless grind their *Shorte Introduction* inflicted on pupils, but also at the docility it was designed to inculcate through strict instruction in the rules of the *sermo patrius* or 'father tongue'.

Despite Evans's best endeavours to reinforce those rules by grilling Shakespeare's namesake, the *sermo patrius* is no match for the instructor's wacky accent or Mistress Quickly's misconstructions. Lewd connotations multiply as the most innocent words divulge double meanings, transforming a dull grammatical exercise into a salacious exchange about genitalia, whores and copulation. In this scene, though, it's vital to stress that ribald equivocation is a means of doing more than letting language off the leash of propriety that restrains it in polite public speech. It's a way of cocking a snook at a conception of language that authorizes its use as an instrument of subjection, a device for schooling citizens in fixed principles of hierarchy and order. In the light of Evans's hapless Latin lesson it's possible to see how much is at stake in the 'abusing' of 'the King's English' (I.iv.5) – the dutiful son of the 'father tongue' – in which the whole comedy is engaged.

The person accused of abusing the version of the vernacular that bears the royal imprimatur is Dr Caius, and his accuser is – of all people – Mistress Quickly. But the French physician is not the only character at whom the charge is levelled. After being buttonholed by Nim and browbeaten with every permutation of his catchword, Page remarks: 'The humour of it, quoth a? Here's a fellow frights English out of his wits' (II.i.130–1). The 'ranting Host of the Garter' (II.i.179), himself no mean abuser of his native tongue, calls for Caius and Evans to drop their swords and butcher the language instead: 'Let them keep their limbs whole, and hack our English' (III.i.71–2). And at the end of the play Falstaff vents his dismay at being obliged to endure Evans's asinine gibes: ' "Seese" and "putter"? Have I lived to stand at the taunt of one that makes fritters of English?' (V.v.141–2). The word 'English', with reference to the language and its misuse, appears more often in *The Merry Wives of Windsor* than in any other Shakespearean play, because abusing, deranging, hacking and shredding the English language are at the gleeful heart of it, and the zany gang of linguistic terrorists who sabotage the King's English are its unsung heroes.

Shakespeare has more than mutiny in mind, however, when he lets Evans, Quickly, Caius & Co. run off at the mouth and play havoc with authorized usage. The life of this play is in its language rather than in any moral lesson, whether conventional or subversive, that can be drawn from it. And that phenomenal verbal vitality, the quintessence of the comedy's festive spirit, finds its most effusive expression when the characters speak utter nonsense and poppycock becomes poetry.

G. K. Chesterton rightly congratulated the English on giving the world the art of nonsense, crediting Edward Lear and Lewis Carroll above all with its invention. Nonsense he defined as 'humour which has for the moment renounced all connection with wit. It is humour that abandons all attempt at intellectual justification; and does not merely jest at the incongruity of some accident or practical joke, as a by-product of real life, but extracts and enjoys it for its own sake.' He even went so far as to describe nonsense as 'the literature of the future' with 'its own version of the cosmos to offer; the world must not only be the tragic, romantic, and religious, it must be nonsensical also.' One can see what Chesterton was driving at: in a world whose present conduct makes no sense, sheer nonsense becomes the only thing that does make sense, releasing us from the limits of the world as it is by releasing us from the limits of its language, and thus transporting us to worlds that do not yet exist. The only objection to be levelled at Chesterton's thesis is that Shakespeare got there long before Carroll and Lear.

In the opening lines of *The Merry Wives of Windsor* we can hear intelligibility being kissed goodbye as Slender, that 'very potent piece of imbecility' as Hazlitt called him, turns Latin legal terms into twaddle: 'Coram', 'Custalorum', 'Ay, and Ratolorum too' (I.i.5–7). Perhaps it was his recognition of something sublime in Slender's inanity that led Hazlitt to call him 'the only first-rate character in the play'. Be that as it may, by the time Evans invites his companions to leave their 'pribbles and prabbles' (I.i.50) – the phrase he echoes at the end of the play while upbraiding Falstaff – we know that we're already in the land where the Jumblies live and the people speak Jabberwocky. In the nonsensical nonce-words and idiotic idiolects of *The Merry Wives of Windsor* Shakespeare's language frees itself to speak in tongues that tell of life transformed in times to come.

8
'Strange misprision': *Much Ado About Nothing*

Ghosts

The first strange thing to note about *Much Ado About Nothing* is the fact that it's haunted. The Quarto edition of the play, which was published in 1600 – a year or so after it was written and first performed – begins Act I with the stage direction: 'Enter Leonato, Governor of Messina, Innogen his wife, Hero his daughter, and Beatrice his niece, with a Messenger.' Act II opens likewise with a stage direction that has Leonato entering accompanied by 'his wife' and by 'a kinsman'. Neither Innogen nor the kinsman, however, says or does anything in *Much Ado*; no character refers to them and they are not mentioned in any other stage direction. They are both what Shakespearean scholars call textual 'ghosts' – characters who survive, by accident or design, in the original stage directions that announce their entrance, but who aren't called upon to speak or act, and who are therefore consigned by modern editors to the oblivion of footnotes, and doomed by modern productions never to tread the boards. It's been suggested that the kinsman may be the same person Leonato alludes to when he asks his brother Antonio, 'where is my cousin, your son? Hath he provided this music?' and is assured that 'He is very busy about it' (I.ii.1–3). But Antonio's busy son has evaporated by Act V, in which Leonato emphatically declares Hero to be the sole heir of both brothers (V.i.282), leaving his ghostly kinsman as discarnate as ever. A similar fate befalls the uncle Claudio evidently has 'here in Messina' (I.i.18), although no one goes so far as to deny his existence. The exchange between Leonato and the Messenger that opens the play brings him briefly but vividly alive, dwelling long enough on his tearful joy – 'A kind overflow of kindness' (I.i.26) – at the prospect of his nephew's arrival to create the expectation that he'll turn up in the flesh in due course; but, once again, we never hear another word about him.

Like Shakespeare's King John, each of these phantoms turns out to be merely 'a scribbled form, drawn with a pen / Upon a parchment' (*KJ*, V.vii.32–3). They can all be mundanely explained away as the aborted offspring of authorial revision or negligence. But their spectral presence on the margins of *Much Ado About Nothing* seems peculiarly apt in a play that advertises its preoccupation with insubstantiality in its title. The ranks of the incorporeal in *Much Ado* are swelled, furthermore, by figurative or virtual *dramatis personae*. The most conspicuous of these is the Hero resurrected in the final scene to be reunited with Claudio. Although the fictive status of her strategic demise is never left in doubt, the past tense Hero uses when she says to Claudio, 'when I lived I was your other wife' (V.iv.60), and the present tense Don Pedro uses when he exclaims, 'The former Hero, Hero that is dead!' (V.iv.65), confer an uncanny, posthumous quality on the being who is about to become Claudio's bride. An equally uncanny, disembodied figure of a different kind materializes out of a misunderstanding during the scene in which the Watch overhears Borachio confessing his skulduggery to Conrad. When Borachio says, 'But seest thou not what a deformed thief this fashion is?', one of the Watch whispers aside to his comrades, 'I know that Deformed. A has been a vile thief this seven year. A goes up and down like a gentleman. I remember his name' (III.iii.119–23). So palpable does this figment of misapprehension become that Dogberry can be found fleshing him out while filling Leonato in two acts later:

> And also the watch heard them talk of one Deformed. They say he wears a key in his ear and a lock hanging by it, and borrows money in God's name, the which he hath used so long and never paid that now men grow hard-hearted and will lend nothing for God's sake.
>
> (V.i.299–304)

Far from being eccentric features of the comedy, these textual spectres that haunt it are symptoms of the central insight round which its vision revolves. Whether begotten by compositional glitches or sired by artistic intent, they make manifest the covert ghostliness of the play's substantive characters. They betray the immateriality of what passes for existence in the alienated world of *Much Ado About Nothing*, where thraldom to convention makes men and women strangers to themselves. When Hero, whom Claudio and Don Pedro believe to be dead, is restored to life and stainless maidenhood at the climax of the play, the narrative arc of the high romantic plot is completed, and nuptial rites followed by connubial bliss beckon from the wings. But the wording of the resurrection scene insists, against the grain of the comedy's benign design, that Claudio will be marrying a dead woman, a woman who is a shadow of her former self, which died the moment she was betrothed to him. Leonato may strive to assure the dumbfounded Don Pedro that 'She died, my lord, but whiles her slander lived' (V.iv.66), but Hero's defamation merely sealed her in the coffin that enclosed her from the moment she was robbed of the right to forge her own identity and fate.

Fashion Victims

Who might be responsible for that robbery, the crime of which Hero is far from the only victim in *Much Ado*? Who else but that 'deformed thief' known to Borachio as 'fashion' and to Dogberry as the notorious 'Deformed'? In a manoeuvre to which his drama repeatedly resorts, Shakespeare plants in the comic unconscious of the play the key that unlocks the logic of its vision. Borachio's drunken digression on fashion, and the Watchman's and Conrad's response to it, exploit the apparent irrelevance of their *obiter dicta* to get straight to the point while seeming to stray from it.

Borachio's reflections on fashion serve in retrospect as an oblique prelude to his confession that he has just 'wooed Margaret, the Lady Hero's gentlewoman, by the name of Hero' (III.iii.139–40), thus beguiling the eyes of Don Pedro and Claudio, those 'fashion-monging boys' (V.i.95), and proving how easily people can be fooled into taking the appearance for the reality. The capacity of clothes to conceal character epitomizes the vulnerability of perception and judgement, and it's fashion in the sense of garments that Borachio has in mind when he boozily broaches the subject to Conrad: 'Thou knowest that the fashion of a doublet, or a hat, or a cloak is nothing to a man' (III.iii.113–15). Borachio means that clothes tell us nothing about the wearer, but Conrad thinks he simply means that men don't care about clothes, that clothes are just clothes to men:

> CONRAD.   Yes, it is apparel.
> BORACHIO. I mean the fashion.
> CONRAD.   Yes, the fashion is the fashion.

BORACHIO. Tush, I may as well say the fool's the fool. But seest
thou not what a deformed thief this fashion is?

(III.iii.116–20)

The pains taken to discriminate the concept of 'fashion' from mere
clothing and the emphatic repetition of the term draw attention to it,
advising us that more may be at stake in it than meets the idle ear. Then,
as we've seen, the Watchman's aside seizes on the phrase 'deformed
thief', underscoring and amplifying each term in turn, to make sure we
give full weight to the implications of both. The epithet 'deformed' is
transmogrified by personification into an imaginary character named
'Deformed', 'a vile thief' whose very identity is stolen, since he 'goes up
and down like a gentleman', concealing his criminality beneath the costume and demeanour of the upper class.

The Watchman's aside harbours an encrypted understanding of the
power of fashion to disguise and distort the reality of human beings, to
turn them into someone they are not by stealing the person they are or
the person they might otherwise become. The personification of fashion as an active, independent entity acknowledges the scale and impact
of its power, while its appearance in the guise of 'a gentleman' locates
the provenance of that power in the ruling class. At the same time,
notwithstanding their personification, the terms 'fashion' and
'Deformed' remain abstractions, which preserves the recognition that
their operation is impersonal and endemic, and cannot be attributed to
the conscious agency of individuals. Fashion is the systemic process by
which the appearance and demeanour of individuals are unconsciously
'deformed' – twisted out of their native shape – to fit the current cultural mould, and in the process it becomes 'Deformed' itself, the ubiquitous, animate epitome of self-estrangement. Although its effects are
material and tangible, fashion itself is immaterial and intangible, a
phantom force invisibly intent on stealing people's souls by reducing
them to spectral simulacra.

Borachio is particularly incensed by the way fashion makes a monkey
out of men:

> Seest thou not, I say, what a deformed thief this fashion
> is, how giddily a turns about all the hot-bloods
> between fourteen and five-and-thirty, sometimes fash-
> ioning them like Pharaoh's soldiers in the reechy paint-
> ing, sometime like god Bel's priests in the old church
> window, sometime like the shaven Hercules in the

smirched, worm-eaten tapestry, where his codpiece
seems as massy as his club?

CONRAD. All this I see, and I see that the fashion wears out more
apparel than the man. But art not thou thyself giddy
with the fashion, too, that thou hast shifted out of thy
tale into telling me of the fashion?

(III.iii.126–37)

In a play in which male pride performs such a pivotal role, almost producing a tragic catastrophe through the defamation of Hero, and placing a seemingly insuperable barrier between Benedick and Beatrice, it's
no accident that Borachio's examples constitute a miniature morphol-
ogy of masculine deformation. In the course of his tirade, masculinity
mutates from the martial image of Pharaoh's soldiers, drowned in the
Red Sea while pursuing the Israelites, into the idolatrous high priests of
Baal overthrown by Daniel for worshipping graven images, and lastly
into the supreme image of emasculation, 'the shaven Hercules', which
fuses the shorn Samson of the Book of Judges with Hercules humiliated
in the house of Omphale by being forced to dress in women's clothes
and spin at her command. All three avatars of masculinity portray the
pernicious impact of the 'deformed thief' on men, while indicting art for
its visual complicity in the process of deformation. The painting of
Pharaoh's soldiers, however, is 'reechy' or begrimed with smoke, 'god
Bel's priests' are depicted in an 'old church window' and 'the shaven
Hercules' belongs in a 'smirched, worm-eaten tapestry', which makes it
plain that these types and travesties of manhood are as *passé* as the sport-
ing of a 'massy' codpiece had become by the time of *Much Ado*.

Borachio's compressed conspectus brings into focus the fact that
masculinity is neither innate nor natural, but a mutable cultural construction with its own history. By doing so, it exposes the disparity
between what men happen to be like in the present and what they hap-
pened to be like in the past, and thus implies the prospect of their being
different again in the future. It invites us to adopt its attitude of detachment from modes of manhood that deserve to be discarded as the postures of a bygone era, however tenacious in reality they may be. To
accept that invitation is to glimpse a space in which alternative styles of
masculinity might be fashioned. In the interim, however, it's men's
helpless subjection to the giddy whims of fashioning that's most apparent, as Conrad's reply reminds us: 'I see that the fashion wears out
more apparel than the man.'

By this point it's clear that 'fashion' signifies much more than styles of dress and the sway they can hold over sight. The word serves in *Much Ado* as shorthand for the myriad ways in which human beings are formed and deformed, physically, mentally and emotionally, by the culture in which they find themselves at a particular moment in history. 'Fashion' is the ideal term for this onerous task, because in its routine sartorial sense it's the most obvious, graphic proof of how tightly people are defined by their world and time. By the same token, however, the wider connotations of the word imply that the subtler, unseen ways in which the self is unwittingly fashioned may be just as extraneous and disposable as an ill-fitting, outdated doublet and hose.

Shakespeare keeps our minds focused on the disfiguring effects of fashion by reanimating its allegorical alias at the end of the scene. After the Watch have arrested Conrad and Borachio, the Watchman with the same bee still buzzing in his bonnet butts in to remind us that 'one Deformed is one of them. I know him – a wears a lock' (III.iii.162–3). That the distinguishing mark of Deformed should be a love-lock, a fashionable affectation of the day, is in keeping with his character, of course, but it's also appropriate that this chimerical felon is visualized as a lover – or rather a 'gentleman' posing as a lover – in a comedy that makes so much ado about men and women locked together in love. In case the latter sense of the word 'lock' should be lost on us, Dogberry picks it up and pushes it forward in the fifth-act speech I quoted earlier. In his unwitting wisdom, Dogberry misconstrues the nature of the lock that sets the arch-larcenist apart, taking it to be the kind of lock that requires a key, which duly materializes as an ornament depending from the ear of Deformed.

In his allegorical capacity as fashion personified, Deformed displays in the lock and key with which Dogberry has adorned him the power of fashion to fetter and imprison, but also the possibility of release from its shackles. Fashion binds, but fashion also looses, being mutable by its nature. To be at the mercy of fashion rather than its master is to be a fashion victim, to be 'giddy with the fashion' as Conrad puts it, dizzied by the lack of self-determination that results from being fashioned by something other than oneself. This plight is figured as subjection to an insidious form of theft, a perpetual taking which gives nothing in return, and which ends up robbing human beings of their own humanity: the insatiable leech Deformed 'borrows money in God's name, the which he hath used so long and never paid that now men grow hardhearted and will lend nothing for God's sake'.

'our whole dissembly'

The bungling constabulary breathe so much life into the infamous Deformed that it's easy to forget that he's a fictitious being, whose function is to make concrete and specific a phenomenon that couldn't be more abstract and diffuse. The accidental invention of Deformed creates an individual culprit on whom the short arm of the law in Messina seeks to pin the rap for grand larceny – for the crime of stealing people from themselves and leaving perfect duplicates in their place to walk and talk as if they were the real thing. It's a crime of which the entire populace of Messina, not excluding its police force, has been the victim: when Dogberry marshals that force by asking, 'Is our whole dissembly appeared?' (IV.ii.1), his malapropism ('dissembly' instead of 'assembly') pinpoints the predicament of everyone in the play. The desire to collar the villain responsible for the crime is undeniable: 'You'll be made bring Deformed forth, I warrant you' (III.iii.165–6), says the Watchman to Conrad and Borachio as they are taken into custody. But since the crime is one for which no individual can be brought to book, because everyone is unwittingly complicit in its perpetration, it comes as no surprise that fashion's elusive alter ego, unlike the dastardly Don John, goes unapprehended and is still on the loose at the end of the play.

The real criminal mastermind in *Much Ado*, in other words, is fashion – alias Deformed – rather than the fall guy who takes the rap for him, the morally deformed bastard, Don John. The villainy of Don John, it soon becomes apparent, is perfectly consistent with the values of those whose honour he contrives to violate. In this respect, the Watch's futile quest to arrest and indict Deformed secretes a critique of their betters' belief that their adversities spring from the motiveless malignity of Don Pedro's black-hearted brother. It reveals the myopia of the mentality that seeks to solve in personal, moralistic terms problems whose causes are social and structural. This is not to deny Don John's delinquency, but to understand it as symptomatic of the dispensation that has fashioned him, just as it has fashioned the characters whose antithesis he seems to be.

Much Ado harps on the word 'fashion', in both its narrower and its wider sense, throughout the play, to the point where it becomes apparent that everyone in its world is ultimately, in one sense or the other, fashion's slave. The scene in which Don John's henchmen are overheard and apprehended is preoccupied, as we've seen, with the fashioning of men and masculinity – a preoccupation it shares with the play as a whole, which puts the word 'man' and its cognates to work far more often than any other play by Shakespeare. But the very next scene foregrounds the fact that women are just as 'giddy with the fashion' as Conrad and Borachio made men out to be. The otherwise idle prenuptial exchange between Hero and Margaret about the bride's ruff, tire and gown – 'a most rare fashion, i'faith', Margaret assures her mistress, 'a fine, quaint, graceful, and excellent fashion' (III.iv.13–14, 20–1) – shows the fairer sex in the clutches of the same 'vile thief' who 'wears out more apparel than the man'. However, Hero's reply to Margaret's praise of her bridal gown – 'God give me joy to wear it, for my heart is exceeding heavy' (III.iv.23–4) – is quite unexpected, and all the more disturbing for remaining unexplained. It affords us a glimpse of the gap Hero is concealing between the woman and the wife-to-be, the gap that talk of her bridal gown, the material sign of her impending transformation, has suddenly brought home to her.

Margaret attempts to lighten her mistress's mood with a bawdy quip that plays on the heaviness of her heart: ''Twill be heavier soon by the weight of a man' (III.iv.25). But the joke misfires, earning the maid a rebuke from her mistress – 'Fie upon thee, art not ashamed?' (III.iv.26) – which forces her to backtrack and defend the propriety of her indecent dig:

> Of what, lady? Of speaking honourably? Is not marriage honourable in a beggar? Is not your lord honourable without marriage? I think you would have me say 'saving your reverence, a husband'. An bad thinking do not wrest true speaking, I'll offend nobody. Is there any harm in 'the heavier for a husband'? None, I think, an it be the right husband and the right wife – otherwise 'tis light and not heavy.
>
> (III.iv.27–34)

But this is the eve of a wedding the audience knows to be doomed, and all Margaret manages to do through her disingenuous rhetorical questions is raise genuine questions about whether Hero's 'lord', Claudio, whom we know to be bent on reviling her in public, is indeed 'honourable', and whether marriage to him would be more or less honourable than marriage to a beggar. The levelling alignment of 'lord' and 'beggar' (shades of Christopher Sly) is reinforced by the pointed correction of 'man' to 'husband', which underscores the implication of the original joke that Claudio's gender matters more than his rank or marital role. Moreover, 'Is there any harm in 'the heavier for a husband'?' revises the previous wording only to hark back to Hero's heavy heart and link it to having a husband rather than feeling the weight of a man. The question of whether there's any 'harm' in being 'the heavier for a husband' is raised in order to quash it with 'None', but in the light of the trauma in store on the morrow, the qualification 'an it be the right husband and the right wife' is charged with proleptic irony.

This scene and the one before it are excellent examples of the way Shakespeare exploits auxiliary or incidental episodes to mine the deeper implications of the drama and bring its central issues to light. Time and again, the cloak of comic relief or aimless dialogue allows him to distil the essence of what's at stake in the play, while the audience's mind and his own are off-guard or at ease, distracted from the issues that overtly drive the protagonists' more prominent exchanges. It's as if his relaxing of the conscious authorial control such exchanges demand releases sub-conscious intuitions of what lies beneath them, subliminal insights that find condensed expression in absurd digressions and impromptu quib-bling. The transmission of those insights to the audience is all the more effective for being subliminal and oblique, for steering us inadvertently towards the heart of the matter: 'Tell all the truth, but tell it slant', as Emily Dickinson observed, 'Success in circuit lies.' However, once we're aware of how highly charged such scenes are in *Much Ado*, once we're aware of how much covert work they are doing to tune us to its vision, it becomes possible to trace their concerns back to the start of the play and follow them through to the end.

Strange Bedfellows and Dark Doubles

If we go back to the beginning of *Much Ado* and the badinage between Leonato and his niece in the opening scene, we find that Beatrice is the first to fasten on the word 'fashion'. She employs it to render Benedick risible even before he enters: 'He wears his faith', she says, 'but as the fashion of his hat, it ever changes with the next block' (I.i.71–3). Beatrice's gibe at the fickleness of Benedick's friendship schools us from the outset to take 'fashion' figuratively as well as literally – in this case as a simile for the attitude a man adopts to his own affection. Twenty lines later, Don Pedro extends the term's significance again in formally com-plimenting his host, Leonato: 'The fashion of the world is to avoid cost, and you encounter it' (I.i.92–3). Here 'fashion' denotes the way most people might be expected to behave, which Leonato unfashionably eschews, thereby proving, if only in the realm of etiquette, that the way of the world can be withstood.

The next usage of the word, however, goes straight to the nub of the matter uppermost in Shakespeare's mind in *Much Ado*. The speaker is the pantomime villain of the piece, Don Pedro's illegitimate sibling, Don John, who dismisses Conrad's advice that he court his brother's newly won favour with the words: 'I had rather be a canker in a hedge than a rose in his grace, and it better fits my blood to be disdained of all than to fashion a carriage to rob love from any' (I.iii.25–8). Don John's contempt for anyone who affects a spurious demeanour in order to steal another's affection anticipates Borachio's fulmination against fashion as 'a false thief' in Act III. By his refusal 'to fashion a carriage to rob love' he cynically implies, moreover, that he is the exception to the rule – to what his brother would call 'the fashion of the world' – as far as affairs of the heart are concerned. How accurately Don John's jaundiced phrase describes the conduct of the lovers in Messina is a question *Much Ado* compels us to consider.

The play's resident '*Bastard*' (as Don John is dubbed in the Quarto's speech-prefixes) certainly finds a strange bedfellow – at least as far as 'fashion' is concerned – in Beatrice. When Hero deliberately describes her best friend's faults in her hearing in order to sway her heart towards Benedick, she laments the fact that 'Disdain and scorn ride sparkling in her eyes' whenever a man approaches, and that no handsome, wise and noble man exists 'But she would spell him backward', being perversely determined to turn 'every man the wrong side out' (III.i.51, 61, 68). In short, Hero concludes: 'to be so odd and from all fashions / As Beatrice is cannot be commendable' (III.i.72–3). Beatrice behaves in a way that is eccentrically at odds with the approved conventions of courtship and the dictates of female decorum; she acts as if what everyone else regards as normal and natural were quite foreign to her. Just like Don John, in other words, she refuses 'to fashion a carriage to rob love' from anyone.

The character Beatrice most closely resembles in this regard, however, is the man she mocks with a fencing term as 'Signor Montanto' (I.i.29), her partner, if not her peer, in the cut and thrust of persiflage. Benedick signals his scorn for the prescribed deportment of the dejected lover when he sarcastically asks Claudio to get himself a willow garland, the staple emblem of the forsaken suitor, and doesn't let it go at that: 'What fashion will you wear the garland of? About your neck, like an usurer's chain? Or under your arm, like a lieutenant's scarf? You must wear it one way, for the Prince hath got your Hero' (II.i.178–81). The same satirical detachment from programmed expressions of emotion dictates Benedick's dismay at Claudio's metamorphosis from tough, no-nonsense soldier into mooning bridegroom: 'I have known when he would have walked ten mile afoot to see a good armour, and now will he lie ten nights awake carving the fashion of a new doublet' (II.iii.15–18).

The fact that Benedick's satirical detachment proves no more secure than Beatrice's, and that both renegades are so readily duped into compliance with conventions from which they once recoiled, is a testament to the tenacity of 'The fashion of the world' (I.i.92) in *Much Ado*. Nowhere is fashion's hold on them more intimately apparent than in the sartorial diction that they employ or that others apply to them; like Don John, their fellow rebel against the customary and conventional, Beatrice and Benedick are obliged to define themselves, and their views on love and life, on fashion's terms, whether they are using the word itself or not. One of the most striking instances of this can be seen in Benedick's response to Leonato's lurid repudiation of his daughter's 'foul tainted flesh' after Claudio has denounced her: 'Sir, sir, be patient. / For my part, I am so attired in wonder / I know not what to say' (IV.i.144–6). What's so striking about it is how invasive and involuntary it reveals the fashioning of the self to be. Benedick describes himself as 'attired in wonder': even a state as unforeseen as astonishment is culturally scripted and can't be called his own. Mental and emotional states that seem to be spontaneous and authentic turn out to be rehearsed; the deepest feelings and most natural frames of mind are unwittingly worn and discarded like garments.

This understanding is built into the very plot of *Much Ado About Nothing*. Given that the vile, deformed thief fashion 'goes up and down like a gentleman', it can be no coincidence that both romantic couples in the comedy are inveigled into each other's arms by Don Pedro, Prince of Aragon, the most powerful figure in the play. Having contrived the betrothal of Claudio to Hero by masquerading as Claudio and wooing her on his behalf, Don Pedro turns his attention to the feuding duo embroiled in a perpetual 'skirmish of wit' (I.i.60):

> I will in the interim undertake one of Hercules' labours. Which is to bring Signor Benedick and the Lady Beatrice into a mountain of affection th'one with th'other. I would fain have it a match, and I doubt not but to fashion it, if you three will but minister such assistance as I shall give you direction.

> (II.i.341–6)

It's no coincidence either that Don Pedro's brother, his dark double and sworn enemy of fashioning a carriage to rob love, is the one who drives a wedge between Claudio and Hero; or that his plot to undo them is devised by the play's expert on fashion, Borachio, who employs precisely the same term as Don Pedro while outlining his plan to deceive the eyes and ears of Claudio and the Prince:

> They will scarcely believe this without trial. Offer them instances, which shall bear no less likelihood than to see me at her chamber window, hear me call Margaret Hero, hear Margaret term me Claudio. And bring them to see this the very night before the intended wedding, for in the meantime I will so fashion the matter that Hero shall be absent, and there shall appear such seeming truth of Hero's disloyalty that jealousy shall be called assurance, and all the preparation overthrown.
>
> (II.ii.36–45)

Borachio does indeed 'fashion the matter' for Don John in such a way that the 'seeming truth' appears to be the case, with almost catastrophic consequences not only for Hero and Claudio but for Beatrice and Benedick as well. Yet in doing so he's doing no more than Don Pedro does, when he lets Hero believe the seeming truth that she is being courted by Claudio, or when he fashions it so that Beatrice and Benedick are fooled into believing the seeming truth that each is in love with the other. 'The sport', says Don Pedro, 'will be when they hold one an opinion of another's dotage, *and no such matter*. That's the scene that I would see, which will be merely a dumb show' (II.iii.205–8; my italics). The friar, of course, stages a similar charade:

> Your daughter here the princes left for dead,
> Let her a while be secretly kept in,
> And publish it that she is dead indeed.
> Maintain a mourning ostentation,
> And on your family's old monument
> Hang mournful epitaphs, and do all rites
> That appertain unto a burial.
>
> (IV.i.204–10)

The purpose of this 'dumb show' is to buy time to clear Hero's name and breed remorse in Claudio's heart, in the hope that 'success / Will fashion the event in better shape / Than I can lay it down in likelihood'

(IV.i.236–8). The show and its sequel, Claudio's public rite of contrition at Hero's tomb, amply fulfil that hope, paving the way for revelation and marital reunion at the close of the comedy. But they can deliver that benign denouement only by fashioning yet another 'seeming truth' and making sure the audience it's aimed at falls for it.

It's impossible to cite that tell-tale phrase without recalling its pregnant use in *The Merchant of Venice*, when Bassanio stands before the golden casket, musing on 'The seeming truth which cunning times put on / To entrap the wisest' (III.ii.100–1). But in *Much Ado* it points to something more pervasive and unnerving than mere illusion masking a recognizable reality. The plots concocted by Don Pedro and the Friar – the embodiments of secular and religious authority within the play – manufacture the emotions that entrap both couples in the web of wedlock. They prompt the protagonists to feel and express the desire and the remorse, the empathy and the guilt, required to bind them to each other, and the protagonists respond right on cue by saying and doing what they are supposed to say and do. Through the device of the plots that dupe the lovers, *Much Ado* exposes the mechanisms that manipulate the heart and mind without their knowing; it makes externally apparent as a conscious conspiracy the internalized machinery that unconsciously controls the way people think and feel.

'trust no agent'

The comedy draws its comic energy from exposing that machinery and the vanity of striving to resist it. It generates exuberant humour and sanguine resolutions from situations which, tilted into another light, might well seem sinister. This is especially true of the tragicomic courtship of Claudio and Hero, whose key players are clamped into conventions that condemn them to an ersatz existence of endless misperception. Aptly enough, the stagy melodrama of Hero's indictment and vindication is the only recycled narrative component of *Much Ado*, the tale of Beatrice and Benedick being, like Dogberry and his bumbling Watch, Shakespeare's own invention. For the principal ingredients of the plot that revolves round Claudio and Hero, Shakespeare turned mainly to the versions he found in translations of Matteo Bandello's *La prima parte de le novelle* and Ariosto's *Orlando Furioso*, although the tale of the slandered woman was extremely popular in the Renaissance and its rudiments could have been lifted from any number of works. The debt underscores the derivative nature of the lovers' desire for each other and the predictability of their fabricated plight. Indeed, the one feature of previous versions Shakespeare might be expected to find irresistible – the social inferiority of the traduced heroine – is precisely the one he declines to adopt and exploit, preferring to narrow the gap between his heroine's rank and that of her suitor to the point where it ceases to be an issue. By bringing their births and fortunes into balance, Shakespeare prevents Hero from attracting the tragic empathy excited by flagrant social injustice, and thus deflecting attention from the couple's joint subjection to subtler modes of coercion.

In his characterization of the couple, however, Shakespeare decided to tip the balance emphatically in favour of his heroine. No special appeal to the dramatic conventions of the day can save Claudio from the conclusion that his creator meant us to view him, in marked contrast to his precursors in the story, as a callow, invertebrate cad. Looking back at Claudio's first appearance in the play in light of his subsequent treatment of Hero, the signs of his superficial, second-hand attitude to the most intimate, intense emotions are plainly visible. His immediate response to beholding Hero is to secure Benedick's confirmation of her nubility, to reassure himself that his comrade has seen what he has seen: 'Benedick, didst thou note the daughter of Signor Leonato?' (I.i.154–5). Benedick's reply, 'I noted her not, but I looked on her' (I.i.156), brusquely refuses to supply the required reassurance. Its pointed quibble on the word 'note', which here means not merely to take special notice of, but to observe in a sexually interested way, activates the concern with perception announced in the play's punning title, whose 'nothing' would have been pronounced like 'noting' in Elizabethan speech. It qualifies Claudio's bewitchment by Hero as the effect of a view of her that Benedick 'in sober judgement' (I.i.162) doesn't share. Pressed by Claudio for his true opinion of Hero, 'the sweetest lady that ever I looked on', Benedick has no qualms about declaring his dislike of her looks and her inferiority to Beatrice: 'I can see yet without spectacles, and I see no such matter. There's her cousin, an she were not possessed with a fury, exceeds her as much in beauty as the first of May doth the last of December' (I.i.177–82). That Benedick's motive in this exchange may be simply the ironic ribbing of his friend doesn't detract from the fact that Claudio's view of Hero appears vulnerable by the end of it.

After confessing his love for Hero to Don Pedro, undeterred by Benedick's continued disparagement of 'Leonato's short daughter' (I.i.200–1) and his unflagging, misogamous mockery, Claudio beseeches the Prince to help him. Before confiding fully in his mentor, however, he has one pressing question that makes his priorities plain: 'Hath Leonato any son, my lord?' (I.i.277). Having been assured by Don Pedro that Hero is 'his only heir' (I.i.277–8), Claudio proceeds to explain how, during the military campaign they have just completed, he 'looked upon her with a soldier's eye' (another instance of prescriptive 'noting'):

> But now I am returned, and that war-thoughts
> Have left their places vacant, in their rooms
> Come thronging soft and delicate desires,
> All prompting me how fair young Hero is,
> Saying I liked her ere I went to wars.
>   (I.i.284–8)

The conclusion of the 'rougher task' (I.i.282) of warfare provides the cue for the romance over which it had taken precedence. The syntax Claudio employs to recount the genesis of his love for Hero is revealing. The passive construction 'I am returned' is followed by Claudio's portrayal of himself as the equally passive object of invasive thoughts and desires that determine his perception of Hero and persuade him – in flat contradiction of his own account – that his amorous attachment to her predates his departure for the battlefield. No wonder Don Pedro replies, 'Thou wilt be like a lover presently, / And tire the hearer with a book of words' (I.i.289–90), for Claudio is indeed assuming the semblance of a textbook lover, whose sentiments have been scripted for him.

A man possessed by emotions with a mind of their own, which falsify his memory of the moment he fell in love, Claudio is bereft of the agency that would allow him to be the author of himself. His acquiescence in Don Pedro's plan to woo Hero in his place is entirely consistent with his occupation by extraneous imperatives. The completeness of Don Pedro's proposed usurpation of his *protégé* is nevertheless disturbing:

> I will assume thy part in some disguise,
> And tell fair Hero I am Claudio.
> And in her bosom I'll unclasp my heart
> And take her hearing prisoner with the force
> And strong encounter of my amorous tale.
>   (I.i.304–8)

The Prince's stratagem might be dismissed as a convenient comedic convention, were it not the first of several occasions when another man takes, or is thought to have taken, Claudio's place in relation to Hero.

That we are meant to make more of it than that becomes apparent in the next scene, whose sole function is to breed confusion among both characters and spectators by misreporting Don Pedro's ploy. The 'strange news' (I.ii.4) Antonio relates to Leonato is that his servant has 'overheard' (I.ii.9) the Prince revealing his love for Hero to Claudio. Although this is the exact reverse of what the audience has just overheard, and thus can construe as a misunderstanding, its effect is to arouse suspicion about what purports to be the case. It alerts us to the distortion that hearsay entails, the aural equivalent of the distorted perception to which 'noting' is prone. 'We will hold it as a dream', Leonato wisely decides, 'till it appear itself' (I.ii.18–19), but he instructs his brother nonetheless to prime Hero for the Prince's suit. In the following scene, the fact that Leonato and Antonio are labouring under a misapprehension is clarified by Borachio, who reports a correct version of the exchange between Don Pedro and Claudio to Don John. The clarification is muddied, however, by Borachio's stipulation that he eavesdropped on the exchange indoors behind an arras, while 'Being entertained for a perfumer, as I was smoking a musty room' (I.iii.54–5), for this contradicts Antonio's placing of the conversation misreported by his servant 'in a thick-pleached alley in mine orchard' (I.ii.8–9). These niggling erosions of certainty pave the way for the gross misconception to which not only Claudio but also Benedick falls victim in the wake of the masked dance in Act II.

Benedick at least has the excuse of not being privy to Don Pedro's true motive for winning Hero's heart. When he says to Claudio, 'the Prince hath got your Hero' (II.i.181), he has no reason to believe that he's speaking anything but the truth. Claudio's credulity is far less defensible. The alacrity with which he accepts Don John's assurance that his brother is wooing Hero for himself is the measure of his confidence in both the wooer and the wooed:

> Friendship is constant in all other things
> Save in the office and affairs of love.
> Therefore all hearts in love use their own tongues.
> Let every eye negotiate for itself,
> And trust no agent; for beauty is a witch
> Against whose charms faith melteth into blood.
>
> (II.i.165–70)

In laying the blame for Don Pedro's deceit on Hero's sexual wiles rather than the Prince's treachery, Claudio betrays the same misogynistic assumptions that dictate his readiness to believe the vile slander levelled against his bride on the eve of their wedding. That Claudio delivers this speech in the belief that Don John has mistaken his masked face for that of Benedick intensifies his alienation from himself, rendering the lines 'Let every eye negotiate for itself, / And trust no agent' all the more ironic. Claudio's agency, his capacity to act for himself, has been surrendered from the outset to agents who act in his stead, surrogate selves of whom Don Pedro is merely the most palpable.

When the Prince hands Hero over to him at last with the assurance 'I have wooed in thy name' (II.i.279), Claudio remains curiously impassive and has to be spurred into speech:

> BEATRICE. Speak, Count, 'tis your cue.
> CLAUDIO. Silence is the perfectest herald of joy. I were but little
> happy if I could say how much. (*To Hero*) Lady, as you
> are mine, I am yours. I give away myself for you, and
> dote upon the exchange.
>
> (II.i.286–90)

Once again, Claudio's choice of words is telling. Beatrice's theatrical prompt draws attention to them, highlighting the scripted quality of his performance at this crucial moment. Claudio's trite, laconic defence of his silence is lame, to say the least, but it's the circumspect terms in which he plights his troth to Hero that are most revealing. The declaration 'I am yours' is prefaced by the conditional clause 'as you are mine', which bespeaks a certain wariness on Claudio's part. The wariness may well be warranted in view of the fact that he is giving himself away, just as he has given himself away before, even if this time it's to a prospective wife instead of a surrogate acting on his behalf. But it scarcely explains the odd formality of his claim to dote upon the 'exchange' of himself for Hero rather than upon the woman herself.

Claudio's dispassionate tone and demeanour elicit a corresponding lack of warmth in the newly betrothed Hero, who meets Claudio's silence with a silence so complete that she too must be prodded into action by Beatrice: 'Speak, cousin. Or, if you cannot, stop his mouth with a kiss, and let not him speak, neither' (II.i.291–2). Both lovers seal the promise of their nuptial union at the instigation of others, not in response to an urge that springs spontaneously from within. So unlikely a candidate is Claudio for the role of 'Monsieur Love' (II.iii.34) in which the comedy has cast him that we're obliged to take his transformation on trust from Benedick. The love-sick fiancé Benedick conjures up, the implausible Claudio who now lies 'ten nights awake carving the fashion of a new doublet', and whose 'words are a very fantastical banquet, just so many strange dishes' (II.iii.17–18, 20–1), never materializes on stage.

The Claudio we actually encounter, as opposed to the one concocted by Benedick's soliloquy, is the perfect patsy for Don John, ripe to be duped into believing himself 'cozened with the semblance of a maid' and crediting the 'seeming truth of Hero's disloyalty' (II.ii.34–5, 43). As before, when Claudio fell for the lie about Don Pedro's courtship of Hero, all it takes is hearsay trumped up by 'a plain-dealing villain' (I.iii.30) to destroy Claudio's faith in his bride-to-be. This time, however, firm ocular proof is promised by Don John: 'If you dare not trust that you see, confess not that you know' (III.ii.109–10). The veiled thrust of this tortuous remark is that knowing depends on daring to trust the evidence of one's eyes, which may well be misleading. But Claudio is blind to the devious import of Don John's convoluted syntax and, in sharp contrast to his counterparts in Shakespeare's sources, immediately plots his bride's public disgrace before the allegation has been proved: 'If I see anything tonight why I should not marry her, tomorrow, in the congregation where I should wed, there will I shame her' (III.ii.113–15).

'Which be the malefactors?'

Shakespeare's decision to have the hoax at Hero's chamber window reported rather than staged is designed to stress its insubstantiality. Unfortunately, time and again directors feel obliged to devise a scene in which the deception of Claudio and Don Pedro is enacted (as it is in Kenneth Branagh's screen version, for example), their purpose being to make Claudio's vicious denunciation of Hero at the altar more understandable. In doing so they miss the point as completely as they do when, in order to avoid confusion, they routinely cut the scene (I.ii.) in which the Prince's surrogate love-suit is misreported. By not dramatizing what Claudio is said to have seen, Shakespeare refuses to mitigate his subsequent conduct, insisting on its outrageous irrationality. Denied first-hand corroboration of the incident round which the whole play pivots, the audience is placed in the same position as the characters, at the mercy of what they think they've seen and heard, unable to trust the evidence of their own eyes and ears. This perplexity is deepened by the decision to substitute for the vital window-scene a scene in which Dogberry briefs the constabulary to turn a blind eye to drunks and let thieves go free, and then we overhear them overhearing Borachio's account of his 'amiable encounter' (III.iii.145) with the unwitting Margaret. The displacement of the play's crucial act of deception by clowning mirrors at the level of dramatic structure the displacements of identity that occur when one character impersonates or stands in for another. But it also allows Shakespeare to disclose indirectly, in the guise of illogical codswallop and absurd coincidence, insights too acute to be directly apprehended.

Foremost among these is the recognition of the pervasive pressures exerted on individuals by what the play dubs 'fashion'. The deformed perception – the distorted 'noting' and knowledge – fashioned by the presiding cultural codes are linked in Act III, Scene iii to the forces of law and order that police those codes by regulating conduct and punishing transgression. That those forces take the shape of Dogberry & Co. in Messina makes Shakespeare's contempt for them plain long before Dogberry has demanded to be 'writ down an ass' (IV.ii.84). Moreover, insofar as they 'present the Prince's own person' (III.iii.72), the hapless constabulary personify the supreme figure of authority in the play and thus invite mockery of his power by proxy. And not just mockery: the Prince's appointed surrogates demystify the power he embodies by exposing its complicity in creating the crimes it condemns. Being 'chosen for the Prince's watch' and charged 'to bid any man stand, in the Prince's name' (III.iii.6, 24–5), Dogberry's 'whole dissembly' countenances crime and yet collars the criminals, at once licensing and exposing transgression. Their contradictory behaviour caricatures the absurdity of a law whose violation and enforcement spring from the same source, as the consanguinity of Don John and Don Pedro makes clear.

The idea of legitimacy, personified by Don Pedro, and its apparent antithesis, the idea of illegitimacy, epitomized by his brother, Don John, are symbiotic: they define and reinforce each other. Don Pedro endorses the defamation of Hero as promptly as Claudio and her own father, because he shares with them the assumptions about women's sexuality that Don John activates so adroitly and that his bastardy so blatantly confirms. (The tenacity of those assumptions is testified to at every turn by the relentless gags about cuckoldry that riddle the play.) That's why Dogberry's astute nonsense puts Don Pedro in the frame as a potential felon subject to arrest – 'If you meet the Prince in the night you may stay him', he advises Verges – before letting him off the hook with the rider, 'Marry, not without the Prince be willing' (III.iii.72–3, 76–7). When the Sexton demands at the interrogation of Borachio and Conrade, 'Which be the malefactors?', the same seditious comic logic leads Messina's chief of police, the Prince's deputy, to declare: 'Marry, that am I, and my partner' (IV.ii.3–4).

The malefaction of the Prince and the police who act in his name consists in their prosecution of conduct tacitly condoned by the society they protect and serve. As enforcers of an ethos that created Don John in its own image, there's every reason for them to be brought to book as well, as the foolish wisdom of the Watch implies. The more closely one compares Don John with his sworn enemies, the harder it becomes to tell them apart. His professed motive, unlike theirs, is of course malign: to sabotage the 'intended marriage' of 'the most exquisite Claudio', the 'very forward March chick' (I.iii.41, 46, 52) who has reaped the benefit of Don John's fall from his brother's grace. But the malcontent's hostility to wedlock is indistinguishable from that of Beatrice and Benedick, either of whom could have uttered his line: 'What is he for a fool that betroths himself to unquietness?' (I.iii.43–4). Moreover, the means he employs to achieve his nefarious ends are identical: like his legitimate sibling, whose ploys manipulate both couples in the comedy into marriage, Don John creates and exploits delusion; he makes people take make-believe for truth. His malicious objective does not detract from the fact that the marriage he contrives to destroy through misapprehension is itself founded on duplicity. Having begun the masked dance expecting to be wooed by the Prince, Hero consents to wed the disguised Don Pedro in the belief that he is Claudio, the depth of whose devotion to her could scarcely be more doubtful. The foundations of the romantic rapprochement and marital union of Beatrice and Benedick are no less fraudulent, both of them having been hoodwinked by hearing fictional accounts of each other. The cruel deception practised on the persons of the play by Don John is perfectly at home in Messina, whose denizens are trapped in a maze of radical misperception from the outset.

'Are our eyes our own?'

In Shakespeare's sources the whole plot turns on this single act of deception, contrived by a rival lover rather than by a misogynous bastard created to confound predictable motives and moral distinctions.

But Shakespeare multiplied the occasions of deceit by adding the eaves-dropping and masquing scenes, and by inventing instances of misreporting and mistaking, both visual and verbal, at every opportunity. As a result, the comedy implies that imposture and delusion are not just unfortunate aberrations foisted on its cast by accident or design, but the ubiquitous condition of existence in its virtual world. Identities and relationships in *Much Ado* are constituted by misperception and dissimulation, and their chance misunderstanding or malign distortion merely compounds the more fundamental plight the play exposes: the plight of a world where nothing is what it appears to be and people are not who they think they are. The characters' deliverance from the fleeting comedy of errors in which they've been entangled leaves them stranded in that world, whose maxim might well be Don John's admonition: 'If you dare not trust that you see, confess not that you know' (III.ii. 109–10).

The perceptual bewilderment betrayed by that remark reaches its climax in the scene where Hero is denounced before the altar by Claudio as a 'rotten orange' who is 'but the sign and semblance of her honour' (IV.i.32–3), and by Don Pedro as 'a common stale' (IV.i.65). These scandalous slurs on Hero's character trigger an exchange that brings the play's most profound concern into focus:

> LEONATO.   Are these things spoken, or do I but dream?
> DON JOHN. Sir, they are spoken, and these things are true.
> BENEDICK. This looks not like a nuptial.
> HERO.   'True'! O God!
> CLAUDIO.   Leonato, stand I here?
>   Is this the Prince? Is this the Prince's brother?
>   Is this face Hero's? Are our eyes our own?
>   (IV.i.66–72)

The irony of Claudio's rhetorical questions is lost on him, of course. The last question in particular is rich, coming from a man who has delegated his courtship to a deputy; and the answer the play provides is that our eyes are no more our own than our minds are, insofar as looking and thinking and acting are governed by drives of which we're not conscious and which we therefore can't control. As Claudio puts it shortly before this, oblivious to the real burden of his exclamation: 'What men daily do, not knowing what they do!' (IV.i.19–20).

The revelation that his intended has been the innocent victim of 'John the bastard' (IV.i.190) reveals Claudio to be as remote from the reality of Leonato's daughter as ever: 'Sweet Hero, now thy image doth appear / In the rare semblance that I loved it first' (V.i.243–4). Even his penitential public grieving is an act of ventriloquism: an anonymous lord is enlisted to read Hero's epitaph on Claudio's behalf and promise in his first person: 'Now, unto thy bones good night. / Yearly will I do this rite' (V.iii.22–3). (The regular reassignment of the lord's lines to Claudio by modern editions and productions is an unwarranted 'correction' of the Quarto and Folio texts, which once again misses Shakespeare's point in its misguided attempt to render Claudio's characterization more plausible and sympathetic.) That said, it seems churlish to rebuke Claudio for remoteness from the reality of a woman whose 'image' and 'semblance' constitute the public selves she exhibits from the outset. His mitigating plea, 'Yet sinned I not / But in mistaking' (V.i.266–7), displays a woeful blindness to his real sin, but in a wider sense 'mistaking' is indeed what he's guilty of, though no more guilty than anyone else in the play.

Wounding by Hearsay

The 'strange misprision' (IV.i.187) the Friar imputes to Claudio and Don Pedro is the state in which all the principals of the play exist in one way or another, and not even the cynical intransigence of Beatrice and Benedick can resist its sway. Indeed, the fact that 'Lady Disdain' (I.i.112) and 'Signor Montanto' (I.i.29), the play's vociferous mockers of marriage and the mores of Messina at large, prove as gullible as the butts of their quips and finally succumb to the yoke of matrimony, is the most compelling testimony to the hold convention has over the characters. Compared with Claudio and Hero, of course, Beatrice and Benedick could scarcely appear less conventional. They deploy their remorseless wit on every occasion to insist on the distance that divides them from the norms of their milieu; whereas it's only by reading discomfort and reluctance into the silences of Hero and Claudio, or by scanning every nuance of their speech, that one catches glimpses of a slippage between subject and self. That slippage is more perceptible in Hero than in Claudio. The woman reviled by Don John as 'Leonato's Hero, your Hero, every man's Hero' (III.ii.96–7) shows that she hasn't been entirely dispossessed of herself at several points, most notably just before she is betrothed, when she banters feistily with the masked Don Pedro (II.i.85–90), and just before the wedding, when she answers Ursula's innocent query, 'When are you married, madam?'

with the ominous line, 'Why, every day, tomorrow' (III.i.100–1) and fails to conceal the 'exceeding' heaviness of her heart (III.iv.23–4).

In fairness to both Hero and Claudio, their involvement in the gulling of Beatrice and Benedick, whom they taunt with gusto about their relapse, requires a wry disengagement from the romantic clichés of their culture that one wouldn't expect them to display. But they are totally eclipsed in this regard by Benedick, love's 'obstinate heretic' (I.i.219), and Beatrice, 'the infernal Ate' (II.i.239), who flaunt their scorn for the tender trap and their defiance of custom from the moment they step onto the stage. The long-standing 'merry war' (I.i.59) between them breaks out afresh in the first scene with a fierce 'skirmish of wit' (I.i.60) at the expense of each other, the opposite sex and love. 'I am loved of all ladies, only you excepted', Benedick assures Beatrice, 'And I would I could find in my heart that I had not a hard heart, for truly I love none.' To which Beatrice retorts, 'A dear happiness to women. They would else have been troubled with a pernicious suitor. I thank God and my cold blood I am of your humour for that. I had rather hear my dog bark at a crow than a man swear he loves me' (I.i.118–26).

On one thing the pair are agreed: to avoid at all costs the shackles of wedlock. Benedick reacts to Claudio's wish to wed Hero with an extravagant profession of dismay: 'Is't come to this? In faith, hath not the world one man but he will wear his cap with suspicion? Shall I never see a bachelor of three-score again? Go to, i'faith, an thou wilt needs thrust thy neck into a yoke, wear the print of it, and sigh away Sundays' (I.i.186–90). For his part, Benedick is adamant that he 'will live a bachelor' (I.i.230) come what may, and he dismisses Don Pedro's warning that 'In time the savage bull doth bear the yoke' as inapplicable to him: 'The savage bull may, but if ever the sensible Benedick bear it, pluck off the bull's horns and set them in my forehead, and let me be vilely painted, and in such great letters as they write "Here is good horse to hire" let them signify under my sign "Here you may see Benedick, the married man"' (I.i.245–50).

As for 'my Lady Tongue' (II.i.257), as Benedick dubs her, she's more than a match for her erstwhile beau when it comes to fanatical misogamy. When Hero's uncle says to her, as the masked dance is about to begin, 'Well, niece, I trust you will be ruled by your father' – that is, accept the Prince's proposal if he makes one – Beatrice butts in before she can reply: 'Yes, faith, it is my cousin's duty to make curtsy and say, "Father, as it please you." But yet for all that, cousin, let him be a handsome fellow, or else make another curtsy and say, "Father, as it

please me" ' (II.i.45–50). Hero's father meets this sassy incitement to
filial disobedience with good humour: 'Well, niece, I hope to see you
one day fitted with a husband' (II.i.51–2). But the remark serves only
to goad Beatrice into a scathing diatribe against the domination of
women by men in the prison-house of marriage:

BEATRICE. Not till God make men of some other mettle than
earth. Would it not grieve a woman to be overmas-
tered with a piece of valiant dust? – to make an
account of her life to a clod of wayward marl? No,
uncle, I'll none. Adam's sons are my brethren, and
truly I hold it a sin to match in my kindred.

LEONATO. (*to Hero*) Daughter, remember what I told you. If the
Prince do solicit you in that kind, you know your
answer.

BEATRICE. The fault will be in the music, cousin, if you be not
wooed in good time. If the Prince be too important,
tell him there is measure in everything, and so dance
out the answer. For hear me, Hero, wooing, wedding,
and repenting is as a Scotch jig, a measure, and a
cinquepace. The first suit is hot and hasty, like a Scotch
jig – and full as fantastical; the wedding mannerly modest, as a measure, full of state and ancientry. And then
comes repentance, and with his bad legs falls into the
cinquepace faster and faster till he sink into his grave.

(II.i.53–72)

With this superb condemnation of the marital doom that awaits the
rest of her sex, Beatrice seals her comedy fate as surely as Benedick seals
his by hubristically insisting that he will live and die unwed. Their
nemesis takes the shape of Don Pedro's plot to con them into the belief
that they are secretly mad about each other, and in next to no time the
'Avowed rebels to love', as Schlegel puts it, 'are both entangled in its
net'. Schlegel's choice of metaphor is apt, since entrapment is exactly
what the conspiracy against the couple entails. Both of the eavesdropping traps sprung in Leonato's orchard leave the predatory aspect of
the enterprise in no doubt. 'O, ay, stalk on, stalk on', says Claudio out
of the hidden Benedick's hearing, 'The fowl sits' (II.iii.93); and again,
a few moments later: 'Bait the hook well. This fish will bite' (II.iii.108).
'Let there be the same net spread for her', whispers Don Pedro, switching his attention to Beatrice as Benedick bites, 'and that must your

daughter and her gentlewomen carry' (II.iii.203–5). The latter enlist
the same lexicon when Beatrice's turn to be ensnared comes round.
Ursula likens her delight in 'the dialogue' they have scripted for
Beatrice's benefit to the pleasure of watching a fish 'greedily devour the
treacherous bait' (III.i.31, 28); Hero is equally anxious 'that her ear
lose nothing / Of the false-sweet bait that we lay for it' (III.i.32–3). By
the end of their rigged exchange Ursula is confident that the bait has
been taken: 'She's limed, I warrant you', she assures her mistress *sotto
voce*, 'We have caught her, madam'. 'If it prove so,' replies Hero as they
exit, 'then loving goes by haps. / Some Cupid kills with arrows, some
with traps' (III.i.104–6).

It would be absurd to overstress the sinister side of the trick played
on Beatrice and Benedick, when the spirit in which it's played is so
patently benign, but it would be remiss not to give it due weight too.
After all, the net that's spread for them, the net in which their lives
become irrevocably entangled, is a web of fabrication that makes them
misconstrue not only each other but also themselves. The gulling of
Beatrice and Benedick grants the audience an estranged, disillusioned
view of the phenomenon of falling in love. What's usually viewed as a
subjective, authentic, spontaneous experience is dramatically objectified
as a culturally enforced fiction. The concerted pressure of social attitudes and expectations is projected into a clutch of characters, who
bring a recalcitrant couple into line by inducing them to 'hold one an
opinion of another's dotage, and no such matter' (II.iii.205–6).

Despite the farcical implausibility of the gulling scenes, Shakespeare
is at pains to stress that there's nothing exceptional about the process
Beatrice and Benedick undergo. On the contrary, it illustrates a general
truth, as Hero reminds her accomplice:

> My talk to thee must be how Benedick
> Is sick in love with Beatrice. Of this matter
> Is little Cupid's crafty arrow made,
> *That only wounds by hearsay.*
> (III.i.20–3; my italics)

'Hearsay' is Shakespeare's shorthand for the means by which spurious
emotions are spawned in the heart in a way that makes them seem
authentic. When Beatrice decides to requite the love that she's been led
to believe Benedick feels for her, she does so because, as she puts it,
'*others say* thou dost deserve, and I / Believe it *better than reportingly*'
(III.i.115–16; my italics): in other words, pure hearsay has convinced

her that Benedick's love is credible and genuine on grounds other than hearsay. The most singular individuals become unwitting copycats in love, adopting prefabricated postures and fictitious frames of mind that make them indistinguishable from each other in the throes of infatuation. Not the least pleasure *Much Ado* affords us is the pleasure of recognizing the collective nature of the delusion to which the comedy of love consigns us. To realize that what seems consciously intended is in fact unconsciously acquired is to be absolved of responsibility for a state which is neither innate nor immutable. The laughter that greets the eavesdropping scenes is the laughter of liberation from the illusion that snares Beatrice and Benedick and robs them of themselves.

Just how contagious that illusion is becomes apparent even before these scenes. After venting his amazement that Claudio has become 'the argument of his own scorn by falling in love' (II.iii.11–12), Benedick falls to musing about himself, as if the discourse of romantic desire, whose clichés he has been deriding, has infected him with the same propensity, which he immediately strives to curb:

> May I be so converted, and see with these eyes? I cannot tell. I think not. I will not be sworn but love may transform me to an oyster, but I'll take my oath on it, till he have made an oyster of me he shall never make me such a fool. One woman is fair, yet I am well. Another is wise, yet I am well. Another virtuous, yet I am well. But till all graces be in one woman, one woman shall not come in my grace.
>
> (II.iii.21–9)

The question with which this quotation opens betrays the futility of Benedick's resistance, as compliance with the ways of his world seduces him. It anticipates Claudio's question before the altar, 'Are our eyes our own?' (IV.i.72), alerting us to the alienation of perception that being 'converted' involves. It finds its precise counterpart in Margaret's teasing of Beatrice about her love for Benedick, who 'swore he would never marry, and yet now in despite of his heart he eats his meat without grudging. And how you may be converted I know not, but methinks you look with your eyes, as other women do' (III.iv.82–6). The point is driven home at the denouement, when Benedick declares his love for Beatrice publicly and broaches the matter of marriage with her uncle:

> Signor Leonato, truth it is, good signor,
> Your niece regards me with an eye of favour.
> LEONATO. That eye my daughter lent her, 'tis most true.

BENEDICK.   And I do with an eye of love requite her.
LEONATO.   The sight whereof I think you had from me,
From Claudio and the Prince. But what's your will?
BENEDICK.   Your answer, sir, is enigmatical.

(V.iv.21–7)

Like the woman who is about to become his wife, Benedick remains blind to the fact that the eyes of love through which they see each other at the close are not their own.

'our own hands against our hearts'

Beatrice and Benedick wind up in the same fix as Claudio and Hero, despite their furious struggle to avert the fate prescribed for them by their class and the conventions of comedy. But the intensity of that struggle, and their profoundly ironic attitude to their predicament, amplifies the impact of Beatrice and Benedick to the point where they displace the play's avowed romantic protagonists and, as Auden observes, 'the subplot overwhelms and overshadows the main plot', just as it does in *The Merry Wives of Windsor*. *Much Ado* became synonymous with its subplot as early as 1613, when it was recorded under the title 'Benedicte and Betteris' as having been performed at Whitehall before Princess Elizabeth. Charles I jotted 'Benedik and Betrice' next to the title in his copy of the Second Folio of 1632. And in lines published in a 1640 edition of Shakespeare's poems, Leonard Digges confirmed the source of the comedy's capacity to sustain its popularity right through to the closing of the theatres on the eve of the Civil War: 'let but *Beatrice* / And *Benedick* be seene, loe in a trice, / The Cockpit, Galleries, Boxes, all are full.'

Beatrice and Benedick have remained the true heart of the play to this day, and a byword for the mutual attraction that finds expression in mutual antagonism. This feature of their relationship is not without precedent in Shakespearean comedy, but their difference from their precursors is as striking as their debt, as Auden explains:

The conventions of love-making are criticized in the courtship of Berowne and Rosaline in *Love's Labour's Lost*, in which Rosaline is superior, and in the courtship and marriage of Petruchio and Katherina in *The Taming of the Shrew*, in which Petruchio is superior. Benedick and Beatrice mark the first time that both sides are equally matched.

The belligerent repartee that generates the erotic friction between them also generates a paradoxical reciprocity, and thus a prospect of equality, more vivid than anything displayed by the sparring stars of Shakespeare's earlier comedies.

It would be a mistake, however, to idealize, let alone sentimentalize, a relationship anchored in a shared animosity to intolerable constraints on their disposition and their liberty. The woman born under a dancing star (II.i.314) and the man 'not born under a rhyming planet' (V.ii.38–9) are inveigled into romantic intimacy and marital commitment by exigencies for which they have genuine contempt. After he has been 'converted' and has announced his resolution to be 'horribly in love with her' (II.iii.223), Benedick is described by Margaret as loving Beatrice 'in despite of his heart' (III.iv.83). The phrase is echoed by her mistress in the final act, when Benedick tells her, 'I do suffer love indeed, for I love thee against my will', to which Beatrice responds, 'In spite of your heart, I think' (V.ii.60–2). Both of them are still striving to repress their reluctance in the dying moments of the play. When each of them asks the other in the last scene, 'Do not you love me?', each receives the same guarded answer, 'no more than reason' (V.iv.74, 77), and the protestation that the other's belief in their love rests on the sworn testimony of their acquaintances.

As that allusion to the second-hand source of their relationship might suggest, what finally clinches the matter is a product of involuntary fashioning:

LEONATO. Come, cousin, I am sure you love the gentleman.
CLAUDIO. And I'll be sworn upon't that he loves her,
          For here's a paper written in his hand,
          A halting sonnet of his own pure brain,
          Fashioned to Beatrice.
HERO.   And here's another,
          Writ in my cousin's hand, stol'n from her pocket,
          Containing her affection unto Benedick.
BENEDICK. A miracle! Here's our own hands against our hearts.
          Come, I will have thee, but by this light, I take thee
          for pity.
BEATRICE. I would not deny you, but by this good day, I yield
          upon great persuasion, and partly to save your life, for
          I was told you were in a consumption.
BENEDICK. (*kissing her*) Peace, I will stop your mouth.
                                              (V.iv.84–97)

The phrase 'our own hands against our hearts' says it all: Beatrice and Benedick's love is authenticated by the documentary evidence of writing in their own hands that contradicts their speech; the dead letter of a stock discourse, detached from its author, acquires authority in its own right and silences the living voice of reluctance and doubt. It comes as no surprise to learn that the speech prefix and the stage direction that precede the last line quoted are another instance of gratuitous emendation by Shakespeare's editors, who for centuries have agreed that the line must belong to Benedick and be accompanied by a kiss, despite the fact that both the Quarto and the Folio editions of the play assign the line to Leonato and make no mention of a kiss. Beatrice and Benedick's relationship is being stage-managed by others in spite of themselves ('I yield upon great persuasion') right to the end. The original attribution of the line to Leonato could hardly be more appropriate, given the comedy's consistent concern with estrangement and dispossession. The restoration of that attribution and the loss of Benedick's kiss make the line more disturbing, but not as disturbing as the compulsion to twist the original text to fit the sentimental assumptions the comedy is bent on contesting.

To assume, like most critics and productions, that Beatrice and Benedick are 'really in love' with each other all along, and that the eavesdropping plot forces their true feelings to the surface, is to evade the evidence of the text and the disquieting questions it poses. That their *liaison amoureuse* has a history that predates the events of the play is clear from Beatrice's rueful recollection of the time Benedick 'lent' her his heart 'awhile' and she repaid the loan with interest, 'a double heart for his single one' (II.i.260–1). That they are sexually attracted to each other is likewise beyond doubt, as remarks made by both of them before the orchard scenes explicitly attest, quite apart from the inferences that can be drawn from their bickering. Invited to share Claudio's admiration of Hero, Benedick declares that Beatrice 'exceeds her as much in beauty as the first of May doth the last of December' (I.i.181–2). And in the heat of needling Benedick with her scorn for 'the Prince's jester' (II.i.127) during the masked dance, Beatrice lets slip a tell-tale double entendre: 'I am sure he is in the fleet. I would he had boarded me' (II.i.132–3). But the fact that the couple have been so intimate 'once before' (II.i.262) doesn't make their subsequent involvement any less volatile or questionable, especially when one recalls that their first relationship foundered, if Beatrice is to be believed, on mendacity, on Benedick's playing 'with false dice' (II.i.262). On the contrary, the duplicitous way in which their final attachment is engineered casts doubt on the integrity of their original attachment to each other, suggesting that what's at stake is not so much true love discovered as the illusion of love rekindled. Even if the initial spark of desire between them was spontaneous, the form it was constrained to take from the moment it flared into love divorced them from that desire, rendering it alien to them. The darkest implication of the eavesdropping scenes is that desire itself, however immediate and instinctive it might seem, is activated by cultural imperatives beyond the individual's command.

Beatrice and Benedick have every reason to shrink in horror from the toils of wooing and wedding. Their recalcitrance is the play's most eloquent witness to the oppressive impact of a sexual code that converts people into semblances of themselves and puts words they don't mean into their mouths. Yet that recalcitrance can't claim to be any more authentic than their ultimate capitulation, because it's plainly a studied pose and perceived as such, as Beatrice and Benedick are well aware. When Benedick asks Claudio whether he wants his 'simple true judgement' of Hero or would rather he speak 'after my custom, as being a professed tyrant to their sex' (I.i.159–61), he makes it clear that the role of tyrannical misogynist is one that he can assume at will, and thus can't be identified with completely. The same goes, *mutatis mutandis*, for Beatrice, who takes obvious delight in playing the part of the termagant who must 'sit in a corner and cry "Heigh-ho for a husband" ', because she 'mocks all her wooers out of suit' (II.i.299–300, 327). 'Thou and I are too wise to woo peaceably' (V.ii.65), observes Benedick towards the end of the play, and it's this sardonic consciousness of their conduct, the wisdom of self-awareness, that releases them from the roles they must perform and sets them apart from the other persons of the play. Like most of the characters in this comedy, Beatrice and Benedick end up, in Dogberry's immortal phrase, 'condemned into everlasting redemption' (IV.ii.54–5) as a consequence of being 'opinioned' (IV.ii.65) – Dogberry's inspired confusion of 'pinioned' with 'opinion', which captures perfectly the state of imprisonment by misprision imposed on Beatrice and Benedick by Don Pedro: 'The sport will be when they hold one an opinion of another's dotage, and no such matter'(II.iii.205–6). But, unlike the other characters, Beatrice and Benedick transmute the trance of 'strange misprision' in which *Much Ado* maroons them by their recognition of their quandary and the blithe view they take of it.

'As strange as the thing I know not'

The exchange that takes us to the core of the comedy occurs as
Benedick and Beatrice struggle to confess their love for each other:

> BENEDICK.   I do love nothing in the world so well as you. Is not
> that strange?
> BEATRICE.   As strange as the thing I know not. It were as possible
> for me to say I loved nothing so well as you, but
> believe me not, and yet I lie not. I confess nothing
> nor I deny nothing.
>
> (IV.i.269–74)

The exchange is mined with equivocations, qualifications and contradictions that arm both parties with escape clauses. Its most intriguing
feature, though, is the convergence of the words 'nothing', 'strange'
and 'know' at this critical juncture. Benedick's assertion that he loves
nothing in the world so well as Beatrice can also be taken as a veiled
rebuff, which equates loving Beatrice with loving nothing in the
world – an ambiguous compliment, which Beatrice returns almost
verbatim with further ambiguities attached. Benedick's pensive question, 'Is not that strange?', receives the enigmatic response 'As strange
as the thing I know not', which likens the strangeness of Benedick's
love for Beatrice, which he has equated with the love of nothing, to the
strangeness of something she has no knowledge of. The use of the singular 'thing', coupled with the definite rather than the indefinite article, lends the unknown a queer specificity, moreover, as if Beatrice
knows what the thing she doesn't know is, even though she can't name
it. In this arresting exchange we find Shakespeare grappling through his
characters with the pervasive condition of 'strange misprision' that
Much Ado About Nothing dramatizes. It's a condition in which the
whole world seems strange to its inhabitants because it defies cognition,
because nothing and no one are knowable beyond the forms in which
they are currently 'noted'. Indeed, beyond those forms, the comedy
implies, for as long as they persist, there is literally nothing to be
known.

In retrospect, it's evident that *Much Ado* has been working its
way through to this realization from the beginning, most notably
in emphatic collocations of the words by which its author was patently
transfixed as he wrote it. Take the following outbreak of obsessive
punning on the diverse meanings of 'note', which is immediately

coupled with 'nothing' (the phonetic pun on which the play's title turns) and 'strange':

DON PEDRO.	Nay pray thee, come;
	Or if thou wilt hold longer argument,
	Do it in notes.
BALTHASAR.	Note this before my notes:
	There's not a note of mine that's worth the noting.
DON PEDRO.	Why, these are very crotchets that he speaks –
	Note notes, forsooth, and nothing!
	The accompaniment begins
BENEDICK.	Now, divine air! Now is his soul ravished. Is it not strange that sheep's guts should hale souls out of men's bodies?

(II.iii.51–9)

'Note' and 'noting', particularly when used as nouns, connote knowledge and knowing as well as perceiving and observing, and the word 'know' itself is put on the same rack in the following act. Don John's gnomic advice to his brother and Claudio – 'If you dare not trust that you see, confess not that you know' – has already been quoted. It comes, however, as the culmination of recurrent harping on the word in question in the preceding dialogue. Claudio's response to Don Pedro's conclusion that Benedick is in love is 'Nay, but I know who loves him', to which Don Pedro replies, 'That would I know, too. I warrant, one that knows him not' (III.ii.58–60). Moments later, Don John's question to Claudio, 'Means your lordship to be married tomorrow?' is answered by Don Pedro: 'You know he does.' Don John pounces immediately on the Prince's innocent use of the verb at stake and sends it spinning: 'I know not that when he knows what I know' (III.ii.79–82). And once Claudio does know what Don John knows to Hero's detriment, which is nothing at all, he exclaims, 'O mischief strangely thwarting!' (III.ii.122).

It's Shakespeare's repeated resort to the word 'strange' that offers the best clue to the distinctive mood of *Much Ado*. The first instance occurs in Antonio's misreporting of Don Pedro's intentions towards Hero: 'But brother, I can tell you strange news that you yet dreamt not of' (I.ii.3–4). The frequency increases in the second act, prior to the furious punning on noting and Benedick's wonder at the strange power of sheep's guts. Claudio's conversion from soldier into suitor, Benedick notes, has converted his language into 'a very fantastical banquet, just

so many strange dishes' (II.iii.20–1); while Don Pedro remarks senten-
tiously of Balthasar's false modesty: 'It is the witness still of excellency /
To put a strange face on his own perfection' (II.iii.45–6). Mulling over
Claudio's claim in Act III that Benedick is in love, the Prince observes
that 'There is no appearance of fancy in him, unless it be a fancy that he
hath to strange disguises' (III.ii.29–30). But it's in the fourth act that
the word comes into its own and cashes in the connotations it has
accrued over the previous three. Its full resonance is achieved, as we've
seen, in Beatrice and Benedict's confessional *tête-à-tête*. Its impact there
is amplified, however, by the Friar's description of his plan to 'Change
slander to remorse' as 'this strange course' (IV.i.213–14), which he jus-
tifies with his version of the old saying that desperate diseases require
desperate remedies: 'For to strange sores strangely they strain the cure.
/ Come, lady, die to live' (IV.i.255–6).

When 'The former Hero, Hero that is dead!' (V.iv.65) materializes
in Act V, the onlookers are understandably struck dumb with 'amazement' at the apparition, but the Friar promises to explain all, adding:
'Meantime, let wonder seem familiar' (V.iv.67, 70). Amazement, however, is the appropriate response not only to Hero's startling resurrection, but also to a world so intrinsically strange that the wonder it
provokes can at best merely '*seem* familiar': it could never *be* a familiar
world, because there's nothing natural or normal about it. What passes
for normality in *Much Ado About Nothing*, as Benedict and Beatrice
shrewdly surmise, is a very bizarre affair indeed, though no more
bizarre than the Elizabethan reality the play has transmuted into comedy. *Much Ado* is acutely aware of the absurdity of living, loving, thinking and feeling in these peculiar ways, under these peculiar
circumstances, in a society that happens to be like this at this time, but
could clearly be quite different at another.

The identities and destinies of the persons of the play are fashioned
by forces that Shakespeare shows to be neither natural nor necessary
but artificial and arbitrary. That's why the characters seem like strangers
in a world that persistently deceives them, a world to which they can
never fully belong. That's why they possess the spectral quality of the
dispossessed and their reality appears so unreal, a mirage created by
misconceptions. And that's why the title of this comedy ultimately
means just what it says. Beyond the pun on 'noting' and the sly puden-
dal gag ('nothing' being slang for the vagina), the phrase *Much Ado
About Nothing* distils the play's recognition that the mode of existence
it dramatizes is bogus or, more precisely, *inane* in both the usual

sense of 'fatuous' or 'senseless' and the more recondite sense of 'vacuous' or 'empty'.

Whether that void will be filled one day by a different kind of world in which human beings are at home, the play cannot say. What it *can* do is show that the way things are in *Much Ado* is not the way they have to be and not the way they would be, if they were in harmony with human needs and not at odds with them. The only attitude to be adopted in such a predicament, the play makes plain, is the ironic attitude of genial nonchalance struck by its title and so perfectly embodied in Beatrice and Benedick. Of Benedick, 'the Prince's jester' (II.i.127), Don Pedro says: 'from the crown of his head to the sole of his foot he is all mirth' (III.ii.8–9). Beatrice, too, meets her fate in a world that makes much ado about nothing by speaking 'all mirth and no matter' (II.i.309), as befits one 'born in a merry hour' (II.i.311–12). As Hazlitt observes, 'she not only turns [Benedick] but all other things into jest, and is proof against everything serious'. We have her own father's testimony, moreover, that 'She is never sad but when she sleeps, and not ever sad then; for I have heard my daughter say she hath often dreamt of unhappiness and waked herself with laughing' (II.i.322–5). A dream of unhappiness from which we awaken laughing: it would be hard to better that as a summary of *Much Ado* itself.

9

'Ducdame': *As You Like It*

Empowering the Audience

The title of *As You Like It* tips us the wink from the start about the tone the play intends to take and the response it expects to elicit from its audience. Like the titles of *A Midsummer Night's Dream*, *Much Ado About Nothing* and *Twelfth Night, or What You Will*, whose title closely echoes it, the throwaway phrase that encapsulates this comedy radiates insouciance. What follows, it implies, is a light-hearted confection, whose chief aim is to please the audience by giving them the sort of play the playwright knows they like. The direct address to the audience in the title, including them and anticipating their response, is unique to *As You Like It* and *Twelfth Night, or What You Will*, Shakespeare's last great romantic comedies, and is a testament to the extraordinary intimacy that had developed between the dramatist and his public, to whose tastes he could confidently appeal. Such intimacy inevitably entailed a licence to tease, which Shakespeare fully exploited in his titles for comedies of this kind. In the case of *As You Like It*, the title begs to be construed as deliberately ambiguous. If the stress falls on '*You*', it becomes the author's wry comment on the conventional yarn he's been constrained to spin, and an invitation to knowing spectators to approach the play in the same ironic spirit. But the whole phrase can also be read as a warrant to make of the play whatever we wish and an expression of the dramatist's indifference to our judgement.

The more one mulls over the title, the more slippery and elusive its connotations become. Whichever way one reads it, though, what's undeniable is the power it accords the playgoer and the attention it draws to the way the play is received, to the impact it has on its audience rather than to its subject matter. Indeed, insofar as the title does serve as an index of the theme, it suggests that how the audience responds to the play may be what *As You Like It* is really about. Unlike *The Two*

198

Gentlemen of Verona, *The Taming of the Shrew* or *The Merry Wives of Windsor*, *As You Like It* advertises its concern with its status as a work of dramatic art up front. It does so, moreover, by employing a casual, inconsequential phrase, which belies its innocence by equivocation and thus puts us on our mettle as an audience before the actors have set foot upon the stage. The title plainly holds out the promise of theatrical pleasure through the fulfilment of the spectators' expectations. It also intimates, thanks to the saucy double entendre lurking in '*It*', that libidinal delight will be inseparable from the pleasure we derive from the play. At the same time, the playful indeterminacy of the expression, which owes as much to the indefinite '*As*' as it does to the unspecified '*It*', leaves the way in which, and the extent to which, our desires will be satisfied uncertain. In fact, it remains to be seen whether we will like what *As You Like It* has in store for us at all. Whatever response we finally arrive at, the title has primed us to feel empowered by the authority it confers on the audience, but to be prepared for its import to change as our understanding of the play evolves.

Beyond Belief

The opening scene ensconces us in the familiar, fairy-tale realm of wish-fulfilment adumbrated by the title, establishing the twin stock predicaments from which the initial conflicts and the closing resolutions of the comedy will spring: the brutal repression of the noble young Orlando by his evil elder brother Oliver, and the banishment of the good Duke Senior to the forest of Arden, following the usurpation of his dukedom by his equally evil younger brother, Frederick. Duke Senior's beloved daughter Rosalind, we also learn, has been restrained from joining her father in exile only by the love of her cousin, Duke Frederick's daughter Celia, who has prevailed on her to remain at court. The key components and the entire trajectory of a plot as old as storytelling itself are already there in embryo. So are the staple features of characterization and topography required by such scenarios: the clear-cut extremes of oppressed innocence and irrational malevolence; the stark contrast between deadly fraternal enmity and idyllic female amity; and the parallel polarization of the treacherous court that must be fled and the sylvan sanctuary sought and found in the uncorrupted country.

Orlando begins the play in the midst of a speech bemoaning the fact that Oliver has inexplicably denied him the schooling his other brother Jaques enjoys, preferring to treat him like a common farm-labourer: 'He lets me feed with his hinds, bars me the place of a brother, and as much as in him lies, mines my gentility with my education' (I.i.17–19). Within moments of Oliver's entrance, Orlando's urge 'to mutiny against this servitude' (I.i.21–2) has him literally at his brother's throat, demanding his just share of their dead father's will. The assault immediately provokes Oliver to conspire with the Duke's wrestler, Charles, to have Orlando crippled or killed during their bout before the Duke the next day. Yet what Orlando has done to deserve his sibling's murderous loathing Oliver is at a loss to explain:

> I hope I shall see an end of him, for my soul – yet I know not why – hates nothing more than he. Yet he's gentle; never schooled, and yet learned; full of noble device; of all sorts enchantingly beloved; and, indeed, so much in the heart of the world, and especially of my own people, who best know him, that I am altogether misprized.
>
> (I.i.154–60)

In Charles's account of the relationship between Rosalind and Celia we encounter the complete antithesis of this lethal male antagonism: 'being ever from their cradles bred together', Celia would have gone into exile with Rosalind rather than be parted from her cousin, 'or have died to stay behind her', for 'never two ladies loved as they do' (I.i.103–7). And in the wrestler's report of how Duke Senior is faring in the greenwood that now shelters him, we get our first rose-tinted glimpse of the pastoral realm to which Orlando, Celia and Rosalind will shortly be forced to resort as well:

> They say he is already in the forest of Arden, and a many merry men with him; and there they live like the old Robin Hood of England. They say many young gentlemen flock to him every day, and fleet the time carelessly, as they did in the golden world.
>
> (I.i.109–13)

Shakespeare's likening of life in Arden not only to the carefree, communal life of the legendary outlaw and heroic foe of tyranny, but also to the ancient classical myth of the Golden Age, when spring was perpetual, food abundant, toil unnecessary and peace universal, places it in direct opposition to life in Duke Frederick's regime, where injustice, violence, envy and slander hold sway.

Lest *As You Like It*'s cheerful compliance with the fairy-tale format escape us, the characters call attention to it in the following scene.

When Le Beau begins to recount the wrestling bout Rosalind and Celia have just missed by saying, 'There comes an old man and his three sons –', Celia chips in with the quip 'I could match this beginning with an old tale' (I.ii.110–11), which glances at the tale of the three sons of Sir Rowland de Boys with which *As You Like It* has begun. That Rosalind falls instantly in love with the youngest of those sons, as he prepares to grapple with 'The bonny prizer of the humorous Duke' (II.iii.8), and that Orlando is simultaneously smitten with her, chimes perfectly with the unlikely laws of this narrative universe. The play underscores the perfection of the match by stressing the symmetry of their situations and their dispositions. Duke Frederick's unexplained hostility to Rosalind's father, the brother whom he has ousted, is replicated in his unexplained hostility to Orlando's late father and consequently Orlando himself:

> I would thou hadst been son to some man else.
> The world esteemed thy father honourable,
> But I did find him still mine enemy.
> (I.ii.213–15)

Conversely, Duke Senior held Sir Rowland in the highest regard, as Rosalind is quick to attest: 'My father loved Sir Rowland as his soul, / And all the world was of my father's mind' (I.ii.224–5). And Rosalind, Le Beau reveals, has become the object of Duke Frederick's animosity with as little justification as Orlando has become the object of Oliver's:

> of late this Duke
> Hath ta'en displeasure 'gainst his gentle niece,
> Grounded upon no other argument
> But that the people praise her for her virtues
> And pity her for her good father's sake.
> (I.ii.267–71)

The gratuitous aggression Rosalind and Orlando attract from 'tyrant Duke' and 'tyrant brother' (I.ii.278) combines with the unqualified affection the people feel for both of them to confirm their moral affinity and seal their romantic fate.

Le Beau's prediction that Duke Frederick's 'malice 'gainst the lady / Will suddenly break forth' (I.ii.272–3) is fulfilled within minutes of his making it. Rosalind is banished from the court by her wicked uncle on pain of death and on a trumped-up charge of treason, for which the

Duke doesn't even pretend to adduce evidence: 'Thou art thy father's daughter', he declares to Rosalind's astonishment, 'there's enough' (I.iii.57). By the end of Act I, she and Celia are headed for the woodlands of Arden, having resolved to seek asylum there in the guise of Ganymede and Aliena, and in the company of 'The clownish fool' (I.iii.129) Touchstone. Three scenes later, Orlando and Adam, the family's faithful old retainer, are on the run and, unbeknownst to Rosalind and Celia, inexorably bound for Arden too, driven by 'the malice / Of a diverted blood and bloody brother' (II.iii.37–8) – now hell-bent on homicide – from the place they can no longer call home: 'this house is but a butchery', Adam warns Orlando, 'Abhor it. Fear it, do not enter it' (II.iii.28–9).

Act II, Scene i has already introduced us to the Arcadian haven that awaits the refugees, and to the exiled Duke and his entourage of loyal lords, who dwell there in rustic contentment. In Act II, Scene iv Rosalind, Celia and Touchstone arrive in Arden, making Rosalind's reunion with her father merely a matter of time, and in Act II, Scene vi Orlando and Adam turn up there too, making Rosalind's reunion with the youngest son of Sir Rowland de Boys a cast-iron certainty as well. For the rest of the play, apart from one fleeting flashback to Duke Frederick's palace, whence Oliver is dispatched to bring his brother back dead or alive, we remain in Arden, while its denizens converse, versify and sing about love and life, killing time with masquerades and battles of wit until the cue to conclude the comedy intervenes.

That cue takes the shape of Oliver's arrival in Arden at the end of Act IV, which triggers the final act's flurry of revelations, metamorphoses and multiple marriages, and thus the long-deferred resolution of the conflicts created in the opening scenes of the play. The means by which the resolution is achieved are as arbitrary and implausible as the problems it purports to solve just the way we like it. Magnanimously rescued by his noble younger brother from the jaws of a 'sucked and hungry lioness' (IV.iii.127), Oliver undergoes an instant transformation from murderous sibling into Aliena's devoted suitor. ''Twas I, but 'tis not I', he assures Rosalind in her guise as Ganymede. 'I do not shame / To tell you what I was, since my conversion / So sweetly tastes, being the thing I am' (IV.iii.136–8). Orlando's disbelief in the speed of his brother's bewitchment by Aliena is dismissed by Oliver with a plea for blind acceptance of their love and a promise to surrender their father's legacy to Orlando:

Neither call the giddiness of it in question, the poverty of her, the small acquaintance, my sudden wooing, nor her sudden consenting;

but say with me, 'I love Aliena'; say with her, that she loves me; consent with both that we may enjoy each other. It shall be to your good, for my father's house and all the revenue that was old Sir Rowland's will I estate upon you, and here live and die a shepherd.

(V.ii.5–12)

The comedy's brazen resort to the incredible to induce a denouement is underlined by Rosalind's alter ego a dozen lines later, when she comments to Orlando:

There was never anything so sudden but the fight of two rams, and Caesar's thrasonical brag of 'I came, saw, and overcame', for your brother and my sister no sooner met but they looked; no sooner looked but they loved; no sooner loved but they sighed; no sooner sighed but they asked one another the reason; no sooner knew the reason but they sought the remedy; and in these degrees have they made a pair of stairs to marriage, which they will climb incontinent, or else be incontinent before marriage. They are in the very wrath of love, and they will together. Clubs cannot part them.

(V.ii.28–39)

The comical acceleration of Celia and Oliver's passage from wooing to wedding flaunts the play's conscription of shameless clichés to ensure an equal distribution of suitable spouses among the romantic protagonists.

All Rosalind has to do to dissolve her own romantic dilemma is drop the male persona she could have ditched much earlier, if verisimilitude had been what Shakespeare had in mind. In a trice the barrier both to marriage with Orlando and reunion with her father is removed, the quandary created by Phoebe's crush on Ganymede is unravelled, and the stage is set for a quadruple wedding as Phoebe settles for her doting swain Silvius, and Touchstone joins 'the rest of the country copulatives' (V.iv.55–6) by tying the knot with the goatherd, Audrey. The last vestige of plausibility vanishes when Hymen, the god of marriage, materializes from nowhere to conduct the nuptial ceremony and shift the whole denouement into another dimension. Not content with this flagrant capitulation to fantasy, however, Shakespeare crowns it with the advent of a further *deus ex machina* in the mortal form of Jaques de Boys, the hitherto unseen second son of Sir Rowland. The glad tidings he brings lift the last remaining shadow from the marital festivities and from the prospect of future happiness: the threat still posed by the villainous

Duke Frederick. While en route to Arden with 'a mighty power' (V.iv.154) and the aim of putting Duke Senior to the sword,

> to the skirts of this wild wood he came
> Where, meeting with an old religious man,
> After some question with him was converted
> Both from his enterprise and from the world,
> His crown bequeathing to his banished brother,
> And all their lands restored to them again
> That were with him exiled.
>
> (V.iv.157–63)

The sole obstacle to a cloudless fairy-tale finale succumbs as promptly to the miraculous powers of the 'wild wood' as his malign precursor, Oliver. To the restoration of identity, which released the possibility of fourfold wedlock and family reunion, is added the restoration of rank and lands, which secures the future of Duke Senior, Rosalind, Celia and their bridegrooms in the dukedom to which they are now free to return.

Rosalynde Revamped

The resistance that reality would otherwise offer collapses under the pressure of the play's need to keep the promise inscribed in its title. Antagonisms, estrangements, betrayals and injustices that would have proved insuperable in the actual world are effortlessly overcome in the fantasy world of Shakespeare's most amenable comedy. Far from masking the timeworn devices deployed to this end, *As You Like It* takes palpable delight in highlighting them and stretching credulity beyond breaking point over and over again. Indeed, after the unheralded, anachronistic theophany of Hymen and Arden's second Damascene conversion, it's hard to suppress the suspicion that the blatant improbability of the formulaic plot is crucial to the play's covert design.

That suspicion is confirmed by a glance at the amendments Shakespeare made to his source in order to heighten rather than mitigate the implausibility of the action. In Thomas Lodge's *Rosalynde or Euphues' Golden Legacy*, the Elizabethan prose romance that furnished Shakespeare with the core characters and basic storyline of *As You Like It*, the hatred of the eldest son, Saladyne, for the youngest son, Rosader, is strongly motivated by the fact that their father has bequeathed to the latter a larger portion of his estate, which Saladyne decides to annex. In *As You Like It* Shakespeare removes this motive by having Oliver inherit the bulk of the estate and having Orlando allotted 'but poor a thousand crowns' (I.i.2), in which Oliver displays little interest. Oliver is thus left baffled by his groundless detestation of his brother and forced back upon the after-thought that Orlando's popularity has put him in the shade. Shakespeare pulls the same trick when required to explain Frederick's abrupt banish-ment of Rosalind. 'The Duke is humorous' (I.ii.256) Le Beau has already warned Orlando, prompting us to ascribe whatever villainy Frederick is about to perpetrate to the caprice of a moody despot. Nor does the despot disappoint us. When Rosalind challenges him in the next scene to justify his charge of treason, he retorts that being Duke Senior's daughter is reason enough. In *Rosalynde*, however, Lodge supplies the usurping ruler, Torismond, with a perfectly credible political reason for getting rid of Rosalynde, the daughter of the man he has deposed: the fear that a peer of the realm may strike an alliance with her through marriage and stake a claim to the kingdom in his wife's name.

Lodge is likewise at pains to render the love that blossoms between the counterparts of Celia and Oliver understandable. In *Rosalynde*, Alinda falls more gradually and circumspectly in love with Saladyne, after he rescues her from a band of brigands who had planned to turn her over to the lecherous Torismond – her own father – to satisfy his lust. Her love for Saladyne is rooted partly in the gratitude she feels and partly in her growing admiration for his virtue and his gallantry. Saladyne in turn takes his time being captivated by Alinda, falling first under the spell of her wisdom before allowing her beauty to snare him. Shakespeare, in sharp contrast, insists on the suddenness and inexplica-bility of Celia's and Oliver's love, which flares up out of nothing and defies rationalization. He also strips Oliver's 'conversion' of the con-vincing explanation Lodge gives for the corresponding event in *Rosalynde* in order to make it more startling. Lodge's Saladyne comes to repent of abusing his brother not after his arrival in the forest, but after pro-longed reflection while languishing in Torismond's prison. He vows to seek Rosader and do penance for his past transgressions, unlike Oliver, who reaches Arden still in the grip of fratricidal wrath and executes his moral *volte-face* after seeing Orlando risk his own life to save him. Shakespeare does provide an occasion for Oliver's change of soul, but the overriding effect of his revisions is to enhance rather than diminish the miraculous immediacy of Oliver's transfiguring epiphany. As for Duke Frederick's no less astounding conversion upon encounter-ing 'an old religious man' in Arden, the incident is entirely Shakespeare's invention. Lodge disposes of Frederick's prototype more realistically and violently by having him defeated and slain in a climactic battle.

The impact of these deliberate deviations from the source of *As You Like It* is complex, pervasive and subtle. By reducing or destroying the psychological credibility of the characters' actions and rendering their behaviour surprising and inscrutable, Shakespeare rules out realistic criteria of believability as irrelevant to understanding *As You Like It*. To engage with this play is to enter a world where the laws of likelihood do not apply, or apply only until they are broken. Here the conduct of characters and the course of events are dictated by the benign laws of improbability, over which the *dramatis personae* have no control. Relieved of rational motivation and autonomy by the strictures of an omnipotent plot, the characters are likewise relieved of the moralism to which Lodge subjects their counterparts in *Rosalynde*. The 'golden legacy' of moral instruction that Lodge's narrator, Euphues, bequeaths with his tale holds no appeal for Shakespeare, who transmutes an edifying pastoral fable into the vehicle for another kind of vision altogether. The fabulous aspects of Lodge's romance are what ignite Shakespeare's imagination, because they license its detachment from empirical reality past and present, and its departures from the mimetic fidelity required to dramatize that reality convincingly. It's these aspects of his source that Shakespeare locks onto and intensifies, because in *As You Like It*, to an extent hitherto matched only by *A Midsummer Night's Dream*, his gaze is levelled at the far horizon of what could be, rather than fixed on the intractable facts of former times or the actual world around him.

Back to the Future

By purging Lodge's already far-fetched romance of its residual realistic psychology and humanly explicable events, Shakespeare frees the basic story to house a play tuned to the frequency of futurity. *As You Like It* becomes as a result a consummate instance of the way in which, to quote Dr Johnson, 'Shakespeare approximates the remote and familiarizes the wonderful; the event which he represents will not happen, *but if it were possible*, its effects would probably be such as he assigned' (my italics). In the course of its transformation from pastoral prose romance into pastoral romantic comedy, the plot of *As You Like It* acquires the power to make wonder seem familiar, by bringing what appears to be impossibly remote in time and space within the imaginative reach of the present; the power to make the *as yet* improbable imaginable, by treating it *as if it were possible* and inviting us to watch it transpire in the theatre before our very eyes. The comedy acquires that power not only from the providential narrative arc built into romance, but also from its fusion of romance with pastoral, which resonates with echoes of the golden age and recalls the ancient dream of a *locus amoenus*, an Edenic elsewhere, sequestered from the tribulations of the court and urban life. In *As You Like It*, however, Shakespeare activates these utopian associations to underpin a *prospective* rather than a retrospective vision of alternative possibilities. The comedy harks back in order to look forward, discerning in past fantasies premonitions of a transfigured world.

The pastoral dimension of *As You Like It* also serves Shakespeare's purpose insofar as it solicits an active interpretive response from the audience. The virtue of pastoral from Theocritus and Virgil down to Spenser and Milton was its capacity to smuggle social critique into its refined pining for lost perfection and bucolic innocence. As Shakespeare's contemporary, George Puttenham, observed in *The Arte of English Poesie*, the aim of pastoral was 'not of purpose to counterfeit or represent the rusticall manner of loves and communication: but under the vaile of homely persons, and in rude speeches to insinuate and glaunce at greater matters, and such as perchaunce had not been safe to have been disclosed in any other sort'. The point is not that *As You Like It* is really a veiled political satire on contemporary Elizabethan mores, although satirical thrusts can certainly be discerned in it, but that Shakespeare's enlistment of pastoral invites us to expect this comedy to mean more than it affects to say, to 'insinuate and glaunce at greater matters', which we are required to decipher. In this respect it compounds the sense of mystery created by the characters' subjection to a genial destiny whose accomplishment is ultimately out of their hands. Even Rosalind, who takes the initiative both in courting and in deploying her masculine persona, and who plays such a pivotal role in orchestrating the denouement, must await the cue to conclude along with the rest of the cast, and bend her will to the subsuming design of the comedy.

Shakespeare's decision to call his version of Lodge's romance *As You Like It* rather than follow his source in naming it after the heroine accords with the quite different focus of the comedy. Like most of his Elizabethan comedies, notably *A Midsummer Night's Dream*, *Much Ado About Nothing* and *Twelfth Night*, *As You Like It* takes for its title a phrase that focuses attention on the experience of the play as a whole and encapsulates the attitude it invites us to adopt to that experience. Unlike history plays such as *Richard III* or *Henry V*, tragedies such as *Titus Andronicus* or *Romeo and Juliet*, and comedies such as *The Two Gentlemen of Verona* or *The Merchant of Venice*, all of which spotlight an individual, or a pair of individuals, as the fulcrum of the play, *As You Like*

It reflects in its title a more diffuse concern with matters of common application. Its fundamental preoccupation is not so much with the lives of individuals at odds with their circumstances as with the overarching, collective pattern of development to which individuals' lives are subject. Nothing could be more alien to characters such as Rosalind or Orlando than the self-scrutinizing soliloquies in which Shakespeare's great tragic protagonists grapple with acute moral quandaries. The play is a perfect illustration of Charlie Chaplin's dictum, 'Life is a tragedy when seen in close-up, but a comedy in long-shot.' Rosalind's predominance among the cast and intimacy with the audience notwithstanding, the viewpoint of *As You Like It* remains emphatically external and detached.

In Shakespeare's hands, Lodge's moralistic fiction becomes a dramatic parable that prefigures the emergence of a new dispensation. Shakespeare exploits romance's phenomenal powers of abstraction and compression to trace within the compass of a comedy the transition from despotism to a time of true community, 'When earthly things made even / Atone together' (V.iv.107–8). The inconceivable means and tracts of time needed to accomplish this transition are condensed into the symbolic action of *As You Like It*. There is, after all, 'no reason', as Johnson reluctantly conceded, 'why an hour should not be a century in that calenture of the brains that can make the stage a field', since 'Time is, of all modes of existence, most obsequious to the imagination; a lapse of years is as easily conceived as a passage of hours.' The action proper of the play, however, is not continuous but split into two telescoped sequences, divided from each other by the long interlude of aimless talk and amorous tomfoolery to which most of *As You Like It* is devoted. Between the brisk unfolding of the events that banish the romantic leads to Arden and the swift succession of disclosures and conversions that conclude the play, the compressed, accelerated plot of *As You Like It* is put on hold, while the characters divert themselves with less oppressive problems, as if there were world enough and time for everything.

That protracted parenthesis is the catalyst that changes the significance of the plot, and the impact of the play, completely. By stranding the cast of the comedy in Arden, and leaving them in a state of suspended animation until the reformation of Oliver and Duke Frederick releases them, Shakespeare creates the time and space to undermine assumptions that would otherwise pass unchallenged, and thereby transforms the import of the ending and our understanding of *As You Like It*. During the privileged period of exile in Arden, beyond the jurisdiction of the state and normal social constraints, the comedy finds room to question the necessity of roles, relationships and beliefs that seem natural, and to reveal the potential for different, more desirable ways of living, loving and thinking.

As a consequence, when we return to the plot after this extravagant digression, its resolution is charged with a powerful utopian resonance, which it would not have possessed had the comedy not taken such a lengthy detour through the licensed domain of Arden. For the persons of the play, the denouement may signify a reinstatement of the *status quo ante*, the just restitution of lands and rights, and the reaffirmation of family bonds and sexual norms through nuptial celebrations; but for the audience watching those celebrations in the wake of what Arden has revealed, it means much more than that.

The Making of a Gentleman

Just how much more it means becomes apparent if we go back to the opening scenes of the play, which pave the way for the revelations that await us in Arden. In the first speech Orlando's complaint about Oliver's mistreatment of him raises the question of conditioning, of the parts played in a person's development by class, the patriarchal family and native disposition. Orlando's outrage at being denied the upbringing due to a man of his rank and forced to endure a servile 'keeping' which 'differs not from the stalling of an ox' (I.i.8–9) dramatizes the vital importance of nurture in the shaping of social identity. While his other brother, Jaques, profits 'goldenly' from being kept 'at school' (I.i.5–6), Oliver treats Orlando like a serf and thus, as Orlando laments, 'mines my gentility with my education' (I.i.19). The assumption on which Orlando's outrage rests is that his acquisition of the status of gentleman, to which his paternity entitles him, depends on his receiving the appropriate schooling, without which his claim to 'gentility', and hence superiority to the 'hinds' (I.i.17) he now feeds with, collapses. It's an assumption plainly at odds with the notion that 'gentility' is an inviolable quality bred in the bone. That notion surfaces too, however, in Orlando's allusion to 'the something that nature gave me' (I.i.16) which Oliver deprives him of, and again towards the end of the speech, when Orlando assures Adam that 'the spirit of my father, which I think is within me, begins to mutiny against this servitude' (I.i.20–2).

The same conflict between the claims of nature and culture breaks out again, when Orlando reproaches Oliver in person for letting the 'tradition' of primogeniture, a convention framed by 'The courtesy of nations', ride roughshod over 'the gentle condition of blood' they share as brothers (I.i.42–5). 'My father charged you in his will to give me good education', Orlando reminds the brother whose power over him derives from mere accidents of birth and custom: 'You have trained me like a peasant, obscuring and hiding from me all gentleman-like qualities' (I.i.64–6). If Oliver isn't prepared to let him acquire those qualities, he should at least give him 'the poor allottery' their father left him. 'With that I will go buy my fortunes' (I.i.68–70), declares Orlando, complicating the scene's latent debate about the determinants of identity by pointing out that rank and position can be purchased, if they can't be secured by birth or education. The issue is further complicated by Oliver in the speech he delivers *solus* to close the opening scene. Oliver has submitted Orlando to systematic degradation: 'Yet he's gentle', a perplexed Oliver reflects, 'never schooled, and yet learned; full of noble device' (I.i.156–7). As even his worst enemy is forced to attest, Orlando's 'gentility' – the qualities of cultivation and refinement that distinguish him as admirable – appears to be innate.

The question of what qualifies a man to be a gentleman was undoubtedly close to the heart of the glover's son from the sticks, whose native talent had turned him into the nation's leading dramatist. In 1596 – just a couple of years before penning *As You Like It* – Shakespeare had applied successfully for the coat of arms his father had earlier failed to secure. Its half-defensive, half-defiant motto, '*Non sanz droict*' ('Not without right'), speaks volumes about how much the right to be called a gentleman meant to the self-made dramatist. Nor does it leave much doubt about his view of the idea that true gentlemen are born, not made, and that gentility can't be purchased. In the first scene of *As You Like It*, however, the question is posed but left open. Oliver may tilt the balance at the end in favour of native nobility and the notion that breeding will out, but he himself, like the wicked Duke Frederick, is the living proof that a. noble pedigree is no guarantee of probity or distinction. Orlando repeatedly ascribes his refusal of servitude to his inheritance of his father's spirit, but rails at Oliver for depriving him of the 'good education' that would give him the very 'gentleman-like qualities' his brother believes him to possess already. Whatever one makes of these vexed issues, it's clear that Shakespeare has gone out of his way to start the play by driving a wedge between birth and worth, and between nature and nurture.

Mocking Fortune from her Wheel

Nor is Shakespeare disposed to let these matters drop. On the contrary, no sooner has Oliver left the stage than Rosalind and Celia enter to resume the debate in their first exchange and make its importance explicit. This ostensibly idle bout of badinage conceals the key to the contention round which the rest of the comedy will revolve: that the way things happen to be now is not inexorably determined by nature or by culture, but contingent, fluid, and mutable. To Celia's plea that she 'be merry', notwithstanding her father's banishment, Rosalind replies, 'From henceforth I will, coz, and devise sports. Let me see, what think you of falling in love?' (I.ii.21–4). Her suggestion foreshadows what's about to become their chief preoccupation in the play: falling in love, yet taking love lightly and treating it as a game. Celia's riposte reminds Rosalind of the risks such games involve and prompts her to think again:

ROSALIND. What shall be our sport, then?

CELIA. Let us sit and mock the good housewife Fortune from her wheel, that her gifts may henceforth be bestowed equally.

ROSALIND. I would we could do so, for her benefits are mightily misplaced; and the bountiful blind woman doth most mistake in her gifts to women.

CELIA. 'Tis true; for those that she makes fair she scarce makes honest, and those that she makes honest she makes very ill-favouredly.

ROSALIND. Nay, now thou goest from Fortune's office to Nature's. Fortune reigns in gifts of the world, not in the lineaments of nature.

Enter Touchstone the clown

CELIA. No. When Nature hath made a fair creature, may she not by Fortune fall into the fire? Though Nature hath given us wit to flout at Fortune, hath not Fortune sent in this fool to cut off the argument?

ROSALIND. Indeed, there is Fortune too hard for Nature, when Fortune makes Nature's natural the cutter-off of Nature's wit.

CELIA. Peradventure this is not Fortune's work, neither, but Nature's, who perceiveth our natural wits too dull to reason of such goddesses, and hath sent this natural for our whetstone; for always the dullness of the fool is the whetstone of the wits. How now, wit: whither wander you?

(I.ii.29–54)

To 'sit and mock the good housewife Fortune from her wheel, that her gifts may henceforth be bestowed equally' is a perfect summary of what *As You Like It* sets out to do. The play deploys every means at its disposal to loosen the grip of attitudes that prevent the equal distribution of the 'gifts of the world' to humankind at large and womankind in particular. Its first step towards achieving that goal is to fasten on the fundamental concepts of Fortune and Nature and undermine both by confounding the distinction between them. The notion that the unjust constitution of the human world, whose 'benefits' are 'mightily misplaced', is predestined gets short shrift as the goddess Fortune dwindles into a 'good housewife' ripe for debunking. Her power is further circumscribed by Rosalind's insistence on restricting it to the worldly circumstances in which people find themselves, and distinguishing it from the primary power of Nature to dictate the physical substance and form of people and things. But no sooner has this distinction between the province of Fortune and the province of Nature been drawn than it dissolves in the heat of the disputants' compulsive quibbling.

Inspired by the timely entrance of Touchstone, the dialogue takes another turn, as both parties conspire to argue that Fortune can change what Nature has made, but that what they are ascribing to Fortune should perhaps be attributed to Nature. The border between the two realms is blurred, making it impossible to tell where nature ends and nurture begins. The calculated confusion of the terms redefines them as inextricably implicated in each other, as they vie for control of human life. It's only too easy to slide like Celia 'from Fortune's office to Nature's' and back again, because the line that divides them is constantly shifting, and what might seem from one angle a natural creation might seem from another to be the work of culture, and vice versa. Things that appear stubbornly natural, moreover, can be transmuted by cultural intervention, while the transient contrivances of society are subject to subversion by the facts of nature. The upshot of this dizzying dialectic is that the forces forging the human condition emerge as flexible instead of fixed, which means that the prevailing ways of the world, and the beliefs that keep them in place, are equally malleable.

'Nature's natural'

The scintillating disputation with which Rosalind and Celia enter the comedy serves as a mock-philosophical preface to the main business of the play in Arden, where assumptions that hold in the cultivated sphere of the court lock horns with the laws that preside in the kingdom of nature. It's no coincidence that Touchstone, the licensed court fool, makes his debut in the midst of this dialogue, and that Rosalind's line,

'Fortune reigns in gifts of the world, not in the lineaments of nature', provides his cue, for the mercurial figure of the fool inhabits that fluid zone where the two realms collide and converge. At once 'Nature's natural' and the quintessence of theatrical artifice, the fool personifies the point at which the faultlines between Nature and Fortune, and thus the space for movement and change, appear. As such, he's the automatic choice to accompany Celia and Rosalind to Arden, where his privileged status and singular powers are enhanced: 'Ay, now am I in Arden; the more fool I' (II.iv.14).

The fool's name contains the clues to his principal functions in the play. The fact that 'stone' is Elizabethan slang for 'testicle', makes Touchstone a walking bawdy gag, a lewd pun that puts in a nutshell his job of boiling everything down to biology. But his brief is not confined to puncturing pretension and humbling the exalted by recalling the primal imperatives that make every member of the human species tick, regardless of rank or rearing. A touchstone is also a substance used to test the quality of gold and silver alloys rubbed upon it, and the fool in *As You Like It* serves figuratively as a touchstone for the credibility and value of the diverse viewpoints the play presents us with. His task, as the *spiritus rector* of the comedy, is to spearhead its endeavour to free the audience from the mind-forged manacles that chain them to the status quo and stop them from seeing and having things otherwise.

That much is already implicit in his first round of repartee with Celia and Rosalind. Touchstone's opening stab at a jest is routinely excoriated as a prime example of Shakespeare's outmoded wit at its worst. But on closer inspection it reveals concerns as crucial to the comedy as the debate about Nature and Fortune, and it shows Touchstone to be as adept as Rosalind and Celia at logic-chopping sophistry that plays havoc with received ideas. The fool tells Rosalind that he learned the inane oath he has just used 'Of a certain knight that swore "by his honour" they were good pancakes, and swore "by his honour" the mustard was naught'; but he offers to prove that 'the pancakes were naught and the mustard was good, and yet was not the knight forsworn' (I.ii.60–4). He offers to demonstrate, in other words, like the comedy that contains him, that what appears to be impossible is perfectly possible after all.

He begins the demonstration by asking Celia and Rosalind to do in fancy what Rosalind will shortly be doing in fact – pretend to be a man:

TOUCHSTONE. Stand you both forth now. Stroke your chins, and swear by your beards that I am a knave.

CELIA.   By our beards – if we had them – thou art.
TOUCHSTONE.   By my knavery – if I had it – then I were; but if
                          you swear by that that is not, you are not for-
                          sworn. No more was this knight, swearing by his
                          honour, for he never had any; or if he had, he had
                          sworn it away before ever he saw those pancakes
                          or that mustard.

                                                                   (I.ii.68–76)

The first scene's agitation about gentility resurfaces in a joke, whose
punch-line is designed to puncture aristocratic self-aggrandizement by
trivializing the knight's oath and then dismissing his claim to honour
completely. The thrust of the joke is in line with the play's declared aim
of mocking Fortune from her wheel, 'that her gifts may henceforth be
bestowed equally'. It achieves its objective by transposing the matter
into the realm of supposition ruled by 'if' and exposing the basic premise of the knight's superiority as false. Truth-claims are only as secure as
the assumptions on which they rest; demolish those assumptions and
the truth-claims collapse with them, clearing the way for propositions that
might otherwise seem preposterous – such as women behaving, and
being treated, as if they were men.

   Touchstone's first comic turn serves as his calling card, anticipating
the transvestite involutions of identity that await us in Arden and his
own fifth-act aria on the virtues of 'if'. Above all, it displays the strategies that he and the play as a whole will employ to inculcate in us a radical scepticism about whatever seems self-evident, and a readiness to
contemplate counterfactual realities, to give credence to what is not, or
is not yet, the case. To put it another way, we are advised by
Touchstone's impromptu overture not to mistake such absurd ratioci-
nation for twaddle, but to take the hint dropped straight after it and pre-
pare to be taught the topsy-turvy wisdom of folly. Warned by Celia that
he'll be 'whipped for taxation one of these days' if he doesn't watch his
lip, Touchstone laments, 'The more pity that fools may not speak wisely
what wise men do foolishly'; and Celia is quick to concur: 'By my troth,
thou sayst true; for since the little wit that fools have was silenced, the
little foolery that wise men have makes a great show' (I.ii.80–6).

Semblances: Ganymede and Aliena

Celia's and Rosalind's budding impersonation of men for the sake of
Touchstone's argument blossoms by the end of the first act into the

decision to transform their identities by masking their rank and Rosalind's gender for their own protection in Arden:

CELIA.   I'll put myself in poor and mean attire,
And with a kind of umber smirch my face.
The like do you, so shall we pass along
And never stir assailants.
ROSALIND.   Were it not better,
Because that I am more than common tall,
That I did suit me all points like a man,
A gallant curtal-axe upon my thigh,
A boar-spear in my hand, and in my heart,
Lie there what hidden woman's fear there will.
We'll have a swashing and a martial outside,
As many other mannish cowards have,
That do outface it with their semblances
(I.iii.110–21)

Swapping a gown for 'poor and mean attire' and daubing on a sunburnt complexion are all it takes to put a Duke's daughter on a par with the hinds Orlando has been forced to feed with. Switching gender, too, is all about manipulating 'semblances': to be suited 'all points like a man' and equipped with masculine accoutrements is to magically acquire the status and prerogatives of the male. Having already driven a wedge between birth and worth, Shakespeare now drives another between class and clothing, and yet another between sex and gender, exposing both class and gender as unstable fictions that can't be anchored in appearance or anatomy. By masquerading as a man, Rosalind sheds the subservience imposed on her sex, and is free to prove, as the masquerade proceeds, that 'the bountiful blind woman doth most mistake in her gifts to women' by proving herself more than a match for men.

As if unmasking the mobility of gender were not enough, Shakespeare gives Rosalind's transformation another twist by retaining the loaded alias conferred on her by Lodge: the name of 'Jove's own page' (I.iii.123), Ganymede, the beautiful youth carried off by Jupiter in the form of an eagle to become his cupbearer. In Shakespeare's day the word was a euphemistic term for a catamite, a boy who was the object of pederastic desire. So by adopting this name Rosalind activates associations that add erotic ambiguity to androgyny, associations that would have been amplified on the Elizabethan stage by the physical presence of a boy in the role of Rosalind. The homoerotic potential of

Rosalind's pseudonym is exploited fully in the convoluted love-games she contrives for Orlando later in the play. But by settling on 'Ganymede' for his heroine's alias Shakespeare is already serving notice that the spectrum of human desire displayed by *As You Like It* will not be exclusively heterosexual, and that heterosexuality itself need not be viewed as either innate or normative.

Celia's adoption of the name Aliena (I.iii.127), which Shakespeare lifted likewise from Lodge, is also highly charged. It underlines the alienation of both Celia and Rosalind from the court they grew up in and their prospective status as strangers in Arden. That their very next thought is 'to steal / The clownish fool' (I.iii.128–9) from the court to accompany them only confirms how vital Touchstone is to the comedy's wider project of estrangement. Revealing the strangeness of familiar ideas and normal behaviour in order to break their spell is, after all, the wise fool's forte, to which the alien milieu of the forest, unfettered by coercive social conventions, gives free play. The ringing exit-rhyme on which the first act ends makes the essential quality of Arden clear and its reversal of the court's perspective unambiguous: 'Now go we in content', declares Celia, 'To liberty, and not to banishment' (I.iii.136–7).

The establishment of Arden as a privileged zone, liberated from the rules that govern Duke Frederick's grim regime, had begun earlier in the act, when life in the forest was likened to that of 'the old Robin Hood of England' (I.i.111) and the carefree world of the golden age. The utopian note was struck again in Le Beau's pointed farewell to Orlando after the wrestling match: 'Hereafter, in a better world than this, / I shall desire more love and knowledge of you' (I.ii.274–5). And the antithesis between oppressive court and carefree countryside that forms the axis of the comedy is prefigured in the distinction Rosalind and Celia draw between 'this working-day world' which is 'full of briers' and the festive period of 'holiday foolery' (I.iii.12, 14) that they will shortly enter. So that by the time the first act's closing couplet, with its promise of freedom and contentment in exile, brings us to the threshold of Arden itself, the audience is primed for the perceptual revolution that awaits it in the following four acts.

'let the forest judge'

The indeterminate character of the forest of Arden is essential to the comedy's cultivation of a transfigured vision. *As You Like It* plays fast and loose with the spatial and temporal parameters of everyday experience in order to create an environment in which the 'working-day world' can be viewed from a vantage point beyond its comprehension. On the face of it, the play's setting is plainly French: Oliver calls Orlando 'the stubbornest young fellow of France' (I.i.133–4), Robin Hood is referred to as 'the old Robin Hood of England', and characters like Le Beau and 'the melancholy Jaques' (II.i.41) who attends Duke Senior are addressed as 'Monsieur' rather than 'Master'. On the strength of such evidence, in a misconceived quest for consistency, The Oxford Shakespeare changes the 'Arden' of the First Folio to 'Ardenne' to fix the location of the forest in the Ardennes, on the border between modern France and Belgium. But the original Folio spelling highlights the geographical ambiguity of the play's greenwood, designating as it does a real stretch of woodland in Shakespeare's Warwickshire, and carrying, as it must have done for the dramatist, an affectionate echo of his mother's maiden name. The speech and characterization of the old shepherd Corin, and of the local yokels Audrey and William, strengthen Arden's partial anchorage in a palpably English rural milieu, in much the same way as the mechanicals in *A Midsummer Night's Dream* transport us from ancient Athens to Elizabethan England every time they appear. That said, one need only note that the flora and fauna of Arden include palm-trees (III.ii.171–2) and olive trees (III.v.76) as well as lions to realize that Arden is not confined to England either, but belongs to a never-never land not to be found on any map.

The denizens of this unlocatable land are equally anomalous. Corin dwells in a prosaic dimension of Arden where the hard realities of agricultural life prevail: 'I am shepherd to another man', he explains to Celia and Rosalind, 'And do not shear the fleeces that I graze' (II.iv.77–8). But, as his bucolic name suggests, he can also slip unfazed into the imaginary universe of pastoral poetry inhabited by the scornful shepherdess, Phoebe, and her tormented swain, Silvius. The transient inhabitants of 'this uncouth forest' (II.vi.6), those who have sought asylum within its bounds, must become equally adept at shuttling between incongruous domains. The Arden they encounter is in many respects a realistic woodland, where human flesh feels 'The seasons' difference, as the icy fang / And churlish chiding of the winter's wind' (II.i.6–7) and hunger compels them 'To fright the animals and to kill them up / In their assigned and native dwelling place' (II.i.62–3). But in other respects Arden is a frankly fictitious terrain cultivated by the literary imagination, and as such it requires virtually all its residents to compose or quote poetry, both romantic and ribald, off the cuff, or to break into song, both festive and plaintive, at a moment's notice. This Arden is the artificial enclave in which one may see 'a pageant truly played / Between the pale complexion of true love / And the red glow of scorn and proud disdain' (III.iv.47–9), and in which a deity from ancient Greece can take command of the wedding rites without anyone turning a hair. The more familiar with the forest of Arden we grow, the harder it is to define its identity, and the plainer its symbolic, theatrical character becomes.

Touchstone's appeal to the audience when Rosalind ribs him makes a point of making it plainer: 'You have said; but whether wisely or no, let the forest judge' (III.ii.119–20). Arden is not so much a place as an imaginary space, coextensive with 'This wide and universal theatre' (II.vii.137) in which we sit and watch; an emancipated state of mind in which we dawdle with the *dramatis personae* for the rest of the play. This freedom from the customary constraints of a definite, stable location is inseparable from Arden's gift of freedom from the tyranny of strictly regulated clock-time, which governs workaday life beyond 'the purlieus of this forest' (IV.iii.77). There is indeed 'no clock in the forest' (III.ii.295), as Orlando reminds Rosalind at their first encounter, giving her the perfect excuse to expatiate on the way 'Time travels in divers paces with divers persons' (III.ii.301–2), a slave to circumstance and subjective perception. Her demonstration of the relativity of time by showing 'who time ambles withal, who time trots withal, who time gallops withal, and who he stands still withal' (III.ii.302–4) emphatically refutes the clock-bound conception of time to which the melancholy moralist Jaques is wedded, and which Touchstone, holding an actual 'dial' drawn from his 'poke' (II.vii.20), has already spoofed in the previous act:

'Tis but an hour ago since it was nine,
And after one hour more 'twill be eleven.
And so from hour to hour we ripe and ripe,
And then from hour to hour we rot and rot;
                              (II.vii.24–7)

Oblivious to the fact that the joke's on him, Jaques's reaction to seeing 'The motley fool thus moral on the time' is to 'laugh sans intermission / An hour by his dial' (II.vii.32–3). For Jaques, not even laughter, notoriously the most unruly of emotions, is allowed to escape precise temporal measurement. The moralistic mentality that makes Jaques mistake Touchstone for the satirist Jaques himself aspires to be – 'Give me leave / To speak my mind, and I will through and through / Cleanse the foul body of th'infected world (II.vii.58–60) – goes hand in hand with submission to the normative regime that clock-time is contracted to enforce. The same mentality informs Jaques's reduction of human life, in the play's most famous speech, to 'seven ages', which he portrays as seven stages of inexorable decline from 'mewling and puking' infant to the senile decrepitude of 'second childishness and mere oblivion, / Sans teeth, sans eyes, sans taste, sans everything' (II.vii.139–66).

By setting the plot aside in Arden and stalling narrative progression, *As You Like It* creates a sense of timelessness designed to deliver the mind from the closed, deterministic outlook to which the clock consigns it. Relieved of the need to make decisions and take action to push the plot forward, and unfettered by their former identities, Arden's interlopers are at liberty to 'fleet the time carelessly' (I.i.112–13), to 'Lose and neglect the creeping hours of time' (II.vii.112) in chance encounters and unscheduled exchanges, which turn curbs and binds into pastimes that mock Fortune from her wheel. 'Caprice and fancy reign and revel here', remarks Hazlitt, 'and stern necessity is banished to the court'; as a consequence, in Arden 'the interest arises more out of the sentiments and characters than out of the actions or situations. It is not what is done, but what is said, that claims our attention.' The effect of what is said, moreover, is that 'The very air of the place seems to breathe a spirit of philosophical poetry', as Hazlitt puts it. For Arden provides a breathing space, a privileged interval of footloose detachment from the daily round, during which entrenched ideas and practices are exposed to playful questioning and sceptical critique.

'sit you down in gentleness'

From the natural perspective of the forest, where the seasons, not sovereigns, hold sway and quite different laws apply, nothing appears more unnatural than the divisive principles of social organization human beings have inflicted on themselves. The unequal distribution of Dame Fortune's gifts, which the powerful and propertied conspire to preserve, and which the powerless and dispossessed are constrained to endure, stands revealed as groundless and irrational when viewed from the vantage point of a life 'exempt from public haunt' and thus 'more sweet / Than that of painted pomp' and 'More free from peril than the envious court' (II.i.2–4, 15). Such sentiments are all the more striking for being uttered by a duke, in the speech which immediately follows the couplet with which Celia concludes Act I: 'Now go we in content / To liberty, and not to banishment.' Even more arresting, however, is the opening line of that speech — the first words spoken in Arden — in which Duke Senior addresses the courtiers attending him as 'my co-mates and brothers in exile' (II.i.1). The use of the word 'co-mates' in this phrase is unique in Shakespeare, who employs it to signal the displacement of degree and the ethos it breeds in 'the envious court' by the communal ethos rooted in 'old custom' and fostered by life in 'these woods' (II.i.2, 3).

The Duke's allusion two lines later to 'the penalty of Adam, / The seasons' difference' (II.i.5–6), which he is happy to pay in Arden, reinforces this shift by evoking the Edenic epoch before the advent of class society and reminding us of our undivided origin in our common ancestor. As the legendary rhyme ascribed to John Ball, the leader of the Peasants' Revolt, puts it: 'When Adam delved and Eve span, / Who was then the gentleman?' The allusion to Adam at this juncture is by no means of merely incidental significance, since it also echoes the name of the loyal old servant addressed by Orlando in the first speech, indeed in the first sentence, of *As You Like It*. That Shakespeare intended the aged retainer to embody something of 'the old Adam' popularly believed to lurk in everyone, irrespective of rank, seems more than likely in light of his decision to drop the surname 'Spencer' (i.e., 'steward') attached to Lodge's Adam in *Rosalynde*. The levelling resonance of the name, latent though it may be to begin with, grows as the first scene's fixation on gentility unfolds. It's hardly an accident that Orlando's protest at the injustice of the law of primogeniture, which flies in the face of natural law, is directed, like his fury at being robbed of his rank, at a servant of humble birth who personifies not only 'The constant service of the antique world' (II.iii.58), but also common humanity. Adam's own outrage at Oliver's betrayal of his filial and fraternal obligations strengthens the moral authority of that protest: 'Your brother – no, no brother – yet the son – / Yet not the son, I will not call him son – / Of him I was about to call his father' (II.iii.20–2).

Given the symbolic significance of the 'good old man' (II.iii.57), Orlando's decision to bring Adam with him into Arden, whose very name carries an echo of Eden, is as apt as the decision of Rosalind and Celia to transport 'The clownish fool' (I.iii.129), their fellow flouter of Dame Fortune, into the woods where, as 'Nature's natural', he is free to be 'the more fool' (I.iii.129, I.ii.47, II.iv.14). The moment when Orlando returns to Duke Senior, bearing on his shoulders the 'old poor man / Who after me hath many a weary step / Limped in pure love' (II.vii.129–31), acquires added poignancy if Adam's fundamental identity is borne in mind. As critics routinely observe, Orlando's entrance with Adam is a powerful visual refutation of the words that immediately precede it – Jaques's dismissal of old age as 'second childishness and mere oblivion, / Sans teeth, sans eyes, sans taste, sans everything' (II.vii.165–6). Exhausted and hungry he may be, but we've no reason to doubt Adam's earlier claim: 'Though I look old, yet I am strong and lusty' (II.iii.48). Far more important, though, are the egalitarian implications of seeing Orlando carry his 'venerable burden' (II.vii.167), the incarnation of our primal precursor, into Arden upon his back. These implications are accentuated by the image of the master carrying his servant, in an extraordinary reversal of the usual relationship.

That reversal springs from the tender concern for Adam shown by Orlando in the previous scene (II.vi), when he puts his servant's need for rest and sustenance before his own. The tenderness of his solicitude and the primacy of the old man's needs are stressed again when Orlando begs Duke Senior to delay the meal he has disrupted, 'Whiles, like a doe, I go to find my fawn / And give it food', because 'Till he be first sufficed, / Oppressed with two weak evils, age and hunger, / I will not touch a bit' (II.vii.128–9, 131–3). And after he has returned with Adam, and they have been invited by the Duke to eat, Orlando's expression of gratitude makes a point once more of putting Adam first: 'I thank you most for him' (II.vii.169).

In the course of this sequence Orlando enacts a new conception of 'gentility', of what it means to be 'gentle', that is quite different from what it meant at the start of the comedy. The word 'gentleness' occurs more often in *As You Like It* than in any of Shakespeare's plays, and most frequently in this first exchange between Orlando and the Duke. When Orlando bursts in on the Duke and his courtiers, sword in hand, as they are about to dine, crying 'Forbear, and eat no more!', the Duke subdues him by asking, 'What would you have? Your gentleness shall force / More than your force move us to gentleness', and welcomes him to their table (II.vii.88, 102–3). 'Speak you so gently?' (II.vii.106) replies the chastened Orlando, who asks their forgiveness for his discourtesy, and reaches for the comedy's favourite conjunction:

> If ever you have looked on better days,
> If ever been where bells have knolled to church,
> If ever sat at any good man's feast,
> If ever from your eyelids wiped a tear,
> And know what 'tis to pity, and be pitied,
> Let gentleness my strong enforcement be.
>
> (II.vii.113–18)

We have indeed done all these things, the Duke assures the abashed intruder, 'and wiped our eyes / Of drops that sacred pity hath engendered. / And therefore sit you down in gentleness' (II.vii.122–4).

What's fascinating here is the semantic sea-change the word 'gentle' and its derivatives have undergone by the end of this exchange. Initially 'gentleness' means essentially what Orlando meant by 'gentility' in Act I, Scene i: the possession of the 'gentleman-like qualities' (I.i.65–6) befitting his rank, which his lack of a 'good education' (I.i.63–4) has denied him. But, as it travels back and forth between Orlando and the Duke, the word sheds its class-bound connotations and is used instead to signify a compassionate disposition rooted in mutual empathy, the capacity 'to pity, and be pitied', which owes nothing to birth and everything to recognizing the claims our fellow human beings have upon our kindness, simply by virtue of being human. It's not by chance that the meaning of 'gentleness' undergoes this transmutation in a 'desert inaccessible' (II.vii.110), where 'The thorny point / Of bare distress' (II.vii.94–5) exposes the physical vulnerability that binds people together, regardless of their social station or their gender. Nor is it fortuitous that Adam disappears from the play at this point, never to be heard from or mentioned again, for the perspective he embodied outside Arden is fostered henceforth within Arden by diverse characters and dramatic strategies, which render Adam's role as its special avatar redundant.

Cross-Dressing and the Cure for Love

Patriarchal assumptions about the supremacy of the male in the family and society, about the inherent distinctions that divide the sexes, and about the inviolable norm of heterosexual love are subjected to the same process of sceptical subversion in *As You Like It* as the principles that underpin class division and social inequality.

The precedence over women ubiquitously enjoyed by men is turned upside down by Rosalind, who dominates the play to a degree unmatched by the heroines of the other comedies. (Charles I jotted 'Rosalind' beside the title on the contents page of his copy of the 1632 Folio.) Rosalind's is the longest female part in all Shakespeare's plays – longer even than Cleopatra's, and more than twice as long as Viola's in *Twelfth Night*. A full quarter of the lines in *As You Like It* are spoken by her. The fact that her part was originally taken by a boy detracts not one iota from the boldness of Shakespeare's decision to privilege his leading female character to such an extent, let alone endow her with such coruscating wit and theatrical power. In the guise of Ganymede, Rosalind initiates the courtship of the man she loves, defines its terms and controls its course from start to finish. A self-styled 'magician' who 'can do strange things' (V.ii.57, 68), and thus a female prototype of Prospero, she orchestrates the denouement in such a way as to resolve the romantic dilemmas in which her androgynous identity in Arden has embroiled her. The temptation to view her as an authorial figure, a surrogate for the dramatist himself, becomes overwhelming when Shakespeare gives her the last word in the dazzling epilogue she delivers to the audience, and places the fate of the play in her hands. To create a stage heroine possessed of such charisma and authority at all at this time, and then put her in command of the comedy with the lion's share of the lines, constitutes in itself a provocative theatrical statement, which puts the thrust of the play's sexual politics beyond doubt.

But Shakespeare doesn't leave it at that. The male persona Rosalind adopts allows him to devise situations of vertiginous complexity, which undo the customary distinctions between masculine and feminine, and between homosexual and heterosexual, creating a space beyond them in which more fluid, less repressive forms of sexual identity and desire can be floated and explored. At its most involuted, *As You Like It* confronted its first audiences with a boy playing the part of a woman (Rosalind), who is posing as a young man (Ganymede), who is pretending to be a woman on whom Orlando can practise his courtship of Rosalind, and who is fending off the amorous advances of Phoebe, whose infatuation with the 'pretty youth' is clearly kindled by his feminine features – the 'pretty redness in his lip' , 'the constant red and mingled damask in his cheek' (III.v.114, 121, 124) – rather than by any semblance of virility. The sexual confusion would have been compounded, moreover, by the confounding of class lines this pretty pass entails: an actor, commonly regarded as belonging to the same underclass as vagabonds and peddlers, playing the part of an aristocrat, the daughter of a duke, who is masquerading as a shepherd and winds up wedding another actor cast in the role of a knight's son, a *déclassé* gentleman, who is her social inferior by birth and education, despite the 'potent dukedom' (V.iv.167) he stands to inherit as a result of his marriage.

Shakespeare had already employed female cross-dressing as a theatrical strategy in *The Two Gentlemen of Verona* and *The Merchant of Venice*, and he would employ it again to equally complex effect in *Twelfth Night*. Cross-dressed male characters had featured too, of course, in the Induction to *The Taming of the Shrew*, in 'Pyramus and Thisbe' in *A Midsummer Night's Dream*, and most memorably in *The Merry Wives of*

Windsor, when Falstaff is constrained to impersonate the old woman of Brentford. But what sets the use of sexual disguise in *As You Like It* apart from its use in Shakespeare's other plays is that Rosalind's assumed persona, Ganymede, provides her with a platform on which to perform *her own identity* as Rosalind. By detaching the character from her primary identity as exiled Duke's daughter and romantic heroine, and revealing it to be as much a role as Ganymede, Shakespeare prises open a dimension independent of both masculinity and femininity as they are currently perceived, and reducible to neither. Likewise, when the disguised Rosalind finds herself wooed as a woman by Orlando, who thinks she's a man, and wooed as a beautiful youth by Phoebe, who is unaware that she's really a woman, a current of desire flows between the three characters that is impossible to pin down, because it keeps both heterosexual and homosexual propensities in play, defying us to tease them apart.

Cross-dressing in *As You Like It* creates opportunities for the playful mimicking of both sexes in the throes of love, unfixing gender stereotypes and placing them between quotation marks that question their validity. It also contrives erotic quandaries which suggest that the sexuality of women and men is more various and volatile than the standard definitions and prescriptions can afford to admit. As a result, Rosalind's resumption of her original identity as the daughter of Duke Senior, and her formal submission of herself to her father and her husband at the wedding ceremony – 'To you I give myself, for I am yours (V.iv.114–15) – can't be so readily dismissed as a capitulation to patriarchal conventions, since the premises on which those conventions rest have been kicked away in the course of the play. The credit for kicking them away doesn't belong to the comedy's transvestite convolutions alone, though. Rosalind may end up giving herself in marriage to the man she fell in love with at first sight, but not before love between men and women, and the state of matrimony, have run the gauntlet of her blunt realism and Touchstone's lewd cynicism.

The cure for love that Rosalind administers to Orlando is designed to divest him of the clichéd postures and predictable discourse that make love 'merely a madness', which 'deserves as well a dark house and a whip as madmen do' (III.ii.386–8). She is equally scathing about the equally absurd 'pageant truly played' (III.iv.47) between Phoebe and Silvius. 'Who might be your mother', enquires Rosalind of Phoebe, 'That you insult, exult, and all at once, / Over the wretched?' (III.v.36–8). 'Sell when you can', she advises her with brutal frankness, 'You are not for all markets' (III.v.61). The pity Celia feels for Phoebe's forlorn suitor, Rosalind assures her, is wasted on Silvius, whom she scolds for tolerating such abuse: 'Wilt thou love such a woman? What, to make thee an instrument, and play false strains upon thee? – not to be endured' (IV.iii.68–70). So much for the rarefied fantasies of pastoral romance.

Orlando fares no better when he declares that the imaginary Rosalind's rejection of him is his death warrant: 'Men have died from time to time, and worms have eaten them', retorts Rosalind, 'but not for love' (IV.i.99–101). She then persuades a reluctant Celia to conduct a make-believe marriage ceremony, in which she and Orlando pronounce the legally binding words and thus pre-empt the official, public wedding conducted by Hymen at the end of the play. (In Shakespeare's day, a declaration of intent to marry by two people before a third constituted a binding contract, provided it was made '*per verba de praesenti*', i.e., in the present tense.) Hardly have they uttered those potent words, whose full import escapes Orlando, when Rosalind dashes the romantic illusions they have conjured up in the mind of her unwitting spouse. Once his love has been consummated, it will last, Orlando pledges, reaching for the nearest cliché, 'For ever and a day'. To which Rosalind replies:

> Say a day without the ever. No, no, Orlando; men are April when they woo, December when they wed. Maids are May when they are maids, but the sky changes when they are wives. I will be more jealous of thee than a Barbary cock-pigeon over his hen, more clamorous than a parrot against rain, more new-fangled than an ape, more giddy in my desires than a monkey. I will weep for nothing, like Diana in the fountain, and I will do that when you are disposed to be merry. I will laugh like a hyena, and that when thou art inclined to sleep.
>
> (IV.i.138–48)

Well before the 'genuine', formal marriage of Orlando and Rosalind takes place, this cross-dressed rehearsal robs it of any unrealistic expectations they or the audience might have of it. Prefaced and qualified by this unclouded view of wedlock, the four weddings before Hymen in the final act are free to serve not only as versions of a repressive patriarchal institution, but also as symbols of the more desirable relationships that might supervene in a transformed reality, 'When earthly things made even / Atone together' (V.iv.107–8).

'That thou mightst ioyne his hand with his'

It's not just the implausible presence of Hymen that exhorts us to read the connubial climax of the comedy symbolically rather than cynically.

Because of Rosalind's disguise as Ganymede and Orlando's ignorance
of Ganymede's true identity, their exchange of vows in Act IV also
enacts, under the aegis of mere pretence, the marriage of a man to a
man, a fact less likely to have been lost on the play's first audiences, who
would have seen one boy dressed as a woman being married to an adult
male playing a man by another boy dressed as a woman. The pervasive
sexual ambivalence of the scene is betrayed by Rosalind's diction, too,
when she warns Orlando that, as his wife, she will be more jealous of
him than 'a Barbary cock-pigeon over *his* hen' (IV.i.141–2; my italics).
Small wonder that the Puritan enemies of the stage perceived it as a
hotbed of illicit proclivities devised to corrupt actors and audience
alike. They would scarcely have been appeased, moreover, by the 'real'
fifth-act marriage before Hymen, since there's every reason to conclude
that the play's original audiences were meant to behold in it a mirror-
image of the earlier mock-marriage.

Not for the first time in this study we find serious distortions
inflicted on the original printed version of Shakespeare's text by med-
dling editors, anxious to correct what they mistakenly assume to be self-
evident authorial errors, erroneous transcriptions of his manuscript, or
misprints. The problem being that, once these emendations are generally accepted and regularly reproduced by subsequent editors, they displace the original text and obliterate the quite different interpretive
possibilities it offered.

In the First Folio edition of *As You Like It* (1623) the last two lines
of Hymen's song read as follows: 'That thou mightst ioyne *his* hand
with his / Whose heart within his bosome is' (2689–90; V.iv.112–13;
my italics). The Second Folio (1632) preserves this wording. From the
Third Folio of 1664 onwards, however, editors have amended the first,
and occasionally the second, 'his' to 'her'. Following the Restoration,
women were permitted to play women's parts in the public theatre, as
a result of which this amendment became set in stone in the productions of subsequent centuries – eighteenth- and nineteenth-century
Rosalinds in particular being keen to conclude the performance in
fetching feminine attire. The trouble is that a female Rosalind in a dress
makes no sense of the line in the epilogue that begins 'If I were a
woman' (16–17), which is consequently often cut in performance.

At no point in *As You Like It* does Orlando say anything to suggest
that he realizes Ganymede, the youth he has been wooing in place of
Rosalind, is really Rosalind herself. Julia in *The Two Gentlemen of
Verona* and Viola in *Twelfth Night* are both explicitly identified while
still in masculine garb by Proteus and Orsino respectively, and in *The*

Merchant of Venice Bassanio and Gratiano finally grasp that the learned doctor and his clerk who saved Antonio were actually their own wives. But Orlando is given no such moment of recognition at which to draw a clear distinction between Ganymede and Rosalind, so that his line in response to the latter's reappearance with Hymen and Celia, 'If there be truth in sight, you are my Rosalind' (V.iv.117), leaves ample scope for visual ambiguity, which the conditional clause ('*If* there be truth in sight') underscores.

In the First Folio, the stage direction for Rosalind's re-entrance in the final scene reads simply: 'Enter Hymen, Rosalind, and Celia'. Having accepted the amendment of Hymen's song in the 1664 Third Folio, however, most later editors incorporated the revised version of the stage direction in Nicholas Rowe's 1709 edition: 'Enter Hymen, Rosalind, and Celia, *Rosalind in Woman's Cloths*' (my italics). This revision in turn provided further authority for what remains the standard approach to staging this scene down to the present day, notwithstanding the less prescriptive, more flexible formulations preferred by recent editions, including the Oxford Shakespeare (2005), which has Rosalind and Celia entering 'as themselves', and the Arden Shakespeare (2006), which adopts Edward Capell's phrase 'both undisguised'.

The First Folio, however, does not presuppose, let alone stipulate, that Rosalind sheds the doublet and hose of Ganymede offstage in order to re-enter in a gown that restores the character's primary gender. When Rosalind re-enters, the reactions of Duke Senior, Orlando and especially Phoebe make it clear that her female identity must be apparent to them at this point, although in all three cases that tell-tale conjunction 'If' betrays disbelief in the evidence of their own eyes. But their realization does not necessitate a complete change of costume by the actor or actress, who can readily indicate Rosalind's return by a change in posture, manner, voice and gait, or by the simple expedient of removing the hat that hides her hair. Indeed, the response of Phoebe – who literally doesn't know Rosalind from Adam because she has never met her – is inexplicable if Rosalind is not simultaneously recognizable to her *as Ganymede as well*: 'If sight and shape be true, / Why then, my love adieu!' (V.iv.118–19).

There's more than a scholarly quibble at stake here. If the pronouns in Hymen's song are allowed to stand as printed in the First and Second Folio, and Rosalind remains dressed as Ganymede throughout the recognition scene and wedding ceremony, then what we also witness in the latter is a re-enactment of the make-believe marriage between two male characters, Ganymede and Orlando. Performed like this, the celebration

of 'high wedlock' (V.iv.142) that crowns the comedy turns into an altogether more expansive grand finale, embracing as it does not only a
quartet of couples who span the entire social scale, from Duke's daughter to goatherd, but also a richer, more diverse spectrum of sexual identity and desire than an unequivocally heterosexual marriage between
Rosalind and Orlando allows.

The Last Word: 'If I were a woman'

Leaving Rosalind garbed like Ganymede has the further virtue of letting her segue seamlessly after the nuptial dance into her tantalizing
epilogue, whose seductive wit and wording plainly depend on her possessing an androgynous appearance:

> It is not the fashion to see the lady the epilogue; but it is no more
> unhandsome than to see the lord the prologue. If it be true that good
> wine needs no bush, 'tis true that a good play needs no epilogue. Yet
> to good wine they do use good bushes, and good plays prove the bet-
> ter by the help of good epilogues. What a case am I in then, that am
> neither a good epilogue nor cannot insinuate with you in the behalf of
> a good play! I am not furnished like a beggar, therefore to beg will not
> become me. My way is to conjure you; and I'll begin with the women.
> I charge you, O women, for the love you bear to men, to like as much
> of this play as please you. And I charge you, O men, for the love you
> bear to women – as I perceive by your simpering none of you hates
> them – that between you and the women the play may please. If I were
> a woman I would kiss as many of you as had beards that pleased me,
> complexions that liked me, and breaths that I defied not. And I am
> sure, as many as have good beards, or good faces, or sweet breaths will
> for my kind offer, when I make curtsy, bid me farewell.
>
> *Exit*

In this astonishing valediction, addressed directly to the audience,
we have the only instance in Shakespeare of a female character explicitly
calling attention ('If I were a woman') to the male actor playing her
part. In fact, what we are presented with, more precisely, is the character Rosalind *playing the part of the boy who has played her*, and delivering, as both 'the lady' and the boy actor, an epilogue in which she
appeals to the women on behalf of the men, and to the men on behalf
of the women. As the opening sentence of the epilogue makes clear,

Shakespeare is well aware that, by giving 'the lady', the heroine of the piece, the last word, he is breaking with theatrical convention. But his defence of his upending of the patriarchal pecking order on stage is couched in symmetrical syntax, whose perfectly balanced clauses enact the tacit aim of that upending, which is to make ladies equal with lords. Like his favourite philosopher Montaigne, Shakespeare recognized that, beyond the artificial discriminations that divide the sexes, 'both male and female are cast in one same moulde; instruction and custome excepted, there is no great difference betweene them' ('Upon Some Verses of Virgil'). The entire cross-dressed courtship of Rosalind as Ganymede by Orlando has been devoted to dramatizing this understanding in concrete, theatrical terms, and the epilogue is expressly designed to drive the point home before the audience leaves the theatre.

The epilogue's scrambling of gender distinctions and androgynous flirtation with both sexes converge with its flouting of the class-distinctions customarily observed in such speeches. With *As You Like It*'s transvaluation of 'gentility' in mind, the manner in which Rosalind addresses the spectators is revealing. In the only other Elizabethan play in which a female character delivers the epilogue, John Lyly's *Gallathea*, the eponymous heroine deferentially addresses the court audience, for which the play was written, as 'ladies and gentlemen'. In Lodge's *Rosalynde* the moralizing epilogue is directed solely at the book's 'gentlemen' readers. And at the end of *A Midsummer Night's Dream*, Puck, whom Rosalind resembles in many respects, not least in her capacity as onstage director of the play, addresses the audience in his epilogue as 'Gentles'. But Rosalind, in a move that epitomizes what Hymen meant by making matters 'even', speaks to them informally, whatever their station might be, as simply 'men' and 'women', and she makes a point of beginning with the women – putting them once again before the men – when she starts to 'conjure' each sex to find the play pleasing. In Rosalind's conjuring of the men, moreover, she slides slyly from heterosexual innuendo ('that between you and the women the play may please') into homoerotic coquetry, laying bare the boy beneath the role: 'If I were a woman I would kiss as many of you as had beards that pleased me'.

The epilogue reprises, in short, the key preoccupations of the comedy and projects them from the stage into the audience. Its aim is to conjure up in the audience the attitude its speaker incarnates and articulates: to infect them with its contagious theatricality and leave them in the unfettered frame of mind the play has been at pains to cultivate throughout. In so doing it reactivates, too, the complex connotations of the play's title, which it recalls when it charges the women 'to like as much of this play as please you', and couples liking again with pleasure – this time of the erotic kind – in the phrases 'beards that pleased me, complexions that liked me'. By this point, though, it should be apparent that the principal pleasure *As You Like It* affords the audience is the pleasure of being endowed with a dramatically different perspective on their lives and times, a perspective liberated, for as long as the play's spell lasts, from the convictions and expectations that imprison their hearts and minds in the 'working-day world' to which they are about to return.

If

To put it another way: the epilogue completes the audience's induction into the wisdom of folly personified and promulgated by the play's own consummate wise fool, Touchstone, the first fully-fledged wise fool in Shakespeare. At the heart of that wisdom is a wry detachment from the ways of the world as it stands, a refusal to succumb to any one view of life it offers, and an awareness of the alternative views and ways of life that can materialize at any moment.

Jaques's delighted account of his first meeting with Touchstone pinpoints the distinctive stance the latter adopts towards the times in which he finds himself and the types of people the world throws in his path. 'A fool, a fool, I met a fool i'th' forest, /A motley fool', cries Jaques, 'a fool, / Who laid him down and basked him in the sun, / And railed on Lady Fortune in good terms' (II.vii.12–16). Being as implacable a foe of Lady Fortune as Rosalind and Celia, Touchstone is also 'an enemy to the prejudices of opinion', as Hazlitt puts it, since such prejudices serve by their very partiality to buttress the man-made causes of misfortune. He therefore wastes no opportunity to expose, by contradiction or by parody, the partiality, and hence the relativity, of whatever point of view confronts him. His parody of Jaques is lost, of course, on the latter, who mistakes the 'liberty' (II.vii.47) that wise fools enjoy for a licence to be merely satirical and indulge his own jaundiced penchant for castigating the vices of the day. Nothing could be further from Touchstone's mobile mind than such a righteous, inflexible objective. His mind is as motley as his multi-coloured costume because, like the comedy he inhabits, he prefers to shuttle back and forth across the play's spectrum of perspectives without coming to rest anywhere. Touchstone epitomizes the play's relaxed, amused detachment from the diverse perspectives it surveys, a detachment which it invites the audience to share.

Smack in the middle of the play, at the point on which it turns, Touchstone demonstrates the stance *As You Like It* commends to us in his reply to Corin's innocent query, 'And how like you this shepherd's life, Master Touchstone?':

> Truly, shepherd, in respect of itself, it is a good life; but in respect that it is a shepherd's life, it is naught. In respect that it is solitary, I like it very well; but in respect that it is private, it is a very vile life. Now in respect it is in the fields, it pleaseth me well; but in respect it is not in the court, it is tedious. As it is a spare life, look you, it fits my humour well; but as there is no more plenty in it, it goes much against my stomach. Hast any philosophy in thee shepherd?
>
> (III.ii.11–22)

Shakespeare compresses into Touchstone's compulsive catchphrase 'in respect of' and its variants the restless, multivocal dynamic of the entire play, which seeks to disengage us from unqualified commitment to any particular identity or standpoint we may be inclined to adopt. That structural dynamic is inherently democratic, inasmuch as it disperses authority impartially across the full range of *dramatis personae*, refusing to grant sovereignty to any of the positions dramatized. This is, perhaps, the most powerful way in which the comedy articulates its utopian commitment to the common interests of humanity, and to the prospect of a form of community that serves those common interests rather than the interests of one class or kind of human being at the expense of the others.

As You Like It's profound estrangement from the actual and imaginative absorption in the possible are reflected in its repeated deployment of that tiny but formidable word 'if'. It crops up far more frequently (138 times) in *As You Like It* than in any other Shakespeare play, acquiring so much prominence along the way that Touchstone feels entitled to treat it as a noun in his tribute to its potency. The fool's fondness for the word first becomes apparent, as we've seen, in his defence of 'a certain knight that swore "by his honour" they were good pancakes, and swore "by his honour" the mustard was naught' (I.ii.60–2). He resorts to it obsessively again at the end of the play in his absurd disquisition on the 'seventh cause' of quarrelling and 'the degrees of the lie' (V.iv.65–94), which concludes thus:

> All these you may avoid but the Lie Direct; and you may avoid that, too, with an 'if'. I knew when seven justices could not take up a quarrel, but when the parties were met themselves, one of them

thought but of an 'if', as 'If you said so, then I said so', and they
shook hands and swore brothers. Your 'if' is the only peacemaker;
much virtue in 'if'.

(V.iv.94–101)

Touchstone's eulogy focuses our attention on the syllable that floods
the last three scenes of *As You Like It* and becomes, in effect, the watch-
word of the play. Well before he launches into his encomium, Rosalind
triggers a minor avalanche of 'ifs' in the ritualistic exchange between
Orlando, Phoebe, Silvius and herself, which she initiates when she
assures Orlando: 'if you will be married tomorrow, you shall; and to
Rosalind if you will' (V.ii.69–70). Rosalind concludes the scene by
promising to solve the problems of all four of them at a stroke by means
of marriage the following day, and the pledge she makes to each in turn
is prefaced by the same indispensable conditional conjunction. She
enlists its services once again at the start of the final scene, when – still
in the guise of Ganymede – she secures promises from Duke Senior,
Orlando, Phoebe and Silvius that they will abide by their agreement to
act as she stipulates, once she has made Rosalind materialize. When the
'real' Rosalind does appear, 'if' qualifies not only the responses in
which Duke Senior, Orlando and Phoebe acknowledge her identity, but
also Rosalind's replies to them and Hymen's conclusion of the formal
wedding ceremony:

ROSALIND. (*to the Duke*) I'll have no father if you be not he.
           (*to Orlando*) I'll have no husband if you be not he,
           (*to Phoebe*) Nor ne'er wed woman if you be not she.
HYMEN.   Peace, ho, I bar confusion.
          'Tis I must make conclusion
            Of these most strange events.
          Here's eight that must take hands
          To join in Hymen's bands,
            If truth holds true contents.

(V.iv.120–8)

The cumulative impact of this barrage of conditional clauses, which
continues right to the end of the epilogue, is to transpose the entire
denouement from the indicative into the subjunctive mood. As it draws
to a close, *As You Like It* confesses that a resolution in which 'earthly
things made even / Atone together' – in which true equality and unity
are realized – is as yet achievable only in the virtual reality of fiction. In so

doing, it reminds the audience of the vast distance that still separates the divisive dispensation they currently endure from the genuine community prefigured by the denouement.

To hasten the demise of that dispensation, *As You Like It* affords its audience a vision of the way they would like it to be, disguised as the way it had to be for those who were living at that moment in history, in late Elizabethan England. It allows the audience to view Shakespeare's world and time from the vantage point of a potential future that still lies beyond our world and time: a future in which Dame Fortune's gifts have at last been 'bestowed equally'. That vantage point is the vantage point of the wise fool, Touchstone, whose laughter is the laughter of the future at the past. In acquiring his perspective, which is the perspective of the play, we acquire the wisdom of folly: the wisdom of those who are fools in the eyes of the world as it is, because they are wise to the ways of that world and fooled by it no longer. As Touchstone remarks to Shakespeare's namesake, the rustic simpleton William (in whom we perhaps behold a mocking self-portrait): 'I do now remember a saying: "The fool doth think he is wise, but the wise man knows himself to be a fool"' (V.i.30–1).

When Amiens and the other exiled lords sing the first of the play's many exquisite songs, 'Under the greenwood tree', with its chorus summoning all who shun ambition to Arden –

> Come hither, come hither, come hither.
>> Here shall he see
>> No enemy
> But winter and rough weather.
>>> (II.v.5–8, 39–42)

– Jaques can't resist supplying a sarcastic parody:

> If it do come to pass
> That any man turn ass,
> Leaving his wealth and ease
> A stubborn will to please,
> Ducdame, ducdame, ducdame.
>> Here shall he see
>> Gross fools as he,
> An if he will come to me.
>>> (II.v.47–54)

'What's that "ducdame"?' asks Amiens, walking right into Jaques's trap along with the others now gathering round him. ''Tis a Greek invocation to call fools into a circle', replies Jaques, springing the trap (II.v.55–6). But once again the joke is on Jaques, who yearns to be 'a motley fool' like Touchstone, but is doomed to spurn the 'dancing measures' of the denouement and 'To see no pastime' (V.iv.191, 193). For the fact is that, long before 'good Monsieur Melancholy' (III.ii.287–8) disappears into Duke Senior's 'abandoned cave' (V.iv.194) at the end of *As You Like It*, the audience has fallen, like the exiled lords, under the spell cast by the 'Greek invocation', having heard in the cryptic cry 'Ducdame, ducdame, ducdame' the play's summons to dwell as wise fools in 'the circle of this forest' (V.iv.34), the charmed circle of Shakespeare's 'wide and universal theatre' (II.vii.137), where the impossible comes to pass.

10
'Nothing that is so, is so':
Twelfth Night

The End of the Affair

Probably written in 1601, either just before or just after *Hamlet*, *Twelfth Night, or What You Will* marks by common consent the end of Shakespeare's affair with the kind of comedy he had made his own during his first decade as a dramatist. After *Twelfth Night* his attention turned to other kinds of comedy, indeed to the creation of plays so different from his previous ventures into the genre that few critics have felt comfortable calling them comedies and they have become better known as problem plays and romances. Insofar as they mask the generic features these comedies share with their precursors, the aliases they have acquired are undeniably misleading. As the first chapter of this book began by pointing out, an unbroken genealogical line connects the concerns and conventions of Shakespearean comedy from *The Comedy of Errors* through to *The Tempest*, and plays as disparate as *A Midsummer Night's Dream*, *Measure for Measure* and *The Winter's Tale* reveal at their core under close analysis the same dramatic DNA. From this point of view it might be more accurate to regard *Twelfth Night* as a turning point in the fortunes of Shakespearean comedy, a Janus-faced play which looks back to the farcical and the festive romantic comedies that preceded it, and forward to the darker, disenchanted vision of the problem plays and the romances' miraculous, bittersweet tales of shipwreck, grief and kindred reunited.

Be that as it may, from the standpoint of this study the first striking feature of *Twelfth Night* is its brazen plundering of virtually all Shakespeare's previous comedies for characters, predicaments, theatrical devices and motifs. Shakespeare almost certainly filched the main ingredients of the play's romantic plot from Barnaby Riche's story of

235

Apollonius and Silla in *Riche his Farewell to Military Profession*, published 20 years earlier: a shipwrecked girl, who serves a young Duke in
the guise of a boy and courts on his behalf a noble lady, who falls in love
with the girl and marries her twin brother by mistake. The comical
revenge-plot grafted onto this amorous imbroglio – the duping of the
straitlaced steward into believing the noble lady is in love with him –
was forged in the dramatist's imagination along with the members of
the lady's household who conspire to take the steward down a peg or
two. Both plots, however, provided Shakespeare with opportunities to
recycle and reconfigure the components of his first nine comedies that
he found most resonant. As a result, *Twelfth Night* reads like a virtuoso
reprise of Shakespearean comedy in its Elizabethan prime, a valedictory
compendium of scenarios, tropes and ploys, which Shakespeare would
never resort to again in quite the same way. It's no accident that
Hazlitt's attempt to define the distinctive qualities of Shakespearean
comedy in *Characters of Shakespear's Plays* was prompted by his contemplation of *Twelfth Night*, in which he found all those qualities
encapsulated. Nor does it come as a surprise to find most critics two
centuries on from Hazlitt agreeing that *Twelfth Night* is Shakespeare's
consummate, quintessential comedy.

The play's most prominent debt to Shakespeare's own comedies was
pinpointed in the first recorded critical comment on *Twelfth Night*, the
sole surviving allusion to it in Shakespeare's lifetime. On 2 February
1602, John Manningham, a law student at the Middle Temple in
London, noted in his diary:

> At our feast wee had a play called 'Twelve Night, or What You Will',
> much like the Commedy of Errores, or Menechmi in Plautus, but
> most like and neere to that in Italian called *Inganni*. A good practise
> in it to make the Steward beleeve his Lady widdowe was in love with
> him, by counterfeyting a letter as from his Lady in generall termes,
> telling him what shee liked best in him, and prescribing his gesture
> in smiling, his apparaile, &c., and then when he came to practise,
> making him beleeve they tooke him to be mad.

Manningham may have mistaken the grieving sister Olivia for a grieving
widow, but he made no mistake in identifying the principal
Shakespearean source of *Twelfth Night* as well as the Italian plotline
transplanted by Shakespeare from Barnaby Riche. (By '*Inganni*'
Manningham meant *Gl'Ingannati*, or *The Deceived*, the anonymous
play of 1531 from which the tale of Apollonius and Silla ultimately

derives.) The identical twins Viola and Sebastian, torn apart by shipwreck, lost in a maze of mistaken identity and finally reunited in a
poignant moment of mutual recognition, are clearly direct descendants
of the identical Antipholus twins and the identical twin Dromios who
attend them.

Close parallels abound between the plights and the speeches of the
characters in both plays. When Adriana addresses Antipholus of
Syracuse as her husband and berates him for abusing her, the latter
exclaims aside, 'What, was I married to her in my dream? / Or sleep I
now, and think I hear all this?' before deciding to 'entertain the offered
fallacy' (II.ii.185–6, 189) and play along with the madness that seems
to surround him. Likewise, when Olivia mistakes Sebastian for Cesario,
his sister's alter ego, and makes her passion for him plain, Sebastian
muses, 'Or I am mad, or else this is a dream' and concludes, 'If it be
thus to dream, still let me sleep' (IV.i.60, 62), before surrendering to
the situation and marrying the apparently deranged woman he's just
met. Orsino's astonished response to the sight of Sebastian and Viola
together – 'One face, one voice, one habit, and two persons, / A natural
perspective, that is and is not' (V.i.213–14) – is prefigured by Adriana's
'I see two husbands, or mine eyes deceive me' and the Duke's bewildered question, 'which is the natural man, / And which the spirit? Who
deciphers them?' (V.i.333, 335–6), when 'These two Antipholus', these
two so like, / And these two Dromios, one in semblance' (V.i.349–50)
stand together at last before them. And Doctor Pinch's decision to have
Antipholus of Ephesus 'bound and laid in some dark room' (IV.iv.95)
to exorcise the devil he believes has driven him insane is echoed in
Sir Toby's decision to have Malvolio 'in a dark room and bound'
(III.iv.133), where Feste, in the guise of 'Sir Topas the curate' (IV.ii.2),
undertakes by means of a mock exorcism to convince the steward
that he's possessed by Satan and thus 'make him mad indeed'
(III.iv.131).

Malvolio himself is a reincarnation of scapegoat figures victimized in
previous comedies, most notably Falstaff in *The Merry Wives of Windsor*
and Shylock, whose antipathy to music and revelry Malvolio shares:
'Let not the sound of shallow fopp'ry enter / My sober house', Shylock
warns Jessica, 'I have no mind of feasting forth tonight' (II.v.35–7).
(The venerable theatrical tradition of having the same actor play
Shylock and Malvolio in rep is a testament to the close kinship of the
characters.) Olivia's stony-faced steward also bears more than a passing
resemblance to two other notorious killjoys: the malcontent Don John
in *Much Ado* and the morose Jaques, who prefers the pious company of

'convertites' to the 'dancing measures' (V.iv.182, 191) with which *As You Like It* concludes. There's a touch of *The Taming of the Shrew*, too, in the way Malvolio is conned into indulging his fantasy of social eleva-tion through marriage to his mistress, Olivia, which recalls Sly the tin-ker's fleeting delusion that he is a noble lord and the page by his side a beautiful gentlewoman and his doting wife. The action replay of Sly's apotheosis, *mutatis mutandis*, in Bottom's brief sojourn as the asinine consort of the fairy queen, which is also the upshot of a cruel practical joke, shows just how hard-wired into Shakespeare's imagination this comedic motif was. Petruchio's brainwashing of Kate into calling the sun the moon and vice versa at his whim, and at the risk of proving her-self mad, finds its counterpart in *Twelfth Night* as well, when Feste insists that Malvolio prove his sanity by admitting that the pitch-dark house in which he's locked is flooded with light. Nor need one look far to find precedents for the eavesdropping scene in the garden, where Malvolio is gulled by a counterfeit *billet-doux* into believing that Olivia adores him: the scene in the King's park in *Love's Labour's Lost*, when three of the four lords are overheard proclaiming their secret love in verse, springs at once to mind, as does the prank played on Benedick and Beatrice in Leonato's orchard, when they are hoodwinked into overhearing conversations contrived to persuade them of their mutual infatuation.

As for the architects of Malvolio's undoing, the figure who bulks largest among them, Sir Toby Belch, has long been pegged as a clone of plump Jack Falstaff, who would undoubtedly applaud Sir Toby's sat-urnalian creed, 'I am sure care's an enemy to life' (I.iii.2), and his con-tempt for the dictates of the clock: 'Not to be abed after midnight is to be up betimes' (II.iii.1–2). A shameless sponger, tosspot and braggart, just like his peerless prototype in *The Merry Wives of Windsor* and the *Henry IV* plays, Olivia's uncle also winds up, just like Falstaff, getting the worst of it instead of getting his own sweet way. Sir Toby's emaci-ated sidekick and witless stooge, Sir Andrew Aguecheek, whose dream of wooing Olivia is doomed from the start, is an obvious avatar of the hapless nincompoop Slender, whose courtship of Anne Page founders on his own ineptitude in the first scene of *Merry Wives*. And a suitor of a different persuasion, whose love is fated to remain as unrequited as Sir Andrew's, relinquishes his starring role in *The Merchant of Venice* as Bassanio's ardent friend for a bit part in *Twelfth Night* as Sebastian's devoted companion, leaving his name, Antonio, unchanged to under-score the emotional affinity of the two characters. Even without that clue, so conspicuously planted by Shakespeare, it wouldn't be hard to see the similarities between the binds in which they find themselves as men prepared to put their money and their lives at risk for the sake of a man they love.

Far more striking, however, is the correspondence between Viola's romantic predicament and that of Julia in *The Two Gentlemen of Verona*, who also masquerades as a boy and serves the man she loves by wooing the woman he loves on his behalf. Julia, moreover, adopts as her alias the name Sebastian, which seems, like the name Antonio, to have been subliminally linked in Shakespeare's mind with sexual ambiguity and homoerotic liaisons. In the guise of the page Sebastian, Julia speaks to her beloved Proteus of herself and her feelings for him – 'She dreams on him that has forgot her love; / You dote on her that cares not for your love' (IV.iv.79–80) – and in doing so anticipates Viola's oblique disclosures of her feelings for Orsino and her musings on the impasse at which love has left her. Wooing by proxy while identities are concealed also features prominently, of course, in *Love's Labour's Lost* in the masque of the Muscovites, in Don Pedro's courting of Hero for Claudio in *Much Ado*, and in *As You Like It*, when Rosalind dupes Orlando into wooing her unwittingly in the shape of Ganymede.

It's the sustained exploitation of cross-dressing, however, that links *Twelfth Night* most intimately with the latter play. Shakespeare had already employed the device briefly in *The Taming of the Shrew* (to supply Sly with a wife) and in *The Merry Wives of Windsor* (to trick Falstaff out as 'Mother Pratt'), and for more protracted purposes in *Two Gentlemen*, where Julia morphs into Sebastian, and *The Merchant of Venice*, where Portia, Nerissa and Jessica resort to masculine attire to conceal their gender and divest themselves of its constraints. But in *As You Like It* and *Twelfth Night* the pretext of protective male disguise is soon rendered redundant and sexual impersonation becomes a structural device integral to the vision of the play. *Twelfth Night* emulates *As You Like It* in its multiplication of the ironies and misunderstandings the device entails. Both plays revel in the cross-purposes and cross-talk that cross-dressing engenders, not least when it allows them to make matters more bewildering by having one young woman smitten with another in the belief that she's a beautiful youth. Olivia's bewitchment by Viola in the shape of Cesario is a transparent reworking of Phoebe's crush on Rosalind as Ganymede, with the added complication of an identical male twin to give the gender-bending double-bind an extra twist. It would be nearly a decade before Shakespeare resurrected the cross-dressed heroine just once more in *Cymbeline*, at the close of his theatrical career. But Innogen's adoption of men's apparel over halfway through that play is a purely practical ploy, whose androgynous implications and homoerotic potential Shakespeare was not inclined to develop. *Twelfth Night* is the swansong of Shakespeare's fascination with sexual disguise as the focal conceit of a comedy, employed to play havoc with hidebound conceptions of identity and desire.

'the melancholy god'

As a comedy quarried so intensively from its author's previous comedies, the play also begs to be seen more broadly as the swansong of a whole genre, which Shakespeare had adopted and transfigured, but which he clearly knew he was done with, at least in its current form. The feeling that *Twelfth Night* is an elegy for comedy itself is insistent and inseparable from the strange sadness that suffuses it. That sadness is partly engendered by the disposition and the discourse of the characters trapped in the romantic plot. The languid atmosphere of amorous reverie and exquisite yearning created by Orsino's opening speech defines the emotional climate of Illyria right at the outset:

> If music be the food of love, play on,
> Give me excess of it that, surfeiting,
> The appetite may sicken and so die.
> That strain again, it had a dying fall.
> O, it came o'er my ear like the sweet sound
> That breathes upon a bank of violets,
> Stealing and giving odour.
>
> (I.i.1–7)

Orsino's melancholy coupling of desire with disease and death proves contagious. Moments later we learn that the object of his doomed desire, Olivia, who 'purged the air of pestilence' (I.i.19) when he first saw her, is transfixed by inconsolable grief for the loss of 'A brother's dead love, which she would keep fresh / And lasting in her sad remembrance' (I.i.30–1). But her resolution to abjure 'the sight / And company of men' (I.ii.36–7) lasts no longer than it takes her to fall for Viola's adopted persona, Cesario: 'How now? / Even so quickly may one catch the plague?' (I.v.284–5). Vain pining for 'A brother's dead love' is immediately superseded by vain pining for the love of Viola, whose grief for the loss of her own brother, whom she believes to have drowned, has been eclipsed by her secret love for

Orsino, a love that seems as futile as Olivia's infatuation with the illusory Cesario:

How will this fadge? My master loves her dearly,
And I, poor monster, fond as much on him,
And she, mistaken, seems to dote on me.
(II.ii.33–5)

Viola's desperate state makes her as 'addicted to a melancholy' (II.v.196) as Maria perceives her mistress Olivia to be and as Feste perceives Orsino to be: 'Now the melancholy god protect thee' (II.iv.72), says the fool to the Count, after feeding the latter's addiction with a plangent dirge lamenting love denied. Shortly before this, when Orsino bemoans the transience of female beauty, and ruefully observes that 'women are as roses, whose fair flower / Being once displayed, doth fall that very hour', Viola concurs, echoing Orsino's bleak conflation of sexual maturity and mortality: 'And so they are. Alas that they are so: / To die even when they to perfection grow' (II.iv.37–40). When Orsino insists that 'There is no woman's sides / Can bide the beating of so strong a passion / As love doth give my heart' (II.iv.92–4), he provokes the disguised Viola to refute him with a riddle, which transfers her own repressed love for Orsino to the fictitious sister of Cesario:

She never told her love,
But let concealment, like a worm i'th'bud,
Feed on her damask cheek. She pined in thought,
And with a green and yellow melancholy
She sat like patience on a monument,
Smiling at grief. Was not this love indeed?
(II.iv.110–15)

But nowhere is the *tristesse* that *Twelfth Night* exudes more sharply focused than in the haunting songs of Feste, whose lyrical impact is rendered more elusive by fusing meaning with melody. 'Then come kiss me, sweet and twenty. / Youth's a stuff will not endure' (II.iii. 50–1): from his first song in the play to his last, with its doleful refrain 'For the rain it raineth every day' (V.i.388), Feste keeps calling to mind the shadows cast by decline and death on the fleeting delights of love and life. Indeed, in the song Orsino bids him sing in Act II, death itself is sought and embraced as fervently as the forlorn lover had pursued his beloved, becoming the object rather than the enemy of desire:

> Come away, come away death,
>   And in sad cypress let me be laid.
> Fie away, fie away breath,
>   I am slain by a fair cruel maid.
>   (II.iv.50–3)

So sweet does the prospect of the 'shroud of white' in the 'black coffin' seem (II.iv.54, 59) that it's hard not to believe that the longing for the 'fair cruel maid' harboured a longing to be slain and a hunger for oblivion all along.

Diverse manifestations of melancholy are to be found in the comedies Shakespeare wrote before *Twelfth Night*. The opening scene of *The Merchant of Venice* revolves round the unsolved enigma of Antonio's sadness, which appears to be motivated neither by an affair of the heart nor by the fear of financial disaster. On her first appearance in the same play, Portia professes herself to be in thrall to a similar mood, a nebulous ennui, which Nerissa is quick to diagnose quite plausibly as a disease endemic to the wealthy, the luxury of those who have too much (I.ii.1–9). In *As You Like It*, the state of mind that afflicts Antonio and Portia is personified by 'the melancholy Jaques' (II.i.41) and debunked as a self-indulgent affectation by both Touchstone, who wickedly parodies its morbidity ('And so from hour to hour we ripe and ripe, / And then from hour to hour we rot and rot' (II.vii.26–7)), and by Rosalind, who gives its epitome equally short shrift when they meet: 'I had rather have a fool to make me merry than experience to make me sad' (IV.i.25–7). Undeterred by such gibes, 'good Monsieur Melancholy' (III.ii.287–8) has the penultimate if not the last word of the play proper, when he rejects dancing and nuptial revelry for a reclusive life of religious contemplation. His vision of the seven ages of man as a cheerless chronicle of inexorable decrepitude (II.vii.139–66) resonates strongly with the glum view of the male life-cycle offered by Feste's final song at the end of *Twelfth Night*.

It's perhaps in *Love's Labour's Lost*, though, that the closest parallels with the distinctive mood of *Twelfth Night* are to be sought. A direct precursor of Viola's imaginary sister, who 'never told her love' and 'pined in thought', succumbing to 'a green and yellow melancholy', may be discerned in the fate of Katherine's real sister, who fell victim, as she recalls, to Cupid: 'He made her melancholy, sad, and heavy, / And so she died' (V.ii.14–15). Death proceeds to disrupt the festive finale of the whole play too, when sudden news of her father's death causes the Princess and her ladies to depart and their wooing by the lords to be left in limbo for twelve months and a day. 'The scene begins to cloud' (V.ii.714), as Berowne observes, and it remains overcast till the very end, when the cuckoo's song of spring evokes the fear of cuckoldry that blights marriage, and the owl's song of winter evokes the bitter cold that cramps domestic life 'When icicles hang by the wall' (V.ii.897). The discordant note on which the comedy closes is amplified by the terse, enigmatic speech that follows the songs: 'The words of Mercury are harsh', says Armado, 'after the songs of Apollo. You that way, we this way' (V.ii.913–4).

In *Twelfth Night* the spectre of death haunts the romantic protagonists' lives and loves from the start, and the scene begins to cloud toward the end from the moment the hoaxing of Malvolio turns into mental torment. It grows darker still when physical violence erupts into the play and the hitherto slap-happy sidekicks Sir Toby and Sir Andrew both stagger on with 'a bloody coxcomb' (V.i.173) inflicted by Sebastian, calling for 'Dick Surgeon' (V.i.195), who is too drunk himself to see to them. As in *Love's Labour's Lost*, the resolution of the comedy is deferred, not for twelve months and a day but until some indeterminate point beyond the time-frame of *Twelfth Night*, when Viola's 'maiden weeds' (V.i.253) have been recovered and her female identity restored. Until then, she must remain Cesario and a man, barred from both the fraternal embrace of her rediscovered twin and the nuptial embrace of Orsino by her 'masculine usurped attire' (V.i.248).

The suspended resolution in reunion and wedlock is rendered even more precarious by the fact that Viola has left her own clothes in the keeping of the captain who rescued her after the shipwreck, and that the latter 'Is now in durance, at Malvolio's suit' (V.i.274). This places the means of releasing the heroine from her plight in the hands of the outraged steward, who has indeed been, as Olivia concedes, 'most notoriously abused' (V.i.375), and who exits swearing 'I'll be revenged on the whole pack of you' (V.i.374). No wonder Orsino urges someone to 'Pursue him, and entreat him to a peace', because 'He hath not told us of the captain yet' (V.i.376–7). For, as he stipulates in the final speech of the play, the 'solemn combination' (V.i.379) of his soul with Viola's, which will make her 'Orsino's mistress, and his fancy's queen' (V.i.384) at last, can take place only when she is seen 'in other habits' (V.i.383) and ceases to be Cesario.

Like *Love's Labour's Lost*, *Twelfth Night* leaves the desired denouement of the comedy undramatized, stranding it forever in the twilight zone of the imagination. And like *Love's Labour's Lost*, it ends the play with an enigmatic song, whose relationship to the scene it follows is oblique, but whose effect is to juxtapose the 'golden time' (V.i.378) of nuptial celebration Orsino anticipates with the disillusioned realism of a rake's progress from boyhood innocence to adult transgression, marital misery and boozy dissipation. Viewed from Feste's final perspective, that of human lives perpetually battered by 'the wind and the rain' (V.i.386) since the beginning of the world, the 'golden time' we are left to imagine appears even more intangible.

Yet in order to understand fully the profound sadness that pervades *Twelfth Night*, it's patently not enough to point to the characters in the comedy who exude or cultivate melancholia, or to trace the melancholy motif back through comparable characters and scenes in Shakespeare's earlier comedies. For the whole play is possessed by a mysterious, impalpable *Weltschmerz* which is all its own, and which its languishing lovers alone can't account for. As John Middleton Murry observes:

> *Twelfth Night* is, to my sense, the most perfect example of the way in which Shakespeare could make his mood override his fable. Than the actual story of *Twelfth Night*, what could be happier? There are no disturbing villainies as there are in *Much Ado* and even in *As You Like It*. The plot is as innocent as that of the *Dream*. Yet the thing is sad: sad, partly with the weight of its own beauty, but sad also with a wistfulness to which Shakespeare could not help giving direct expression.

Murry finds most of that wistfulness invested in Feste and his singing, and to the fool and his last song in particular we shall return. But to get closer to grasping the deeper source and the significance of the elusive mood that permeates *Twelfth Night*, we need first to take the measure of the fable it overrides.

Or

Before the play even begins, its title has tipped us off about the sort of comedy this will be, about the emotional climate it will create, and about the attitude it will strike and invite us to share. *Twelfth Night, or What You Will* is unique among Shakespeare's plays in supplying both a title and an alternative title, which suggests a good deal in itself about the frame of mind the comedy was written in. *Twelfth Night* alludes to the Feast of the Epiphany on 6 January, the twelfth and final day of the Christmas celebrations. By giving the play this title Shakespeare plainly intended to evoke what Twelfth Night signified in Elizabethan England: a brief, licensed period of festive release and frivolity on the last evening of the holiday season, after which the routine burdens of the workaday world had to be shouldered once again.

As we soon discover, however, the events of the play don't actually take place on Twelfth Night, to which no specific reference is made (although Sir Toby does cite an unidentified song, 'O' the twelfth day of December' (II.iii.81)). Indeed, such clues as the text provides to the seasonal setting of the comedy point not to mid-winter but to spring or summer, which is when many productions have therefore felt free to set it. At the end of the first scene, for example, Orsino dismisses his entourage with the couplet: 'Away before me to sweet beds of flowers. / Love-thoughts lie rich when canopied with bowers' (I.i.39–40). Nor is the action confined to any one night, or any one day for that matter. At the beginning of Act I, Scene iv, we learn that three days have elapsed since Viola arrived at Orsino's court, and in the final scene both Antonio and Orsino speak of three months having passed since Viola and Sebastian were shipwrecked on the shores of Illyria, despite the fact that the intervening sequence of scenes seems to span only two consecutive days. Samuel Pepys was predictably irked by *Twelfth Night*'s failure to take place on Twelfth Night, the date on which he saw it performed in 1662, observing in his diary that it was 'but a silly play, and not relating at all to the name or day'. But the literal-minded Pepys missed the whole point of this blatant disjunction between the title and the play, which is that the title should be taken figuratively.

It should be taken, in other words, as Shakespeare's appropriation of the same licence to flout convention as Twelfth Night enjoys. In this comedy, the title implies, we can expect the same topsy-turvy travesty of what passes for normality to prevail, but only for as long as the comedy lasts; once the privileged interlude of performance is over, actors and audience alike must return to coping with the constraints of everyday life on the terms of the world as they find it. In this respect the title of *Twelfth Night* resembles the titles of earlier comedies such as *A Midsummer Night's Dream* and *Much Ado About Nothing*, which implicitly claim a similar provisional licence on the grounds that nothing that transpires in them need be taken seriously. Indeed, Shakespeare has Olivia exclaim at one point, 'Why, this is very midsummer madness'

(III.iv.54). But, unlike those titles, *Twelfth Night*'s title equates the comedy overtly with carnival as an institutionalized interval of transgressive revelry, and it announces, moreover, what will turn out to be the case: that with this play the carnival is truly over, because this is the last festive comedy Shakespeare will write.

There's a distinct air of disenchantment about *Twelfth Night*'s alternative title too. If calling this comedy *Twelfth Night* locates it in the same licensed zone, and solicits the same latitude, as *A Midsummer Night's Dream* and *Much Ado About Nothing*, calling it *What You Will* as well directly echoes the synonymous title of *As You Like It* and activates the same complex connotations. Like the latter title, *What You Will* addresses and involves the audience on the threshold of their encounter with the play, underlining the dramatist's easy, playful intimacy with his public. The intrinsic ambiguity of the phrase allows Shakespeare once again to tease his audience by promising to give them what they want – the kind of comedy he knows they like – while intimating that the play's satisfactions may not be quite so predictable, and that they must make of it what they will. Read one way, *Twelfth Night*'s surrogate title delivers a wry dig at the commercial taste to which Shakespeare is obliged to pander; read another way, it empowers the very punters whose predilection it guys by submitting the play to their interpretation and leaving its import up to them.

Unlike *As You Like It*, however, *What You Will* plays second fiddle to the primary title of the comedy it fronts, which gives the phrase a quite different impact when its role as an alternative name for the play is restored. The full, compound title of the comedy – *Twelfth Night, or What You Will* – captures the spirit of whimsical detachment tinged with lassitude in which it seems to have been written. If you don't care for the title *Twelfth Night*, Shakespeare assures us, you can call it whatever you like, as the title of the play, and by implication the play it describes, is a matter of no more consequence than the transient misrule of Twelfth Night itself. The off-hand disclaimer is disingenuous, of course, a transparent rhetorical feint designed to make us suspect that the comedy is anything but the mere bagatelle it claims to be. But the attitude of laid-back levity struck by the title can't disguise the genuine note of resigned indifference it sounds. The same note is sounded by Feste in the penultimate line of the song he sings at the very end of *Twelfth Night*: 'But that's all one, our play is done' (V.i.403).

Although the main meaning of the word 'will' in the play's title is 'wish' or 'want', in Elizabethan usage it could also signify irrational desire, unbridled passion, as Shakespeare's persistent puns on the word in his sonnets to the Dark Lady testify. This sense lurks in '*or What You Will*' too, adumbrating the play's concern with characters seized by a blind infatuation or consuming emotion. In this respect, the alternative title reinforces the carnivalesque connotations of '*Twelfth Night*': it primes us to expect violations of sexual propriety unleashed by the drive to be and to act *otherwise* than the present dispensation dictates, by the tidal pull of alterity concealed in that crucial conjunction '*or*'. And violations of propriety, not only in the domain of sexuality and desire, but also in the realms of social, cultural and discursive convention, are exactly what the play delivers.

The World Upside Down

The hub of festive mayhem in its staple manifestations is Olivia's household, or rather those backstairs regions of it where the feckless booze-hound Sir Toby Belch, the comedy's resident Lord of Misrule, presides over a permanent, unofficial Feast of Fools. Late is redefined as early, turning night into day; guzzling, dancing and singing are the impulsive rule, not the scheduled exception; scenes of mock wooing and a mock sword-fight are staged, making matters of serious consequence occasions of hilarity; the unpopular figure of authority within the household, the voice of discipline and prudence, is stripped of his dignity and made a laughing-stock; and the full-time fool of the house undertakes a mock exorcism in the garb of a priest, debunking clerical pomposity and mumbo-jumbo by mimicry, just like the Bishop of Fools, who travestied the solemn ceremonies of the medieval church.

The keynote of the anarchic ethos cultivated by Sir Toby and his kitchen cronies is struck at our first encounter with him in the third scene of *Twelfth Night*. Toby enters complaining of his niece Olivia's refusal to cease mourning for her brother on the grounds that 'care's an enemy to life' (I.iii.2), whose hedonistic delights should take priority over piety. In pursuit of those delights, we learn from Maria's response, Toby has been keeping 'ill hours' (I.iii.5), spending his nights on the tiles and incurring his niece's wrath in the process. But he remains unrepentant: 'you must confine yourself within the modest limits of order', Maria warns him, only to be answered: 'Confine? I'll confine myself no finer than I am' (I.iii.7–9). Restraint is not a word in Sir Toby's vocabulary, and Maria's prudent admonition, 'That quaffing and drinking will undo you' (I.iii.13), falls on deaf ears, as does her reproof of him for latching onto Sir Andrew Aguecheek, 'a very fool, and a prodigal' (I.iii.22), and conning him into wooing Olivia in order to con him out of his 'three thousand ducats a year' (I.iii.20).

Aguecheek's idiocy and profligacy go hand in hand with the love of the bottle he shares with Belch, in whose company 'he's drunk nightly' (I.iii.34). Notwithstanding his cadaverous physique, which makes him the perfect comic butt for the corpulent Sir Toby, Aguecheek also professes to be a trencherman like the latter, putting his trouncing in repartee by Maria down to his being 'a great eater of beef' (I.iii.83) and consequently beef-witted. His witlessness is amply demonstrated by his bafflement in the face of the word 'accost', which he takes to be Maria's surname (I.iii.46–56), and the word 'Pourquoi', which gives the lie to Toby's earlier claim that he 'speaks three or four languages word for word without book' (I.iii.24–5). 'I would I had bestowed that time in the tongues that I have in fencing, dancing, and bear-baiting' (I.iii.89–91), laments Sir Andrew. But in confessing his predilection for such idle amusements and his 'delight in masques and revels' (I.iii.109–10), he naturally proves himself ideally qualified for a cameo role in Sir Toby's domestic carnival. In Belch's arsy-versy universe a taste for trivialities or 'kickshawses' (I.iii.111) is a cardinal virtue, and he resolves 'to set about some revels' (I.iii.130–1) in earnest with Aguecheek, whom he cajoles into dancing his way off stage: 'let me see thee caper. Ha, higher! Ha ha, excellent' (I.iii.135–6).

With effortless economy Shakespeare compresses into this brief, incidental scene most of the ingredients of the unbridled buffoonery that animates the subplot of *Twelfth Night*. Apart from the capering, masquerading, music and song that are as *de rigueur* for revellers as overindulgence in food and drink, these include hoaxing and hoodwinking, milking language for laughs, and losing no opportunity to let the sex-drive surface in a double entendre: Sir Andrew's hair, Toby assures him, 'hangs like flax on a distaff, and I hope to see a housewife take thee between her legs and spin it off' (I.iii.98–100). As their very surnames, Aguecheek and Belch – 'A plague o' these pickle herring!' (I.v.116–17) – attest, the body calls the shots while the holiday humour prevails, giving free rein to urges and appetites that are usually curbed, letting gratification ride roughshod over obligation. In this inverted world, where what you will, not what you should, is the motto, the repressed returns to take revenge on the forces of repression, playing fast and loose with the principles and protocols of civil society. Normal values are reversed: recklessness is prized over sobriety; sense surrenders to nonsense; folly becomes wisdom and wisdom becomes folly; materialism trumps morality; and *carpe diem* rather than *contemptus mundi* is the only creed that counts.

As a result of this riot of reversals, the arbitrariness and fragility of the status quo stand revealed: a whole way of life, which might otherwise have seemed permanently entrenched, is exposed as anything but by the alacrity with which it can be abandoned overnight for its antithesis. Not the least virtue of turning the world upside down for a while – and the risk those who rule run by permitting it – is that it serves as a powerful reminder of how close to collapse the facade of normality is at any given moment.

Rousing the Night Owl and Tickling the Trout

Nothing in the play illustrates the frailty of repression's grip on the pleasure principle more vividly than the speed with which Malvolio unknowingly succumbs to the sway of frivolity and self-indulgence. Being by disposition 'cold, austere, repelling; but dignified, consistent', as Charles Lamb observes, Malvolio's 'morality and his manners are misplaced in Illyria. He is opposed to the proper *levities* of the piece, and falls in the unequal contest.'

The would-be nemesis of 'Sir Toby and the lighter people' (V.i.336) is doomed to be undone from the moment he clamps down on their 'uncivil rule' (II.iii.119) in the second act. When Feste, the explicit embodiment of festive licence, joins the dissolute double-act of Belch and Aguecheek and turns it into a trio of fools – 'How now, my hearts. Did you never see the picture of "we three"?' (II.iii.15–16) – the revelry soon reaches its cacophonous climax. Feste has already shown himself in Act I to be a kindred spirit of Sir Toby's and the natural antagonist of Malvolio, whose name ('ill will', 'malevolence') speaks, likewise, for itself. His first skirmish of wit with his mistress is designed to commend to her the same *carpe diem* philosophy advocated by her uncle and put an end to her relentless grieving. 'Those wits that think they have thee do very oft prove fools,' he begins, 'and I that am sure I lack thee may pass for a wise man. For what says Quinapalus? – "Better a witty fool than a foolish wit"' (I.v.30–3). Having established the paradoxical premise of the wisdom of folly, which Touchstone espoused so effectively in *As You Like It*, Feste proceeds to practise what he preaches by proving Olivia to be a fool for forgetting that 'beauty's a flower' (I.v.48) and wasting her life mourning for a brother she knows to be in heaven. 'I wear not motley in my brain' (I.v.52–3), declares the fool, but Malvolio, irked that her ladyship 'takes delight in such a barren rascal' derides him for having been 'put down the other day with an ordinary fool that has no more brain than a stone' (I.v.79–81). The gibe hits home, and the seeds of Feste's revenge on Olivia's frigid, dour retainer are sown.

As Olivia shrewdly perceives, her steward is displaying in his contempt for Feste all the symptoms of chronic egotism, which is the polar opposite of the permissive, tolerant, light-hearted outlook fostered by festivity: 'O, you are sick of self-love, Malvolio, and taste with a distempered appetite. To be generous, guiltless, and of free disposition is to take those things for birdbolts that you deem cannon bullets. There is no slander in an allowed fool' (I.v.86–90). The authoritarian egotist locks horns with the festive foe in the third scene of the following act. Toby, Sir Andrew and Feste kick off what used to be called 'the kitchen scene' in a relatively low key, with an idiotic exchange of gibberish between Aguecheek and the fool:

SIR ANDREW. [. . .] In sooth, thou wast in very gracious fooling last night, when thou spokest of Pigrogromitus, of the Vapians passing the equinoctial of Queubus. 'Twas very good, i'faith. I sent thee sixpence for thy leman. Hadst it?

FESTE. I did impeticos thy gratility; for Malvolio's nose is no whipstock. My lady has a white hand, and the Myrmidons are no bottle-ale houses.

(II.iii.20–7)

'Excellent!' cries Sir Toby, delighted by Feste's transmutation of recondite pedantry into inspired absurdity, 'Why this is the best fooling, when all is done. Now a song' (II.iii.28–9). Having been freed from functionality by nonsense, language is at liberty to fuse with music in song to create an interlude that puts life on hold for as long as the song lasts. The love-song Feste sings is a poignant one, which expands on his earlier advice to Olivia, now utterly besotted with Viola, to gather rose-buds while she may:

What is love? 'Tis not hereafter,
Present mirth hath present laughter.
    What's to come is still unsure.
In delay there lies no plenty,

Then come kiss me, sweet and twenty.
Youth's a stuff will not endure.
(II.iii.46–51)

But no sooner has Feste's 'mellifluous voice' (II.iii.52) died away than
Toby resolves that they will 'make the welkin dance indeed' and 'rouse
the night-owl in a catch that will draw three souls out of one weaver'
(II.iii.56–8). The racket that erupts brings Maria running in to scold
them for their 'caterwauling' (II.iii.69), and moments later Malvolio
materializes to terminate the revelry.

The steward's outraged rebuke pinpoints the defining features of
festive misrule and defines him as diametrically opposed to it in every
respect:

> My masters, are you mad? Or what are you? Have you no wit, man-
> ners, nor honesty, but to gabble like tinkers at this time of night? Do
> ye make an alehouse of my lady's house, that ye squeak out your
> coziers' catches without any mitigation or remorse of voice? Is there
> no respect of place, persons, nor time in you?
>
> (II.iii.83–9)

The raucous conduct of the tipsy triumvirate violates the fundamental
principles on which the decorum of everyday social life depends: the
manor house of a noble lady is transformed into an alehouse; her uncle
and Sir Andrew, both knights of the realm, stand hierarchy on its head
by acting like common tinkers and cobblers; the still of the night
becomes the time for uproar instead of peaceful sleep; and rational,
responsible behaviour gives way to bedlam.

Toby and Feste remain defiant in the face of Malvolio's indignation,
singing snatches of a ballad adapted to needle him further. Then Toby
suddenly rounds on Malvolio, reasserting his rank to put the latter in
his place and reinforcing their hostility to everything he stands for: 'Art
any more than a steward? Dost thou think because thou art virtuous
there shall be no more cakes and ale?' (II.iii.109–11). There's clearly
more at stake in the antagonism towards Malvolio than the natural
antipathy festive indulgence feels for pious abstinence. When Maria
remarks of the steward after he storms off, 'sometimes he is a kind
of puritan' (II.iii.135), she aligns him with the enemies not only of
holiday jollity, but also of the theatre, which paid-up, card-carrying
puritans reviled as a sink of sexual iniquity, indolence and paganism.
Shakespeare is careful to have Maria stress that Malvolio's puritanism

is merely an opportunistic pose: 'The dev'l a puritan that he is, or anything constantly but a time-pleaser' (II.iii.141–2). But the qualification
arrives too late to stop us drawing the obvious inference from the allusion. In the confrontation between the rowdy carousers and the 'affec-
tioned ass', whose 'grounds of faith' are 'that all that look on him love
him' (II.iii.142, 145–6), Shakespeare is staging the conflict between
the untrammelled dramatic imagination epitomized by *Twelfth Night*
and the forces of oppressive rectitude that were to close the theatres at
the start of the Civil War in 1642. The 'revenge' (II.iii.147) that the
adepts of 'uncivil rule' resolve to take on Malvolio by making him 'a
common recreation' (II.iii.131) acquires much wider resonance in this
light, as does Malvolio's infamous exit line at the end of the comedy:
'I'll be revenged on the whole pack of you' (V.i.374) – a line destined
to prove more chillingly prophetic than Shakespeare could ever have
imagined.

What better way to make the po-faced foe of roistering 'a common
recreation' than to exploit his infatuation with himself and fulfil his
secret wish to violate decorum too? Maria's ingenious ruse inflicts
poetic justice on Malvolio by inveigling him into acting the fool, taking
liberties, and displaying 'no respect of place, persons, nor time' in his
speech, his dress or his behaviour. The domestic despot unwittingly
transforms himself 'in the name of jesting' into 'a contemplative idiot'
(II.v.18–19). Scarcely has Maria baited the trap with the forged love-
letter, when 'the trout that must be caught with tickling' (II.v.20–1)
turns up on cue to reveal his fantasy of leaping the class barrier between
himself and his mistress – 'To be Count Malvolio!' (II.v.33) – and taming the titled delinquent Sir Toby with his 'austere regard of control'
(II.v. 65). As he takes up and scans the letter, Malvolio aggravates the
affront to his social superiors by unconsciously cracking an obscene
joke at Olivia's expense: 'By my life, this is my lady's hand. These be her
very c's, her u's, and her t's, and thus makes she her great P's'
(II.v.84–6). Not even the high-born mistress of the manor is spared the
degradation of the dignified, in which Malvolio colludes by spelling out
the slang for vagina and evoking an image of the Countess Olivia pissing copiously from her 'cut'.

The rhyming 'fustian riddle' (II.v.107) that begins the letter is posed
in the ludic spirit of traditional festive pastimes, but with the further
twist that its cryptic final line – 'M.O.A.I. doth sway my life' (II.
v.106) – contains a booby trap for its egocentric interpreter: 'And the
end', Malvolio muses, 'what should that alphabetical position portend?
If I could make that resemble something in me' (II.v.116–18).

In a trice he does just that, confirming Olivia's and Maria's diagnosis of his narcissism, and he resolves to comply with the letter's plea that henceforth he be 'strange, stout, in yellow stockings, and cross-gartered' (II.v.165–6) and exchange his censorious frown for a perpetual smile. What Maria calls 'the fruits of the sport' (II.v.191) are gathered four scenes later when Malvolio fulfils Maria's prediction at the end of Act II:

> He will come to her in yellow stockings, and 'tis a colour she abhors, and cross-gartered, a fashion she detests; and he will smile upon her, which will now be so unsuitable to her disposition, being addicted to a melancholy as she is, that it cannot but turn him into a notable contempt.
>
> (II.v.192–7)

Kissing his hand compulsively and grinning inanely at the dumbfounded Olivia, blissfully unaware that his 'very strange manner' makes him appear 'possessed' and 'tainted in's wits' (III.iv.8, 9, 13), Malvolio has been transmogrified into a Twelfth Night travesty of himself, an unconscious accomplice of the 'uncivil rule' he had denounced so vehemently in Sir Toby, Sir Andrew and Feste; nor will his part in the covert revelry be over until he has played out the role of festive scapegoat in the following act and been baited like an inmate of Bedlam by the fool, who dons the gown and false beard of a man of the cloth to exact revenge for his humiliation before Olivia in Act I.

'midsummer madness'

Although the subplot of *Twelfth Night* furnishes the play's most flagrant instances of the liberties, japes and clowning sanctioned by holiday convention, the principal characters of the main plot prove no more immune to 'midsummer madness'(III.iv.54) than Malvolio. The cross-dressed heroine, Viola, and the motley-clad jester, Feste, a dab hand at disguise himself, commute between the households of Orsino and Olivia, transporting the infectious spirit of inversion and release from one to the other and fusing the two plots together. Both Orsino and Olivia are as vulnerable to the virus of carnival as Malvolio, because they are just as pathologically self-absorbed as he is, and thus ripe for emancipation from the egotism that negates the ethos of the festive community. Olivia's decision to veil her face and sequester herself 'like a

cloistress' (I.i.27) for seven years to mourn her brother is the sterile
counterpart of Orsino's fixation on supplanting her brother as the
object of her exclusive devotion:

> O, she that hath a heart of that fine frame
> To pay this debt of love but to a brother,
> How will she love when the rich golden shaft
> Hath killed the flock of all affections else
> That live in her – when liver, brain, and heart,
> These sovereign thrones, are all supplied, and filled
> Her sweet perfections with one self king!
>
> (I.i.32–8)

The phrase 'one self king' encapsulates not only the egocentric posture that is anathema to communal revelry, but also the deeper delusion
that underpins that posture: the belief in the singularity of the self
and the indivisibility of identity. By the end of the comedy Orsino and
Olivia have been disabused of this belief. Orsino finds himself confronted with 'One face, one voice, one habit, and two persons' (V.i.213),
one of whom he pledges to make 'Orsino's mistress, and his fancy's
queen' (V.i.384) despite his masculine attire and name, which Orsino
insists on using right to the end. Olivia is forced to realize that in marrying the double of the man she took Cesario to be she has, to say the
very least, 'been mistook' and has wound up in effect 'betrothed both
to a maid and man' (V.i.257, 261), emotionally if not physically wedded to two persons in one.

In the guise of Cesario, Viola's catalytic impact on Orsino at the start
of the play is immediate. Scarcely has our first encounter with Sir Toby
and Sir Andrew ended, when Orsino enters and commands Viola to 'Be
clamorous, and leap all civil bounds' (I.iv.21) in her wooing of Olivia,
as if the incipient 'uncivil rule' of the previous scene has seeped through
to contaminate his language. Before this brief scene is over, furthermore, Orsino has betrayed his subconscious sexual attraction to the
androgynous creature before him:

> For they shall yet belie thy happy years
> That say thou art a man. Diana's lip
> Is not more smooth and rubious; thy small pipe
> Is as the maiden's organ, shrill and sound,
> And all is semblative a woman's part.
>
> (I.iv.30–4)

With that, Orsino is inextricably entangled in a sexual charade that blurs gender boundaries beyond recognition and expands the antic assault on conformity spearheaded by Sir Toby's mutinous crew. 'I'll do my best / To woo your lady', Viola promises her master, but then confesses in an aside: 'yet a barful strife – / Whoe'er I woo, myself would be his wife' (I.iv.40–2).

Viola's aside is the cue for the entrance of Feste, whose first task is to provoke levity in the doleful Olivia by proving 'Dexteriously' (I.v.56), in cock-eyed mockery of the Christian catechism, that she, not he, is the fool. This preliminary bout of banter with Feste loosens Olivia up for the main event of the scene, the seductive badinage in which Viola obliges her to engage, despite Olivia's insisting, ''Tis not that time of moon with me to make one in so skipping a dialogue' (I.v.192–3). As a playful display of digressive wit and verbal virtuosity, the skipping dialogue that ensues pulls Olivia inexorably into the orbit of the holiday humour incarnate in her uncle. Within seconds of being left alone with Viola, she lifts her veil of mourning to invite the latter's admiration of her beauty. Their exchange adverts repeatedly to its theatricality: Viola describes the speech she has prepared as 'excellently well penned' and one that she has 'taken great pains to con' (I.v.166–7); Olivia asks, 'Are you a comedian?' and is told 'I am not that I play' (I.v.175, 177). The characters' self-conscious performance of their roles as proxy suitor and refractory coquette gives the audience a teasing glimpse of the male actors concealed by the female characters, reminding them that the entire play they are watching is a form of festive interlude, a brief, beguiling flight from the humdrum and habitual into make-believe and metamorphosis. In so doing, it gives the characters scope to disengage themselves from the stereotyped postures and predictable speech-patterns the situation requires them to adopt, placing every verbal move they make in audible quotation marks.

The effect of this is to open up a space between self and role, between character and speech, in which more mercurial modes of identity and desire can evolve and flourish. Behind the smokescreen of Cesario, Viola undertakes the surrogate heterosexual courtship of Olivia on behalf of Orsino, but in the process snares the heart of the countess, inadvertently creating a liaison whose lesbian overtones are as inescapable as the homosexual subtext of Cesario's love for 'his' master and the latter's budding love for a boy in whom 'all is semblative a woman's part'. The homoerotic charge of the scene between Olivia and Viola, to which the boy actors would have brought a further homoerotic dimension in Shakespeare's day, is redoubled in the next scene, which opens the second act. As Olivia exits, dazed by the sudden passion for Viola/Cesario that has seized her, Viola's identical twin brother enters with Antonio, who wastes no time making his fervent devotion to Sebastian transparent: 'If you will not murder me for my love, let me be your servant', he pleads, and when his plea is rejected and Sebastian departs, he resolves to pursue him incognito to Orsino's court, despite the risk he runs in doing so: 'But come what may, I do adore thee so / That danger shall seem sport, and I will go' (II.i.31–2, 42–3).

The advent of Sebastian at this juncture, just before the full extent of her dilemma dawns on Viola, assures the audience well in advance that the means of resolving that dilemma, and giving the comedy the benign denouement they expect, lie ready to hand. But it also widens the web of conflicting desires and identities the play is weaving. When Antonio asks him earlier in the scene where he's headed, Sebastian replies, 'My determinate voyage is mere extravagancy' (II.i.9–10). By this he means nothing more than 'I've decided to just wander about', but the Latinate way Shakespeare words the line lends it an ulterior import in the context of *Twelfth Night*. For 'extravagancy' in the sense of diverging from himself and deviating from the route relationships are supposed to follow is a fate Sebastian is destined to share with the other principal characters, whose voyage through the comedy is equally 'determinate' in this respect. As if to confirm this reading of the line, Sebastian comes clean to his companion two sentences later about his false identity, splitting himself in two: 'You must know of me then, Antonio, my name is Sebastian, which I called Roderigo' (II.i.13–15).

The compulsion to hide behind an alias and pose as someone else clearly runs in the family. Antonio's exit is the cue for Sebastian's spitting image to enter and grasp the implications of the ring Olivia has sent after her via Malvolio: 'She loves me, sure. The cunning of her passion / Invites me in this churlish messenger' (II.ii.22–3). In contempt of precedence, but in keeping with the festive obligation to stand hierarchy on its head, Olivia has fallen for the servant rather than the master: 'I am the man. If it be so – as 'tis – / Poor lady, she were better love a dream!' (II.ii.25–6). The audience alone has the comfort of knowing that, thanks to her sibling's survival and proximity, the erotic quandary that confronts Viola is not as hopeless as she thinks:

What will become of this? As I am man,
My state is desperate for my master's love.
As I am woman, now, alas the day,

What thriftless sighs shall poor Olivia breathe!
O time, thou must untangle this, not I.
It is too hard a knot for me t'untie.
(II.ii.36–41)

The trick *Twelfth Night* pulls off so adroitly is to untangle the knot in such a way as to keep in play all the permutations of desire it entails right to the end of the comedy. For what Viola, Orsino and Olivia experience as the torments of unrequited love, and the baffled anguish inflicted by sexual disguise, allows the audience to delight in a world where the illusion of the self's singularity has been dispelled, the customary definitions of masculine and feminine no longer apply, and hard and fast distinctions between the varieties of sexual desire have been dissolved.

Making a Good Voyage of Nothing

That world is brought still closer two scenes later, when Feste and Viola converge on Orsino. Feste links the latter's melancholy to mortality by following his song 'Come away death' with an ironic gibe at Orsino's governing humour:

Now the melancholy god protect thee, and the tailor make thy doublet of changeable taffeta, for thy mind is a very opal. I would have men of such constancy put to sea, that their business might be everything, and their intent everywhere, for that's it that always makes a good voyage of nothing.
(II.iv.72–7)

The thrust of Feste's dig is the same as that of the proverbial saying, 'He that is everywhere is nowhere': Orsino's moodiness annihilates him by causing the consistency on which selfhood depends to evaporate, leaving a void in place of the plenitude the melancholic secretly covets. But, like Sebastian's line 'My determinate voyage is mere extravagancy', with which it chimes, Feste's speech harbours another take on its intent. In this case, it's the invitation to draw the opposite inference to the one Orsino is meant to draw, and turn making a good voyage of nothing into the virtue the lustrous image of the opal suggests it might be. Like Sebastian's line, too, when taken this way, that final phrase of Feste's transcends its immediate occasion and taps into the deepest currents of the comedy. A protean intolerance of definition and finality, a restless refusal to be pinned down or to fix anyone or anything anywhere, is as much the hallmark of *Twelfth Night* as it is the mainspring of Orsino's disposition.

After Feste's departure Viola takes up where the fool left off. To defend her sex against Orsino's denigration of their capacity for love, she projects her true feelings for him into a fictitious version of her female self:

> My father had a daughter loved a man
> As it might be, perhaps, were I a woman
> I should your lordship.
>
> (II.iv.107–9)

The 'history' of that phantom daughter Viola describes as a 'blank', because that virtual self, the Viola she might become, 'let concealment, like a worm i'th' bud, / Feed on her damask cheek' and so wound up sitting 'like patience on a monument, / Smiling at grief' (II.iv.109–12, 114–15). But no sooner has Viola's imaginary sister been conjured up to house Cesario's secret self, and that self's potential fate, than she disappears into the discourse of a riddle – the only discourse capable of accommodating the sexual conundrum incarnate in the cross-dressed character of Viola: 'I am all the daughters of my father's house, / And all the brothers too; and yet I know not' (II.iv.120–1).

Viola's masquerade is the most sustained instance of sexual disguise in the whole of Shakespeare: she is unique amongst his transvestite heroines in assuming her masculine attire and persona right at the outset of the play and never appearing in feminine attire and *in propria persona* again. It's certainly arguable, as the last chapter sought to show, that Rosalind never sheds the garb of Ganymede after the recognition scene, and that she weds Orlando and delivers the epilogue still dressed as a young man, in order to protract the androgynous impact of the character. But Orlando and Rosalind first meet and fall in love *before* the latter dons doublet and hose, which makes the subsequent revelation of Ganymede's true identity on the threshold of their marriage reassuring rather than astounding; whereas Viola doesn't meet and fall – unilaterally, in her case – for Orsino until *after* she resurfaces as Cesario: from the beginning to the end of the play Orsino knows her, and physically perceives her, only as a boy, and at the very end, even after Cesario has revealed himself to be Sebastian's sister, and both Orsino and we learn *for the first time* that Cesario's real name is Viola (V.i.239), Orsino insists on maintaining the sexual charade: 'Cesario, come – / For so you shall be while you are a man' (V.i.382).

Orsino's wording is worth pausing over: he says 'while you *are* a man', not 'while you seem a man', or some other phrase to the same effect. Glancing equivocally at the gender of the actor who first played Viola/Cesario, the line suggests that something more than mere impersonation is involved in his future wife's disguise. That suspicion is confirmed by the remarkable exchange between Olivia and Viola in the first scene of Act III:

> OLIVIA. Stay. I prithee tell me what thou think'st of me.
> VIOLA. That you do think you are not what you are.
> OLIVIA. If I think so, I think the same of you.
> VIOLA Then think you right, I am not what I am.
>
> (III.i.136–9)

Once again, Shakespeare chooses not to use the expected verb 'seem', and this time in relation not only to the disguised Viola, but to Olivia as well. The implication is that distinctions between apparent and actual identity simply mask the complexity of the self, which is inherently divided to begin with. The undisguised Olivia is no more self-identical than the Viola veiled by her alter ego and her brother's double, Cesario. And what's true of Olivia is by extension true of the rest of the *dramatis personae*, who are all imposters inasmuch as they are all impersonating themselves. Viola's performance as Cesario is in this sense a metaphor for what all the characters in *Twelfth Night* are up to, whether they adopt a disguise or not: passing themselves off as whoever they are supposed to be by playing parts that don't coincide with them, and thus can't contain them completely. Orsino, Feste, Sebastian, Malvolio, Maria, Sir Andrew: any of them might say like Viola with equal justification: 'I am not what I am.'

'One face, one voice, one habit, and two persons'

It's through Viola, though, that Shakespeare dramatizes the full ramifications of the riddle of the self. The actor who plays Viola plays a woman who masquerades as an imaginary male version of herself, an unsexed youth – 'an eunuch' (I.ii.52) – called Cesario, who is a dead ringer for her identical twin, Sebastian. As a consequence, at any given moment the audience can never be sure if it's watching and hearing

Cesario or Viola, or a character compounded of both of them but reducible to neither, who defies sexual definition. The creation of such a character came readily, no doubt, to the creator of Rosalind and the poet who begins Sonnet 20 to a beautiful young man: 'A woman's face with nature's own hand painted / Hast thou, the master-mistress of my passion.' But *Twelfth Night* takes Shakespeare's fascination with androgyny to another level altogether by giving Viola a sibling of the opposite sex and making her his mirror-image:

> He named Sebastian. I my brother know
> Yet living in my glass. Even such and so
> In favour was my brother, and he went
> Still in this fashion, colour, ornament,
> For him I imitate.
>   (III.iv.371–5)

In *Riche his Farewell* the twins are not identical, which a male and a female twin, for obvious biological reasons, cannot be; so, in departing from his source in this regard, Shakespeare was deliberately raising the stakes, pushing the boundaries of the imaginable even further back than he had in *As You Like It*. It's one thing to have a female character like Rosalind or Viola cross-dressed as a male and stranded in a zone where gender fluctuates continuously and all kinds of erotic liaisons, both latent and overt, can be contemplated. But it's quite another to make that imaginary male self a consubstantial reality in the shape of a flesh-and-blood twin brother, who supplies a *physical* solution to the heroine's sexual dilemma. In *As You Like It*, Phoebe's desire for Rosalind in the guise of Ganymede is thwarted and displaced by marriage to her faithful swain Silvius; but the existence of Sebastian, who conceals his true name from Olivia until after their marriage is consummated, answering happily in the interim to 'Cesario', allows Olivia to be 'betrothed both to a maid and man' (V.i.261) – to possess in Sebastian both Cesario and the Viola within Cesario. By the same token, in making his erstwhile page his 'master's mistress' (V.i.323), but continuing to call her 'Boy' and 'Cesario', Orsino keeps the Cesario within Viola, 'his fancy's queen', alive.

In the final scene of his farewell to festive comedy, Shakespeare stages a secular theatrical epiphany, which gives us a glimpse of the impossible taking place before our eyes, and in so doing brings the utopian within the bounds of plausibility. Through the reunion of perfectly identical male and female twins, each believed by the other to be dead, a figment of the imagination is made flesh, in defiance of natural law and social convention: the dream of the self made whole again and of human desire, in all its diversity, liberated at last. This exquisite state is intensified by its suspension on the brink of fulfilment, which would spell the end of it as surely as the satiety Orsino craves in the play's opening speech would kill the 'spirit of love' (I.i.9) he apostrophizes, as Orsino is acutely aware. Not only must Viola's marital and physical union with her master, and her relinquishment of her surrogate male self, be deferred until she has retrieved her 'maid's garments' (V.i.273) from the captain incarcerated by Malvolio, but her full reunion with her beloved twin brother must also be postponed, at Viola's fastidious insistence, until her true identity has been placed beyond question:

> If nothing lets to make us happy both
> But this my masculine usurped attire,
> Do not embrace me till each circumstance
> Of place, time, fortune do cohere and jump
> That I am Viola [. . .]
>
> (V.i.247–51)

Because the delight of this anticipated moment is never enacted, it never materializes, but by the same token it can never decay. The prospective status of the plot's completion lends the ending an ethereal perfection impervious to time.

Shakespeare takes pains to highlight the miraculous quality of *Twelfth Night*'s deferred denouement. He makes no bones about the fact that the means by which the comedy's resolution has been accomplished beggar belief. When Orsino beholds Sebastian and the servant he calls Cesario together for the first time, he can only exclaim in amazement: 'One face, one voice, one habit, and two persons, / A natural perspective, that is and is not' (V.i.213–14). What he's perceiving, Orsino concludes, is an optical illusion spawned by nature, as opposed to one produced by a 'perspective' device or 'glass' (V.i.263) designed to dupe the eye. In saying that the phenomenon he beholds both 'is and is not', Orsino reinforces the effect of similar phrases already cited, which press beyond the comforting divide between reality and illusion to disclose a perplexing division at the core of being itself. Antonio is equally confounded by the fissiparous powers of his beloved Sebastian:

> How have you made division of yourself?
> An apple cleft in two is not more twin

Than these two creatures. Which is Sebastian?
(V.i.220–2)

But he's no more astounded than Sebastian himself, when he sees in
Cesario the living image of the sister 'Whom the blind waves and surges
have devoured' (V.i.227):

Do I stand there? I never had a brother,
Nor can there be that deity in my nature
Of here and everywhere.
(V.i.224–6)

So when the 'drownèd Viola' (V.i.239) voices her fear that this clone of
the brother buried in 'his watery tomb' (V.i.232) is a spirit posing as
him, Sebastian is inclined to agree, though he is quick to put an ortho-
dox gloss on his ghostly state: 'A spirit I am indeed, / But am in that
dimension grossly clad / Which from the womb I did participate'
(V.i.234–6).

The miracle of Sebastian's resurrection and restoration to his sister is
rendered all the more moving by the reflection that Shakespeare was
himself the father of girl and boy twins, Judith and Hamnet, and that
Hamnet had died in 1596, just five years before *Twelfth Night* was written. It's hard to believe that Shakespeare didn't derive a profound
delight from dramatizing what reality denied him: a twin son and
brother's return from the dead. Judith's bereavement as much as his
own may well account, at least in part, for the striking fact that in
Twelfth Night Shakespeare, unlike Riche, makes the loss and recovery of
the brother frame the whole plot, ensuring thereby that the emotionally charged reunion of the siblings upstages the budding unions of the
two pairs of lovers.

Strangling Propriety

However shallow or deep the biographical roots of the resolution
may be, the marvel it stages is the culmination of the play's assault on
beliefs that bind men and women to the way things are, and to the people they have become, by making the idea of their being otherwise
unthinkable. As Shakespeare had shown a decade earlier in *The Comedy
of Errors*, the blueprint for so many of the comedies and romances he
subsequently wrote, not the least merit of identical twins is that their

sheer existence exposes the instability of the identities on which our understanding of people and things relies, and the vulnerability of our minds and senses to deception – to what Feste calls 'Misprision in the highest degree!' (I.v.51). How solid and secure can the constitution of the world as we perceive it be, if all it takes is a *lusus naturae* – 'a natural perspective' – to show that what we took to be the case is nothing of the sort?

Shakespeare seems to have been brooding on such matters with unusual intensity while writing *Twelfth Night*, for about the same time he was also composing his notoriously cryptic poem, 'The Phoenix and Turtle'. (It's perhaps no coincidence that the name of the Illyrian ship Antonio is accused of capturing is the *Phoenix* (V.i.57), or that this is also the name of the house of the identical twin Antipholus of Ephesus in *The Comedy of Errors*.) Two stanzas at the centre of the poem might almost have been conceived as a philosophical commentary on *Twelfth Night*'s climactic revelation through the reunion of the twins:

> Property was thus appalled
> That the self was not the same.
> Single nature's double name
> Neither two nor one was called.
>
> Reason, in itself confounded,
> Saw division grow together
> To themselves, yet either neither,
> Simple were so well compounded
>   (lines 37–44)

In these lines Shakespeare employs the same riddling idiom that he resorts to in *Twelfth Night* ('I am not what I am', 'A natural perspective, that is and is not') to precisely the same end: to confound the preconceptions that normal reasoning depends upon by insisting that the self, far from possessing a 'single nature', is a diverse, discontinuous entity, and thus a scandalous affront to the belief that a person's distinctive quality – what makes them different – is a fixed, inalienable 'property' that they own. For the truth of the matter is that 'Ourselves we do not owe [i.e., own]' (I.v.300), as Olivia rapidly realizes, and the last thing anyone can claim to be is self-possessed. At the same time, to confound the reasoning that supports the dominant system of differences is also to enable 'division' to 'grow together' without sacrificing diversity to unity.

No mean philosopher – or rather, foolosopher – himself, Feste nails the nub of the matter when he hails the egregious Belch with a spoof citation of vacuous scholastic pedantry, prompted by his impersonation of Sir Topas:

> *Bonos dies*, Sir Toby, for, as the old hermit of Prague, that never saw pen and ink, very wittily said to a niece of King Gorboduc, 'That that is, is.' So I, being Master Parson, am Master Parson; for what is 'that' but 'that', and 'is' but 'is'?
>
> (IV.ii.13–17)

The answer to Feste's mock rhetorical question is that the nature of both 'that' and 'is' is anything but self-evident, let alone self-defining, as his own dual identity as Master Parson and Feste the fool makes plain. At this point, Feste is *not* what he is, inasmuch as he is and is not Feste, a fact that would doubtless appal the fictitious old hermit of Prague by proving that the self is not the same. Olivia coins an apt phrase for what Feste, amongst others, is up to, when she rebukes Viola for denying that she is Olivia's newly-wed husband, Cesario: 'Alas, it is the baseness of thy fear / That makes thee strangle thy propriety' (V.i.144–5). For *Twelfth Night* creates a climate in which strangling propriety, in the sense of killing off the concept of a core identity, a single self, is the order of the day.

But it's again the wise fool Feste who delivers the line that sums up better than any other the liberating insight enshrined in *Twelfth Night*. Mistaking Sebastian for Cesario, and exasperated by what he takes to be the latter's rude rebuffs, Feste vents his irritation in a sarcastic tirade, ironically unaware, for once, that he speaks more truly than he knows:

> Well held out, i'faith! No, I do not know you, nor I am not sent to you by my lady to bid you come speak with her, nor your name is not Master Cesario, nor this is not my nose, neither. Nothing that is so, is so.
>
> (IV.i.5–8)

'Nothing that is so, is so': therein lies the distilled wisdom not just of *Twelfth Night*, but of the whole sequence of comedies it brings to a close. It's the exhilarating revelation that the way people are, and the way things are, is not the way they have to be or the way they are doomed to remain, because selves and situations are manifold and mutable. Which is why, as Shakespearean comedy repeatedly shows, the differences that divide individuals can dissolve as emerging similarities eclipse them, and the most obdurate antagonisms can conceal an unforeseen capacity for rapprochement and consensus.

'A most extracting frenzy'

The play has a word for this veiled state of benign mutability, which materializes under the auspices of Twelfth Night: madness. The word 'mad' and its offshoots crop up more frequently in *Twelfth Night* than in any other play by Shakespeare, with *The Comedy of Errors*, unsurprisingly, running it a close second. The drunken Sir Toby 'speaks nothing but madman', laments Olivia, and Feste exits at her request to attend to him, quipping 'He is but mad yet, madonna, and the fool shall look to the madman' (I.v.102–3, 132–3). 'My masters, are you mad?' (II.iii.83) asks Malvolio, in his vain attempt to bring Toby's alehouse choir of shameless miscreants to heel. 'My lady bade me tell you', he informs the profligate knight, 'that though she harbours you as her kinsman she's nothing allied to your disorders' (II.iii.91–3). But, as his lady herself admits in due course, Malvolio couldn't be more wrong. For when he, too, begins to act like one 'tainted in's wits' (III.iv.13), Olivia allies both her steward and herself to Sir Toby's disorders by declaring, 'I am as mad as he, / If sad and merry madness equal be' (III.iv.14–15). Malvolio's bizarre demeanour may well be 'midsummer madness' (III.iv.54), as Olivia terms it, but when she belatedly remembers, in the dying moments of the play, that the 'poor gentleman' is 'much distract', she recognizes once again in his distraction the reflection of the madness by which she has been possessed: 'A most extracting frenzy of mine own / From my remembrance clearly banished his' (V.i.278–80).

The answer to Sebastian's question 'Are all the people mad?' (IV.i.26) is clearly yes, including possibly Sebastian himself:

> For though my soul disputes well with my sense
> That this may be some error but no madness,
> Yet doth this accident and flood of fortune
> So far exceed all instance, all discourse,
> That I am ready to distrust mine eyes
> And wrangle with my reason that persuades me
> To any other trust but that I am mad,
> Or else the lady's mad.
>
> (IV.iii.9–16)

Sebastian's adoring stalker Antonio strikes Orsino as equally deranged, when they meet face to face in the final act: 'fellow, thy words are madness' (V.i.95). But it's in the second scene of Act IV that *Twelfth Night*'s preoccupation with lunacy becomes most intense, as Malvolio, having been locked up 'in hideous darkness' (IV.ii.31), desperately strives to prove his sanity to Feste's casuistical curate:

> MALVOLIO.   I am not mad, Sir Topas; I say to you this house is dark.
> FESTE.   Madman, thou errest. I say there is no darkness but ignorance, in which thou art more puzzled than the Egyptians in their fog.
> MALVOLIO.   I say this house is as dark as ignorance, though ignorance were as dark as hell; and I say there was never man thus abused. I am no more mad than you are.
>
> (IV.ii.41–9)

When Malvolio tries the same line of defence on Feste as himself, however, the latter is quick to point out the fatal flaw in his contention: 'Then you are mad indeed, if you be no better in your wits than a fool' (IV.ii.91–2). Malvolio scarcely improves his plight by equating his frame of mind with that of a nation whose whole populace appears unhinged, and whose very name suggests a fusion of illusion and delirium: 'I tell thee I am as well in my wits as any man in Illyria' (IV.ii.109–10).

'Madness' is the comedy's code word for the condition that unites the denizens of Illyria by driving them to distraction, the point of utter confusion at which clarity and the promise of resolution appear. In their shared capacity to be dispossessed of themselves by 'A most extracting frenzy', the possibility of a different kind of human community can be discerned – an 'accident and flood of fortune' that does indeed 'exceed all instance, all discourse'. From the perspective of normality such a prospect inevitably appears insane, utopian in the usual sense of absurdly unrealistic, patently impossible. But from the standpoint of Shakespeare's quintessential comedy, which perceives the radical otherness latent in every word and deed, and which is driven by the desire to transfigure the world, to bring the utopian within the realm of the real, it's entirely feasible.

Twelfth Night inducts us into the same inverted understanding that Hamlet voices in the grip of his 'antic disposition' (*H*, I.v.173), the same 'Reason in madness' (*KL*, IV.v.171) uttered by the demented Lear.

It's no coincidence that while in these licensed states both Hamlet and Lear adopt the role and exploit the immunity of a dead court jester – Yorick in *Hamlet* and the fool in *King Lear* – and thus become the counterparts of Feste in *Twelfth Night*. (Lear's fool makes his consanguinity with Feste eerily explicit when he echoes the song the latter sings at the end of *Twelfth Night* (*KL*, III.ii.74–7).) What these tragic protagonists share at these points with Feste is an estrangement from their world so complete that apparent nonsense alone makes sense, because what that world considers sensible is plainly insane. To subscribe to the truly deranged way of the world is to labour under the delusion that 'That that is, is', when in truth the exact opposite is the case: 'Nothing that is so, is so.'

'But that's all one'

Feste acknowledges the affinity of his fool's vision with the mind of the mad when he says, 'the fool shall look to the madman' (I.v.132–3), which is what he literally does when he visits 'Malvolio the lunatic' (IV.ii.22–3), and when he likens himself to 'a mad lad' (IV.ii.132) in the song he sings as he leaves him. Shakespeare leaves us in no doubt, however, about the character's paradoxical perspicacity. 'This fellow is wise enough to play the fool', observes Viola after her first encounter with Feste, adding

> This is a practice
> As full of labour as a wise man's art,
> For folly that he wisely shows is fit,
> But wise men, folly-fall'n, quite taint their wit.
> (III.i.59, 64–7)

As Viola learns in the course of this exchange, acquiring the wisdom of folly commended by the play and vested in Feste means adopting a perspective that stands received wisdom on its head and fosters a sceptical detachment from the language in which that wisdom is couched, and in which *Twelfth Night* itself is written:

VIOLA. Save thee, friend, and thy music. Dost thou live by thy tabor?

FESTE. No, sir, I live by the church.

VIOLA. Art thou a churchman?

FESTE.   No such matter, sir. I do live by the church for I do live at my house, and my house doth stand by the church.

VIOLA.   So thou mayst say the king lies by a beggar if a beggar dwell near him, or the church stands by thy tabor if thy tabor stand by the church.

FESTE.   You have said, sir. To see this age! – A sentence is but a cheverel glove to a good wit, how quickly the wrong side may be turned outward.

VIOLA.   Nay, that's certain. They that dally nicely with words may quickly make them wanton.

FESTE.   I would therefore my sister had no name, sir.

VIOLA.   Why, man?

FESTE.   Why, sir, her name's a word, and to dally with that word might make my sister wanton. But indeed, words are very rascals since bonds disgraced them.

VIOLA.   Thy reason, man?

FESTE.   Troth, sir, I can yield you none without words, and words are grown so false I am loath to prove reason with them.

VIOLA.   I warrant thou art a merry fellow, and carest for nothing.

FESTE.   Not so, sir, I do care for something; but in my conscience, sir, I do not care for you. If that be to care for nothing, sir, I would it would make you invisible.

VIOLA.   Art not thou the Lady Olivia's fool?

FESTE.   No indeed, sir, the Lady Olivia has no folly, she will keep no fool, sir, till she be married, and fools are as like husbands as pilchards are to herrings – the husband's the bigger. I am indeed not her fool, but her corrupter of words.

(III.i.1–35)

This exemplary round of repartee is worth quoting at length, because it captures perfectly the way Shakespeare's comedic mind moves in *Twelfth Night* and the viewpoint the play invites us to share. It kicks off with a quick burst of quibbling, which denigrates both church and state by putting religion on a par with a jester's drum and royalty in bed with a beggar. Having collapsed the basic hierarchical distinctions on which the social order depends, it turns its attention to the stock-in-trade of Feste and Shakespeare himself, and in the same irreverent spirit exposes the instability of language, and thus the instability of the status quo, which conventional discourse is conscripted to lock into place. The labile nature of language is immediately linked to the wilfulness of the libido by the quip about making words wanton, which identifies wordplay in *Twelfth Night* as indivisible from the comedy's demonstration that gender is a fluid concept and sexual desire ungovernable. So unreliable has language in its customary uses become, contends Feste, that truly rational thought is impossible, which is why he describes himself as not so much Olivia's fool as 'her corrupter of words'. If words are the means by which false reasoning creates and preserves compliance, what recourse does the wily foe of such reasoning have but to become a linguistic terrorist, a semantic saboteur? The levelling demolition of difference; the cynical mistrust of marriage as curbing the free play of desire; the mutual refusal of eros and logos to observe propriety in comedy; and the liberation of language to redefine reality: all these staple components of Shakespearean comedy are on dazzling display in Feste's master-class in extemporal wit.

But so too, it must be acknowledged, is a streak of callousness, born of indifference, which doesn't escape Viola. When she says, 'I warrant thou art a merry fellow, and carest for nothing', she hits a nerve in Feste, prompting him to retort, 'Not so, sir, I do care for something; but in my conscience, sir, I do not care for you.' Viola's barbed remark implies, somewhat disconcertingly, that the fool's capacity to make merry is the product of his fundamental indifference, that the fun he generates is fuelled by his not giving a toss about anything or anyone. Feste denies that this is the case, intriguingly insisting that he does care for something, but declining to say what that something is. Notwithstanding his denial, Viola has clearly put her finger on a quality of Feste that reflects a quality of the comedy whose presiding genius he is. Of the role of the fool in Shakespeare, Coleridge remarked: 'We meet with characters who are, as it were, unfeeling spectators of the most passionate situations, constantly in life. The Fool serves to supply the place of some such uninterested person where all the characters besides have interest.' Feste's dispassionate attitude is summed up by the phrase he repeats twice as the comedy draws to its close, the second time in the penultimate line of his final song: 'But that's all one' (V.i.369–70, 403), which is to say: 'But none of that matters' or 'It's a matter of no consequence now'.

We can't take the full measure of *Twelfth Night* without grasping the significance of the fool's disinterested detachment. As Murry observes:

> There is a strange aloofness in Feste: he is attached, as Dr Bradley has remarked, to nobody. He is woven in and out the play like a careless wraith. Nothing matters to him. If he is turned away, 'let summer

bear it out'. His fooling has a different flavour from the fooling of any other fool. It is almost metaphysical in its aloofness.

It is indeed, because Feste embodies the transcendent perspective from which *Twelfth Night* and Shakespearean comedy is written. He is disinterested and attached to nobody in the play, because he does not belong to the world and time of the play: he is a revenant from a future purged of the conflicts that warped the minds and cramped the lives of men and women in Shakespeare's time. As such, he speaks in the common interests of humanity, in the name of a human community which has yet to come into being, and whose advent we still await in our own time. That, I believe, is the unspoken, unspeakable 'something' he does care about. The aloofness of his fooling is 'almost metaphysical', because it's the fooling of an incarnate abstraction, a spectral manifestation of futurity. 'Nay, I am for all waters' (IV.ii.63), Feste says in response to Sir Toby's praise for his impersonation of Sir Topas holding forth on 'the opinion of Pythagoras' (IV.ii.50). It's an apt remark from a character who can no more be pinned down to a single identity or viewpoint than the mind of the playwright who penned it can. It's appropriate, too, that the remark caps a jocular riff on the concept of metempsychosis by a figure who is himself an avatar of the soul of a play obsessed with transformation.

Understood in these terms, as the spirit of humanity abroad in a world that has no home for it yet, the fool's rootless anonymity and uncanny anachronism become easier to comprehend. Feste materializes at the beginning of the fifth scene after a mysterious absence which remains unexplained, and he retains throughout the play an awareness of elsewhere and an air of knowing more than the other characters do. Although Olivia is his mistress, he's not confined to her household, but commutes between it and the court of Orsino as he pleases, behaving the same way in both and allying himself with neither. He participates, to be sure, in the hoodwinking of Malvolio, with whom he has his own bone to pick, but his reluctance to don the garb of Sir Topas is made clear at the start of the scene, and he credits not himself but an impersonal power, 'the whirligig of time' (V.i.373), with exacting his revenge. And at the end of the play it's Feste who steps effortlessly out of the time-frame of *Twelfth Night* and into the audience's to sing his rueful ballad of disenchantment, underscoring the frailty of the comedy's conclusion and placing the whole play in a vast temporal perspective, which reaches back from the present moment of performance to the moment when 'A great while ago the world begun' (V.i.401).

'Prove true, imagination, O prove true'

If we return now to reflect once more on the sadness in which *Twelfth Night* is steeped, and recall Murry's observation that 'most of all it is contained in Feste, and in his singing', the nature and source of that sadness may appear less obscure. As a harbinger of the future for which the play is striving, as a stranger from another place and time, whose values are the reverse of those that prevail in Illyria, Feste is innately at odds with everything and everyone he encounters there. His explicit task as the fool is the implicit task of all Shakespearean comedy: to make the familiar, intelligible conventions of early modern culture seem as alien, puzzling and irrational as they would seem to the citizens of a transfigured world. Hence Feste's compulsion to talk at cross-purposes with everyone he meets, as if what they say makes no sense, or means something else altogether. Hence his hostility to the bonds of matrimony, the vital convention on which romantic comedy relies for its conclusion. And hence his suspicion not only of the words that forge the rationale of this alien world, but also of the resolution secured by the devices of dramatic fiction.

Feste's final, valedictory song is designed to throw the purely imaginary status of that resolution into bold relief by contrasting it with the bitter realities comedy must exclude from its conclusion. No fitter character could have been chosen by Shakespeare to have the last word in the last comedy of its kind he clearly knew he was going to write. Feste's haunting epilogue is not only a farewell to the play that has just ended, but also a lament for a mode of drama his creator had made his own: the extraordinary sequence of comedies begun a decade earlier appears in retrospect as one long Twelfth Night, which is now drawing to a close. The next time Shakespeare would turn his hand to comedy, it would be to put the genre itself on the rack in the problem plays, *Troilus and Cressida*, *All's Well That Ends Well* and *Measure for Measure*.

The bleak disenchantment of those plays is already foreshadowed in *Twelfth Night*, which is under no illusion about the cost of comedy, a cost the dramatist knew from the start it was bound to incur, as *The Comedy of Errors* makes clear. The complicity of comedy with cruelty is unforgettably dramatized in the tormenting of Malvolio, in which the fool, the spirit of the genre personified, is directly involved. 'I would we were well rid of this knavery' (IV.ii.67–8), says Sir Toby, as if speaking Shakespeare's thoughts out loud, for the remark reflects an awareness of what every audience feels, that the comedy has got out of hand and

crossed the line that divides it from barbarity and the pathos of the victimized. Nor is Shakespeare prepared to conjure the cruelty away by
showing Malvolio appeased and reconciled to the rest, as he could so
easily have done at the end. Instead, he leaves the threat of reprisal
hanging over the little society formed at the end of the play, a society
from which the wounded revellers Belch and Aguecheek – 'He's broke
my head across, and has given Sir Toby a bloody coxcomb, too'
(V.i.173–4) – are also conspicuously absent, and which is thus more
fragmented and fragile than the one assembled in Arden at the end of
As You Like It.

Twelfth Night is festive comedy's last stand against the realities the
play has barely managed to keep at bay. The whole comedy cries with
Viola, 'Prove true, imagination, O prove true' (III.iv.367), but is compelled to confess that the gulf between what can already be imagined
and what the present will allow is as yet unbridgeable. That it *can* be
bridged is the conviction that drives Shakespearean comedy up to this
point and enables it to make the incredible tenable. But in *Twelfth
Night* the remoteness of the dream from realization in Shakespeare's
time refuses to be repressed, and floods the play with the melancholy
that finds its consummate expression in Feste's final song. The song
gains its power to move in part from our recognition of the force to
which the comedy must resort in order to wrench the intractable realities the song recalls into a semblance of what we will. But its impact
springs chiefly from its juxtaposition with the final scene of the comedy,
which leaves the principal characters stranded forever in the liminal
realm of Illyria, on the threshold of a fulfilment that can be envisaged
but never enacted. As Keats wrote in his *Ode on Melancholy*, 'Aye, in the
very temple of Delight / Veiled Melancholy has her sov'reign shrine'.

The vulnerability of the delight Shakespeare's utopian imagination affords us in *Twelfth Night* has been apparent from the beginning
of the comedy. It's inscribed, of course, in the play's title, which places
us at the point where the revelry reaches its climax before dissolving in
the cold light of day. It can be inferred, too, from the fact that *Twelfth
Night* opens and ends in the delirious land of Illyria. In marked contrast
to *As You Like It*, no prior province of workaday reality is established,
to which the protagonists are destined to return after the action in the
parallel world concludes. Viola is already shipwrecked on the shore of
Illyria when we first meet her in the second scene, after the first scene
in Orsino's court; to transpose these scenes, as directors frequently do,
in order to establish a more logical sequence of events, is to destroy the
impression, so carefully created by Shakespeare, that everything takes

place within Illyria, which has absorbed Viola and Sebastian before the action commences, and which they have no intention of leaving.

For the romantic protagonists of this comedy there will be no voyage back from the virtual reality in which Shakespeare has marooned them. The completeness of their enclosure in the illusory universe of Illyria is underscored by Viola's continuous disguise, from which she's fated never to emerge to embrace her brother and claim her husband on stage. Only when 'golden time convents' (V.i.378) shall she and Orsino 'have share in this most happy wreck' (V.i.264) and the 'solemn combination' of both couples' 'dear souls' (V.i.379–80) be made. There Shakespeare leaves them, in a perpetual state of elated anticipation, which will never be satisfied, but which can never be disappointed. As for us, we have no choice but to return with Feste to the world outside the theatre, a world whipped by the wind and lashed by the rain, where adversity and dismay rather than delight seem to be the rule, but where, as *Twelfth Night* has been at pains to teach us, nothing that is so, is so, and glimpses of golden times abound.

Works Cited

Shakespeare

All quotations from the plays and poems are from *The Complete Works*, second edition, ed. Stanley Wells, Gary Taylor, John Jowett and William Montgomery (Oxford: Clarendon Press, 2005). I have, however, retained the First Folio's 'distract' in preference to the Oxford edition's modernized 'distraught' in Olivia's line about Malvolio, 'They say, poor gentleman, he's much distract' (*Twelfth Night*, V.i.278). I have also preferred the following spellings of certain proper names to those adopted by the Oxford editors: Petruchio (for 'Petruccio') in *The Taming of the Shrew*; Launce (for 'Lance') in *The Two Gentlemen of Verona*; Berowne (for 'Biron'), Katherine (for 'Catherine') and Moth (for 'Mote') in *Love's Labour's Lost*; de Boys (for 'de Bois') and Arden (for 'Ardenne') in *As You Like It*. The grounds for preferring 'Arden' to 'Ardenne' are discussed in the chapter on *As You Like It*, as are the problems raised by the routine amendment of Hymen's line 'That thou mightst join *his* hand with his' to read 'That thou mightst join *her* hand with his' (V.iv.112), which the Oxford edition incorporates. The chapter on *Much Ado About Nothing* discusses the problems raised by the standard editorial practice, likewise adopted by the Oxford editors, of transferring Leonato's line 'Peace, I will stop your mouth' (V.iv.97) to Benedick and inserting the stage direction '*(kissing her)*' after the speech prefix.

My only significant departure from the chronology proposed by the Oxford editors is dictated by the order in which I assume Shakespeare's first three comedies were written. The Oxford edition contends that *The Two Gentlemen of Verona*, which it dates 1589–91, was the first comedy Shakespeare wrote, followed by *The Taming of the Shrew* (1590–1) and *The Comedy of Errors* (1594), but I see no compelling reason to dissent from the still widespread view that these three plays were composed in the order in which they are discussed in this study. The precise chronology of the comedies' composition is far from crucial, and only occasionally pertinent, to my account of them, but my working assumption is that their sequence and approximate dates are as follows: *The Comedy of Errors* (1592–3), *The Taming of the Shrew* (1593–4), *The Two Gentlemen of Verona* (1594), *Love's Labour's Lost* (1594–5), *A Midsummer Night's Dream* (1595), *The Merchant of Venice* (1596–7), *The Merry Wives of Windsor* (1597–8), *Much Ado About Nothing* (1598–9), *As You Like It* (1599), *Twelfth Night, or What You Will* (1601).

Wherever the title of one of the comedies, or of another play by Shakespeare, is cited after a quotation to avoid confusion about its source, I have used the usual form of abbreviation (*LLL* = *Love's Labour's Lost, KL* = *King Lear*, etc.).

Critical Studies and Other Works

Quotations from Dr Johnson are taken from the *Preface* and the notes to his 1765 edition of Shakespeare's plays in *Samuel Johnson on Shakespeare*, ed. H. R. Woudhuysen (Harmondsworth: Penguin, 1989). The quotations from Coleridge are taken from *Coleridge on Shakespeare*, ed. Terence Hawkes (Harmondsworth: Penguin, 1989), with the exception of his remarks on *The Comedy of Errors*, which can be found in Jonathan Bate (ed.), *The Romantics on Shakespeare* (Harmondsworth: Penguin, 1992). All quotations from Hazlitt come from *Characters of Shakespear's Plays* (1817; numerous subsequent editions), with the exception of the quotation from his *Examiner* review of *The Taming of the Shrew* in Chapter 2 and his observation, apropos of Shylock and the Christians, that 'He is honest in his vices; they are hypocrites in their virtues' (quoted in Chapter 6), both of which can likewise be found in Bate's anthology. The latter is also the source of the quotations from Schlegel in Chapters 2, 6 and 8, the quotation from Heine about *The Merchant of Venice* in Chapter 6, and the quotation from Charles Lamb about Malvolio in Chapter 10. Quotations from commentators and editors before Johnson (Pepys, Dryden, Rowe and Pope) can be found in *Shakespeare: The Critical Heritage*, ed. Brian Vickers (London: Routledge & Kegan Paul, 1974–81), vols 1 and 2.

Quotations from Shaw are taken from *Shaw on Shakespeare*, ed. Edwin Wilson (1961; New York: Applause, 1989). Chesterton's essay on *A Midsummer Night's Dream* can be found in *Chesterton on Shakespeare*, ed. Dorothy Collins (Henley-on-Thames: Darwen Finlayson, 1971); his observations on nonsense quoted in Chapter 7 occur in the essays 'Humour', collected in *The Spice of Life and Other Essays* (Beaconsfield: Darwen Finlayson, 1964), and 'A Defence of Nonsense', collected in

Essays of Today and Yesterday (London: Harrap, 1928). Quotations from John Middleton Murry are from his study *Shakespeare* (London: Jonathan Cape, 1936). Unless otherwise stated, all quotations from Auden are taken from W. H. Auden, *Lectures on Shakespeare*, ed. Arthur Kirsch (Princeton and Oxford: Princeton University Press, 2000).

George Eliot's comment on *The Two Gentlemen of Verona*, quoted in Chapter 3, can be found in *The George Eliot Letters, Volume 2: 1852–1858*, ed. Gordon S. Haight (New Haven: Yale University Press, 1954). The quotation from Stefan George at the end of Chapter 5 comes from the opening line of his poem 'entrückung' ('rapture') in his collection *Der siebente Ring* (1907); the unconventional use of lower-case initial letters for German nouns is George's. The quotation from Wittgenstein on Shakespeare and dreams in Chapter 5 can be found in Ludwig Wittgenstein, *Culture and Value*, trans. Peter Winch (Oxford: Blackwell, 1980); I am indebted for this quotation to Peter Holland, who cites it in the introduction to his edition of *A Midsummer Night's Dream* (Oxford: Oxford University Press, 1994).

Index